# LAND OF THE DRAGON

# LAND

# OF THE

# DRAGON

Published by The Reader's Digest Association Limited

LONDON • NEW YORK • SYDNEY • MONTREAL

WALES IS A LAND OF CRAGGY PEAKS and plunging valleys; dramatic cliffs and wild offshore islands; slate-roofed towns and sturdy castles; expansive lakes and a wealth of wildlife. It is a land with its own language and a distinct culture, rich in compelling history and lore. This potent mix has won the heart of many a visitor to Wales, and we hope this volume will demonstrate the appeal of this magical land to many more.

Our lavishly illustrated volume has at its core a condensation of *Wynford Vaughan-Thomas's Wales*, an 'autobiographical guidebook' in which this companionable author takes the reader on a personal tour of his beloved country. Travel writer Lindsay Hunt, a frequent visitor to Wales, pens an informative introduction to Wynford's book, and dotted throughout the text and complementing it are a number of feature panels. These new features, exclusive to this publication, look in more detail at topics of interest. Rounding off this book is a 'Highlights' section, complete with map, listing specially selected visitor attractions, from castles to religious sites, and from industrial museums to music festivals.

LAND OF THE DRAGON was edited and designed by The Reader's Digest Association Limited, 11 Westferry Circus, Canary Wharf, London E14 4HE

*Wynford Vaughan-Thomas's Wales*
Original full-length version
first published by Michael Joseph Ltd, 1981
© Wynford Vaughan-Thomas, 1981
British condensed version © The Reader's Digest Association Limited, 2000

### CONTRIBUTORS

**Series Editor** Steve Savage
**Volume Editor** Charlotte Rundall
**Assistant Editor/Researcher** Miriam Sharland
**Associate Editor** Hugo de Klee
**Copy Editors** Caroline Arthur, Marion Moisy, Emma Waghorn
**Editorial/Picture Research Assistants** James Alexander, Kate Michell
**Art Editor** Karen Stewart
**Picture Researchers** Helen Ashford, Jenny Barlow
**Additional material by** James Harpur, Henrietta Heald, Lindsay Hunt, John Kahn, Tim Locke, David Owen, Roly Smith, Emma Waghorn
**Cartography** Anthony Sidwell (page 9), Malcolm Porter (pages 140–41)
**Index** Brian Amos

**FRONT COVER** *From Pen-y-Fan, the highest point in the Brecon Beacons, a ridge snakes down towards Brecon.*
**BACK COVER (TOP)** *Welsh rugby fans at Cardiff Arms Park hang out their national flag, depicting a red dragon.*
**BACK COVER (BOTTOM)** *Surrounded by lush plants, Tenby beach is an idyllic spot for sun- or sea-bathing.*
**TITLE PAGE** *A view from Penberi across patchwork fields on St David's Peninsula, looking towards Carn Llidi.*

**THIS PAGE** *A winding engine house at Blaenavon's Big Pit Museum is a reminder of Wales's once-great coal industry.*
**PAGES 6-7** *Two walkers exploring Snowdonia National Park are dwarfed by the majestic scenery around them.*
**PAGES 24-5** *A flock of sheep—an omni-present sight in Wales—high above the Vale of Ffestiniog.*
**PAGES 138-9** *Caernarfon Castle, once a symbol of English military might, is now a popular visitor attraction.*

# CONTENTS

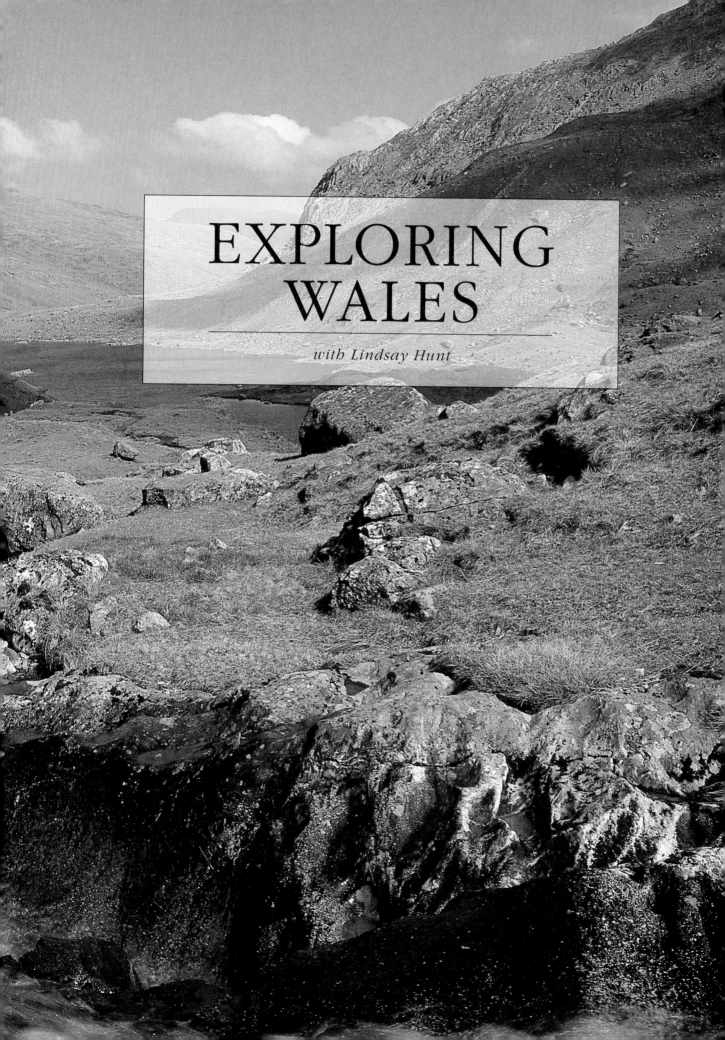

# EXPLORING
# WALES

*with Lindsay Hunt*

# WALES

## *with Lindsay Hunt*

O F ALL THE DOZENS OF APPROACH ROUTES leading from England into Wales, none is more dramatic or sharply defined than the twin suspension bridges carrying the M4 and M48 motorways across the Severn Estuary. The mighty steel support towers loom overhead like the drawbridge gates of giant castles—a fitting entrance to this land of fortresses. It's a majestic boundary, that River Severn. Steel-grey and motionless from a distance, at closer quarters its waters churn into restless whirlpools of café au lait.

Since my student days in Bristol, I've lost count of how many border raids I've made on southeast Wales, but the frisson of crossing the Severn has never waned. Now, more than ever, I am astonished that less than a hundred miles from the landlocked Derbyshire village where I grew up lies a completely different country, whose inhabitants speak a language I am ashamed to say I cannot begin to pronounce, let alone understand.

National differences may become accentuated with Wales's new-found autonomy, but wherever its destiny takes it in the new millennium, I hope the road signs on its frontiers will remain the same for any future invasions. *Croeso i Gymru!* Welcome to Wales.

## A KITE'S EYE VIEW

The River Wye joins the Severn near the older suspension bridge at Chepstow, and its lower reaches form another Anglo-Welsh borderline. If you follow this sparkling salmon run upstream past Hay-on-Wye and the genteel Victorian spa town of Llandrindod Wells you reach the little village of Rhayader, deep in the heart of rural Wales. The Wye races swiftly above the village, tumbling through ever-narrowing banks from its source on the slopes of Plynlimon. West of Rhayader lies a daisy chain of slender reservoir lakes, created amid furious controversy at the end of the 19th century when the Elan Valley was flooded to slake the thirst of Birmingham's rapidly expanding population. Today, the row has died down, though resentment lingers on in these dispossessed communities.

This man-made 'lake district' is now a popular outdoor leisure zone attracting many visitors for walking, pony trekking, mountain biking and fishing. An added bonus, if you're lucky, is a glimpse of its famous red kites. These handsome birds of prey are steadily recolonising central Wales after many years' absence, to the delight of visitors and conservationists. Soaring high over this central moorland plateau, the sharp-eyed kites have a stupendous vantage point. Two-dimensional

**ABOVE** *A red kite in its nest with young; thanks to conservationists' efforts, the bird is recolonising mid Wales.*

road maps show Wales stuck on Britain's western flank like a much-gnawed sandwich with a huge bite out of it. But from the air it must look amazing: its mountainous interior pierced by stately river estuaries and a magical coastline of cliffs, islands and beaches stretching towards the sea. To the north, the Snowdon range rears its splintered crags above winking lakes and waterfalls; southeastwards the rounded hills of the Brecon Beacons loom above densely populated but dazzling emerald valleys. Focusing on man-made glories, an aerial view takes in a host of eye-catching buildings—castles, abbeys, cathedrals, mansions—and spectacular feats of engineering—bridges, aqueducts, railways and canals.

## BORDER COUNTRY

One of the oldest and most impressive of these monumental constructions is Offa's Dyke, dug to keep the Welsh out of the Mercian King Offa's domain. This 8th-century earthwork no longer marks a national boundary, but it makes a

brilliant 170-mile walk along the castle-strewn borderlands, or Marches, between Chepstow and Prestatyn. It's deceptively tough. Attempting just a small section of its hillier bits a few years ago made me acutely aware of an unsatisfactory power-to-weight ratio. No doubt Wynford Vaughan-Thomas, the sprightly author of the centrepiece of this volume, would have tackled it with ease.

The Wye runs parallel to the dyke south of Monmouth, almost disappearing among deep quilts of luxuriant woodland near Tintern. On the Welsh bank, however, the evocative skeleton of the great Tintern Abbey ruins makes an unforgettable landmark. Today's visitors may find the abbey, with its tidy restoration work and the constant parade of tour coaches, less conducive to romantic imaginings than it was to Wordsworth and Turner, with its blurrier 18th-century outline of fallen masonry and sprouting vegetation. Nonetheless, few sights highlight the mindless vandalism of Henry VIII's Dissolution of the Monasteries more starkly than the roofless shell of the West Front.

Monmouth commemorates several national heroes usually claimed by the English side: Henry V, born in Monmouth Castle in 1387; Admiral Horatio Nelson,

**ABOVE** *The Elan Valley—Wales's 'lake district'—was flooded in the late 19th century to create a chain of reservoirs.*

a freeman of the borough; and Charles Rolls who teamed up with a certain Mr Royce to crown Britain's motoring and aviation industries. Upstream, the border town of Hay-on-Wye periodically declares independence from both England and Wales under the rule of its self-styled secondhand-bookshop king, Richard Booth.

The River Dee marks the Welsh border along parts of the Cheshire Marches. Llangollen, on the A5 London–Holyhead route, where narrow boats nudge in single file across Thomas Telford's Pontcysyllte Aqueduct, a breathtaking 126 feet above the Dee, is an obligatory stop for canal-boat fans. An excellent little museum reveals the story behind this daring construction. Llangollen has other claims on visitors' time, particularly its annual International Musical Eisteddfod (Welsh cultural festival) in early July, and a mock-Tudor house called Plas Newydd, home of the eccentric Ladies of Llangollen. Near Wrexham stand the stately homes of Erddig Hall (where the servants' quarters vividly reveal a slice of 'Upstairs, Downstairs' life), and Chirk Castle, a restored Marcher fortress built by Edward I.

ABOVE *Thomas Telford's Pontcysyllte Aqueduct, built between 1795 and 1810, carries the Ellesmere Canal across the River Dee in a cast-iron channel more than 1,000 feet long.*

## THE IRON RING

Many visitors find the magnificent castles that pepper the Welsh landscape its most memorable sights. Even in modern terms, they are awesome structures. Considered in the context of medieval building methods and logistics, they represent an astonishing feat of architectural skill. The greatest of them mark the epic 13th-century struggle between Edward I and his Welsh adversary Llywelyn ap Gruffydd. Repeated rebellions against the English Crown were a constant drain on the exchequer and a worrying diversion of resources from other foreign quarrels. In an attempt to consolidate the territory he had won and quell Welsh uprisings once and for all, Edward ordered the construction of a formidable ring of concentric fortresses on the North Wales coast, each a day's march apart.

The first batch, at Flint, Rhuddlan, Builth Wells and Aberystwyth, are now mostly ruinous. But the second wave, including Harlech, Caernarfon and Conwy, display the genius of Edward's great military engineer, Master James of St George, recruited from Savoy after the last Crusade. His castles were constructed along designs perfected in Gascony, with several layers of moated walls, which surrounded the 'soft target' domestic quarters, a defensive keep or gatehouse, and (on coastal sites) a protected dock which could receive essential supplies during sieges. Below the castle walls, towns were founded which symbiotically supported and received protection from their neighbouring fortresses. These were called English Boroughs, but they were closely based on the French idea of a *bastide* town of gridlike streets with a central marketplace. Though greatly battered in subsequent conflicts, the fortifications Edward built can still be seen much in their original form. The Iron Ring culminated in his last great castle at Beaumaris on Anglesey, constructed in the 1290s, which represents the most sophisticated evolution of the style.

OPPOSITE *Beaumaris was founded as a fortress town for Edward I in the 1290s; the castle is considered the finest achievement of architect Master James of St George.*

Caernarfon, though, is perhaps the most emotionally significant of all Welsh fortresses. Built after Llywelyn's final undoing, it witnessed the birth of the first English Prince of Wales in 1284—and in 1969, the investiture of the current prince. Several exhibitions on military history and royal associations with Wales are housed inside. If you climb to the top of the ramparts you are rewarded by a splendid view of the medieval township and the harbour bristling with yacht masts.

Wales has dozens of other castles. Caerphilly, near Cardiff, is one of the most enormous and impressive of the southern fortresses. Criccieth, Raglan, Kidwelly and Pembroke castles were constructed at various stages between the 13th and 15th centuries. Several, such as Chirk, Cardiff and Castell Coch, were restored as stately homes on a wave of neo-Gothic enthusiasm in the 19th century. Others have crumbled into picturesque decay.

If you are interested in visiting Welsh castles (and it would be a shame not to see at least some of them), it's worth investing in an annual subscription to Cadw, Wales's principal heritage organisation for historic monuments (*cadw* is a Welsh word meaning 'keep' or 'conserve'); membership gives free access to many castles, abbeys and ancient sites.

## HIGH POINTS

Before anyone thought of Snowdonia as a tourist attraction, it provided an impenetrable stronghold for the medieval Welsh princes in their struggle against the English. Far grander and more defensible than any of Edward I's fortresses, these mountain fastnesses sheltered Llywelyn ap Gruffydd and the 15th-century Welsh nationalist Owain Glyndwr (Owen Glendower in English) after their battles, enabling them to fight another day.

In more than one sense, the Snowdon range deserves top billing in the Welsh scenery league. National park status emphasises the region's importance—it was the first such park to be designated in Wales, and encompasses an area of 840 square miles. These impressively glaciated landforms have a long history of tourism; admirers have been coming to gaze at the fissured crags and mare's-tail waterfalls for centuries, and now thousands pour in every summer weekend to scale the heights along a variety of routes. Wynford Vaughan-Thomas tried them all, but lamented the commercialisation that followed the tourist influx.

At 3,560 feet, Snowdon is the highest peak in Wales (and England, too, for that matter), but some of its neighbours have equally spectacular and less crowded and commercialised scenery—including, of course, good vantage points of Snowdon itself. There are fourteen 'Munros' (mountains over 3,000 feet) to choose from in the Snowdon massif. Once in a lifetime, at any rate, everybody should try one.

At least six walking routes lead up the five-fingered massif of Snowdon proper, ranging from the gentle Llanberis Path to the awe-inspiring Snowdon Horseshoe (Wynford's choice), a magnificent ridge walk around ice-gouged cirques. A lazy but entertaining way up Snowdon is via the narrow-gauge rack-and-pinion mountain railway which starts at Llanberis and clambers to the summit café

between March and October. Here you can send your postcard from the highest postbox in Britain and set off down again.

An even more delightful Snowdonian railway journey is the two-foot-gauge Ffestiniog Railway which trundles from Porthmadog harbour along a 13-mile route to the slate town of Blaenau Ffestiniog. Between 1863 and 1946 horse-drawn, and then steam-powered, traction engines carried slate from the quarries directly to the quayside. Volunteers began restoring the route as a nostalgia railway in 1955, and it is one of Wynford's favourite 'great little trains', spiralling tightly in a skittish pirouette near Dduallt.

Myth-chasers may want to track down the stone cairn that marks the romantic site of Gelert's Grave at Beddgelert, one of Snowdonia's most attractive villages. This is the alleged burial place of Prince Llywelyn the Great's faithful hound, left behind while he went out hunting. On finding the dog covered with blood when he returned, Llywelyn slaughtered it, thinking it had attacked his infant son. But then he discovered the carcass of a wolf near the cradle, and, finding his son unharmed, realised that Gelert had been unjustly accused. This touching tale is recounted on a plaque by the cairn near the River Glaslyn, just south of the village. The surrounding landscapes of the Aberglaslyn Pass are some of the finest anywhere in the national park.

**ABOVE** *The summit of Snowdon is crowded with tourists in the summer season.*

**TOP** *The Snowdon Horseshoe is a walk for those with no fear of heights, passing along the ridge of Crib Goch.*

ABOVE *Houses in Blaenau Ffestiniog shelter below mountains scarred with discarded splinters of slate from the quarries.*

## BURIED TREASURE

Since Roman times, and possibly even before that, Wales has been exploited by mining and quarrying. Over the centuries, such vast quantities of rock and soil have been extracted that in some places it's a wonder there's anything left above sea level. The mineral deposits of Snowdonia offered enormous wealth for a lucky few. Slate quarrying gouged huge chunks from the landscape around Blaenau Ffestiniog, where the Llechwedd Slate Caverns opened as a tourist attraction in the 1970s. There are tours of the caverns by tramway and railway, followed by a slate-splitting demonstration. It was an incredibly wasteful industry, and it is estimated that more than twenty tons of rock were quarried to extract a single ton of usable slate. Some reconstituted slate spoil is being used in Cardiff's extensive waterfront development—a commendable recycling effort.

The most exciting find was gold, used by the Celts for their jewellery and systematically mined by the Romans. Gold still exists in the valleys around Dolgellau, and new finds caused a flurry of interest in the 19th century, but the quantities are considered too small for large-scale commercial exploitation. Welsh gold is still a popular choice for wedding rings.

Rich seams of iron ore and plenty of local limestone made Merthyr Tydfil not only the largest town in Wales, but the biggest iron-producing centre in the world in the 19th century, and for over a hundred years its hideously polluted slag heaps and blast furnaces created a major health hazard and fuelled social unrest. The inevitable decline after the First World War was acutely painful in these populous valleys. The Blaenavon Ironworks give some idea of what the Welsh version of dark satanic mills must have looked like. Copper deposits made Anglesey prosperous until the 19th century: the hills near Amlwch still bear the scars of open-cast extraction.

The biggest boom of all, however, was the 'black gold' found in huge quantities in the Rhondda Valley. During the 1920s the 620 mines of South Wales produced a third of the world's coal; a decade later, the misery of the Great Depression struck, to be echoed in the 1980s by another economic collapse and the miners' strike. Since then, every working pit has closed, leaving just two behind (the Rhondda Heritage Park and the Big Pit in Blaenavon) as vividly evocative industrial heritage attractions. A few ex-miners have found employment in familiar, if sanitised, surroundings—as tour guides.

ABOVE *Colliers work in extremely hot and cramped conditions, chipping away at the 'black gold' in a coal mine in Wales, c. 1910.*

The ravaged Rhondda, destabilised by mining activity, wreaked a terrible revenge in October 1966 when a slag heap slid down the hillside and buried a primary school in Aberfan, killing 144 people, mostly children. Their graves make a poignant sight at the top of the village cemetery—a double row of simple arched headstones testifying to the enormous human price of coal. Yet this is a mere handful of casualties in comparison with the relentless toll of those lost in less dramatic mining accidents: more than 100,000 people have died in British mines since 1850. The most frightful disaster took place in the Senghenydd colliery in 1913, with the loss of 440 miners in a single explosion. Today, the tips and slag heaps of South Wales are carefully sculpted into safer terraces, and, surprisingly quickly, the scarred landscapes are turning green again.

## COASTAL HERITAGE

A recent expedition took me along the entire length of the Welsh coast, a fascinating and enormously varied journey. I visited it in winter, a surprisingly enjoyable season, when the resorts and beaches were mostly empty and the seascapes wild. Stripped to the bone, the coastal topography and geology shone out in clear relief, unblurred by flowers or foliage. Wales boasts an enviable number of wonderful beaches, many in exceptionally beautiful settings. Much of the seaside is classified as Heritage Coast, and a large chunk of Pembrokeshire forms Britain's single exclusively coastal national park. Nature reserves, country parks and Sites of Special Scientific Interest (SSSIs) provide havens for wildlife all around Welsh shores, including its offshore islands.

The north coast of Wales has miles of good sand—a feature not lost on the holiday trade. A string of well-known resorts—Prestatyn, Rhyl, Colwyn Bay, Llandudno—lines the seafront west of the Dee Estuary, promising oodles of

**ABOVE** *The southwest coast of Anglesey offers tranquil sandy beaches, such as Newborough, backed by dunes.*

traditional seaside fun, if precious little open space between the caravan parks. Queen of these towns is undoubtedly Llandudno, strung between the scenic limestone headlands of Great and Little Orme. Justly proud of its handsome Victorian esplanade, the town boasts one of Britain's best-preserved piers. Further west, Anglesey's splendid rural beaches regularly win Blue Flags and other seaside gongs. The best include Newborough near the Menai Strait, and Llanddona on Red Wharf Bay, both vast, scenic expanses of quiet dune belts with nature reserves behind. The tides move swiftly over these flat sands, cutting off unwary strollers.

Much of the remote westerly peninsula of Lleyn is designated as Heritage Coast. Here, especially in resorts like Pwllheli, you're bound to hear Welsh spoken. The name of Porth Neigwl (Hell's Mouth), which is deceptively calm in fine weather but exposed to the full brunt of the Atlantic, indicates something of the danger the place poses to shipping. A long chase down minor roads takes you to the isolated, unspoilt strand of Porth Oer, the intriguing Whistling Sands, which squeak as you walk on them.

The Ceredigion Heritage Coast lays claim to several well-known resorts on the huge 'bite' facing Cardigan Bay. Aberporth is a cheerful sailing centre full of rock pools and fine cliff-top walks. Its neighbour Tresaith offers a waterfall as a natural freshwater shower. The fishing town of New Quay was Dylan Thomas's home for a while, and along with Laugharne, was at least a partial inspiration for *Under Milk Wood*, which greatly offended all his neighbours. The lively university town of Aberystwyth dominates the seaside scene, fringed by dark sand beaches. You need a good map, and a good navigator, to trace the secretive but idyllic little cove of Mwnt, tucked amid a maze of lanes below a simple medieval church.

Pembrokeshire is another eternal favourite, its national park traversed by a splendid coastal path. Even its main towns and resorts (Tenby, Pembroke, St David's and Fishguard) are positive attractions rather than urban eyesores. Tenby's elegant, well-preserved Georgian terraces have provided a backdrop for more than one period costume drama, and its beaches stretch clean, spacious and beautiful below dark cliffs or dunes smothered with wild flowers. The spicy vanilla fragrance of sun-warmed gorse lingers on the breeze most of the year, and is captured by the monks of Caldey Island in perfume bottles for the few days when it isn't flowering.

Arriving at Whitesands Bay near St David's one cheerless January afternoon, my attention was drawn to a group of people standing on the beach, all intently watching some creature floundering in the surf. Myopic without glasses, I was alarmed. 'Shouldn't we help that dog?' I asked. But it was an orphaned seal, just being released into the wild by an environmental charity. This was its first experience of waves since it was a tiny pup, and it wasn't too sure about them. A passing surfer, looking slightly seal-like himself in a wet suit, soon gave it some inspiration and in a flash it was off, a receding dot gallivanting through the breakers towards the open sea.

Marloes Sands, a National Trust beach on the Milford Haven peninsula, presents tantalising vistas of the offshore islands that speckle this southwestern section of the Welsh coast. From Martin's Haven, two miles northwest, boats ply to the maritime nature reserve of Skomer Island, haunt of puffins and seals. The Stackpole estate south of Pembroke, now managed by the National Trust, contains some of the most sublime scenery anywhere in the national park. Fascinating oddities include the Bosherston Lily Ponds—a scene Monet might have painted; the Green Bridge of Wales, a huge rock arch; the Elegug Stacks, where seabirds perch; and Huntsman's Leap, a chasm 130 feet deep. Legend says a horseman successfully vaulted it but died of horror when he realised what a risk he had taken. Accessible only to walkers is a deep bay of almost tropical-looking, tide-washed sand in a setting of cliffs, dunes and rock arches. This is Barafundle Bay, the sort of beach you hesitate to tell anyone about in case the magic vanishes. Well, there you are—I've done it now. *Please* take care of it if you track it down.

The medieval historian Gerald of Wales was born in the sturdy Norman castle behind Manorbier's beach, where a stream babbles across mauve and pink coin-shaped pebbles towards low-tide sands. Winter storms show all too clearly the terrible effects of tidal litter on many Welsh beaches. Some of it comes from as far away as Canada, borne on the Gulf Stream, and much is dumped offshore from passing ships. Exceptional tides lodge it high in the dunes from where it has to be picked off painstakingly by hand; besides looking dreadful, it presents a great danger to wildlife.

Southwest of Swansea, the gorgeous beaches of Gower are well documented in the rest of this book. Don't miss the unforgettable Three Cliffs Bay, where streams meander through drifts of sand towards a trio of conical offshore rocks.

The Glamorgan Heritage Coast is best seen near Southerndown, a surprisingly rural place just a short drive from Cardiff's international airport, and minutes from Cardiff itself along the M4. Dunraven Bay is a glittering stretch of sand, pebbles and rock pavements below strange banded cliffs of sallow limestone. The cliffs are unstable here and subject to constant landslides, especially after heavy rainfall.

## UNIFYING FORCES

Lapped by the Gulf Stream, damp, mild Wales effortlessly produces the lush vegetation and rich grazing land that made *How Green Was My Valley* such an apt title for a book about the country. No visitor should arrive without waterproof

**ABOVE** *Bosherston Lily Ponds in Pembrokeshire are freshwater pools covered with expanses of green lily pads and, in summer, their attractive white flowers.*

gear, but don't let the rain put you off—an enterprising hotel in one of Wales's wettest areas (Lake Vyrnwy in Montgomeryshire) now advertises 'Brolly Breaks' complete with an umbrella (which you can keep after your stay), and promises a bottle of champagne if it *doesn't* rain. They must be on to a winner here! The manager is nothing less than frank: 'We do get the occasional shower...'

Neither the hilly terrain nor the high rainfall are much good for cereal crops, but the hardy breeds of Welsh sheep and cattle dominate the agricultural scene, currently outnumbering the human population by well over four to one. But in Wales, as in other parts of Britain, recent events have taken a dreadful toll on traditional hill-farming communities. The aftermath of Chernobyl halted the sale of Welsh lamb for many months, and the outbreak of BSE did the same for some of its beef herds. These disasters, coupled with threats of EU subsidy cuts, make the future of stock raising look very gloomy. As if Wales needed more economic problems, when its mining valleys are still reeling from the catastrophic demise of the British coal industry.

Many of the old workplaces are no longer economically viable and have passed into the realms of 'industrial archaeology', but here hope glimmers as they are turned into marketable products for the heritage trade. Wales figures more and more prominently on the itineraries of foreign visitors. On a recent visit to one of the coal mines recently turned into a popular tourist attraction, I found I was the only English member of the party,

**ABOVE AND RIGHT** *The Lake Vyrnwy Hotel in Montgomeryshire offers holidaymakers a free umbrella so that they can make the most of rainy days in the beautiful surroundings of the lake* (right).

heavily outnumbered by Irish, Australian and New Zealand visitors, and thus the legitimate target of a barrage of good-humoured insults on the subject of rugby.

As in other Celtic parts of the world, team sports are an abiding passion in Wales. Soccer, cricket, ice hockey—all have a keen following, but it is rugby that arouses the strongest emotions in its spiritual home of Cardiff. Souvenirs fashioned from the concrete rubble of the former Cardiff Arms Park stadium are selling like hot cakes. In its place stands the futuristic 72,500-seater Millennium Stadium, complete with retractable roof, host to the 1999 Rugby World Cup.

**TOP AND ABOVE** *The Millennium Stadium in Cardiff is the new home of Welsh rugby; Cardiff Arms Park, which previously stood on the site, was pulled down and its stone fashioned into rugby souvenirs.*

And then, not a million thought processes away from a rugby stadium, there's the singing. Wales is fanatically musical. The oral tradition stems from the ancient bards of the Dark Ages whose epic songs and stories were first recorded in the *Mabinogion*. The love of music lives on most characteristically in today's male-voice choirs. Dating from the hymn-singing days of the Methodist movement in the 17th and 18th centuries, these are still an important part of life in many towns, especially the industrial valleys, but perhaps most visible to visitors during eisteddfods. These are no fossilised folk memories artificially revived for a paying audience, but a thriving part of everyday culture. Visitors are often welcome to listen, or join in if they wish, at rehearsals.

Eisteddfods foster another important aspect of the Welsh sense of identity—its ancient language. The official policy of bilingualism means that all public announcements, notices and signs take up twice as much time and space because they have to be spoken or written in both English and Welsh. Until recently, only about a fifth of the population spoke Welsh, and only in parts of the north and west is it habitually used as a mother tongue. But active and enthusiastic promotion via the media and in many public places now ensures a much greater awareness of the Welsh language—a far cry from the dark days of the 19th century, when schoolchildren were punished for daring to speak it.

Welsh is a language well suited for declamation. From the time of Owain Glyndwr's nationalist rebellion against English rule at the beginning of the 15th century, radical Welsh leaders have set themselves against the status quo at Westminster by using their powers of oratory—men like David Lloyd George and

Aneurin Bevan. Long after the great ages of coal, iron and steel, the Valleys still resound with voice-overs recorded by Neil Kinnock at the Rhondda Heritage Park. In recent decades, Owain's extremist spiritual descendants, *Meibion Glyndwr* (the Sons of Glyndwr), chalked slogans on buildings and bridges and torched holiday cottages to intimidate English settlers. Firebrand socialism of the most unreconstructed kind swirls alongside the rising tide of Welsh nationalism in the fluid political channels of the new Assembly.

## MILLENNIAL CITY

Cardiff became the official capital of Wales only in 1955, but the city's history dates way back to Roman times, and it has a long and proud pedigree as a port. In 1913 it was the world's busiest coal-exporting town, with a burgeoning and cosmopolitan population and considerable wealth. Since then, things haven't been easy. The economic decline of the docks was followed by a comprehensive bombardment by the Luftwaffe in the Second World War.

But Cardiff is a decidedly feisty city, and its increasing importance as a business and administrative centre has given it a hearty injection of confidence and optimism in recent years. Vastly ambitious civic regeneration projects have completely changed the face of the derelict docklands of what used to be called Tiger Bay. The city is now witnessing one of the greatest changes in its history so far: the construction of the Cardiff Bay Barrage which will transform a dismal zone of mud flats into a sparkling freshwater marina. Not everyone approves, not least because there is a large population of estuarine wading birds whose feeding grounds (an ecologically important SSSI) are about to be inundated.

**RIGHT** *The Cardiff Bay Visitor Centre, known as 'the tube', is designed to give panoramic views across the newly revitalised dock area.*

So far, the waterfront scene is patchy, but state-of-the-art buildings are springing up apace. For an overview of what Cardiff Bay will eventually look like, head for the futuristic-looking Visitor Centre, where a huge scale model lights up all the latest landmarks. These provide space for offices, hotels, shops and leisure facilities, as well as many new homes. Flagship projects include the Pierhead Building, the Mermaid Quay, the Oval Basin events arena and the dynamic Millennium Centre, created to provide a showcase for Welsh arts and culture. Pride of place goes to the new Welsh Assembly building with its floating canopy and sky-lit debating chamber, designed by the Richard Rogers Partnership. Constructed in steel, slate and glass, its transparent walls will enable the people of Wales to watch their elected representatives at work—democracy in action indeed.

So far housed in temporary premises, the Welsh Assembly was finally inaugurated in spring 1999. Clouded by the sudden eclipse of its prospective Labour leader, Ron Davies, who was forced to stand down in mysterious circumstances, and subsequent political in-fighting, its first few months have not been a particularly auspicious start to Wales's high hopes. But with massive investment plans still on target, Wales has everything to play for, and, as the new millennium begins, the future looks bright in Cardiff Bay.

## INTRODUCING
## *WYNFORD VAUGHAN-THOMAS'S WALES*

Few people can claim such exemplary credentials to write about Wales as Wynford Vaughan-Thomas. Not only was he (alas, he is now deceased) a trueborn Welshman through and through, but in his lifetime he must have combed virtually every mile of it—mostly more than once. Not in some effete, motorised way as most of us do, but by exploring vast distances on foot, by bike, on horseback, in small boats or dangling precariously from a mountaineer's rope. Some of these adventures he undertook at an age when most people prefer to reminisce by the fireside on a lifetime's accumulated recollections. According to his late widow Charlotte, he went into training for his expeditions by renouncing cakes and ale. Then he would set off from his home in Fishguard, armed with a bag of prunes—sucking the stones to keep his mouth moist—and a packet of jasmine tea.

If you find yourself on the mountain road between Llanidloes and Machynlleth, northeast of Aberystwyth, watch out for a memorial near Dylife and the waterfall of Ffrwd Fawr. Close to one of the most panoramic roadside vantage points in Wales, a slate monument immortalises him against a backdrop of distant peaks.

Fiercely proud of his native land, he sought to share his lifelong passion for Wales with others. Things have changed since Wynford wrote. As we have seen, there are now *two* crossings over the River Severn, for instance, and it's doubtful whether he would immediately recognise the rejuvenated waterfront of his homeland's capital city. But the landscapes, the essence of the place and its people, stay as sharply focused as ever. Those of us old enough to remember his affable radio broadcasts will hear his lilting cadences and generosity of spirit in every line.

# WYNFORD VAUGHAN-THOMAS'S
# WALES

*A condensation of the book by Wynford Vaughan-Thomas*

# CHAPTER ONE

# WELCOME TO WALES

**ABOVE** *The author, pictured here beside the tranquil harbour of Lower Town, Fishguard, where he spent the last years of his life.*

O N SECOND THOUGHTS, I am a little worried about the title of this book. Perhaps it suggests that I actually own the whole of Wales. How I wish I did! I confess that there have been magical moments in my travels through the Principality when I really felt that I possessed it for my own private pleasure.

I remember a few years ago climbing to the top of Carningli, where the lonely Preseli Hills sweep down to the sea in what used to be the delectable county of Pembrokeshire. It was a day of exceptional clarity in early spring, so clear that the tips of the Wicklow Mountains lifted themselves over the horizon far away to the west across the Irish Sea. To the north, I could trace every snow-covered summit from Snowdon down to Bardsey Island on the tip of the Lleyn Peninsula. Below me, the River Teifi wound its way towards its wide estuary through a pattern of dark fields. The first larks of the year sprang up from beneath my feet as I walked, and rose singing into the crisp, clear air. I had a moment of exultation. I said in triumph to myself, 'Yea, Wales really does belong to me.'

I am sure that keen Yorkshiremen will have felt the same possessive emotion as they walked through the beauties of Wharfedale; or Sussex men as they tramped the South Downs, 'so noble and so bare'. As a Welshman born and bred, I am bound to feel it most intensely in my native land. This book is therefore a personal appreciation of the charm, romance and fascination of the land of Wales.

I'll admit that all sorts of problems face the Principality today, and not every valley has been exalted by tourist developments. But how much beauty remains, and how many delights are still hidden among the hills—especially for those who are willing to get out of their cars and walk.

Wales is the surprise packet among the tourist areas of Britain, the last unexploited patch of local colour. Who would expect to find a country speaking its own language, and with its own fiercely defended culture and traditions, within seventy miles of the huge English urban complexes of Birmingham, Liverpool and Manchester? Who could imagine that you might lose yourself in a dangerous

wilderness of moorland and bog after a few hours' drive down the motorway from London and over the elegant steel tracery of the giant Severn Bridge? Yet I'm sure that it is this atmosphere of surprise and mystery that gives such special zest to travel in the Principality.

I claim to know my Wales reasonably well. I've walked the length of the country from south to north, I've ridden over it on horseback and I've pedalled a bicycle the whole way along the border. But I still feel the surprise and excitement of it all. I keep coming across delightful little landscape cameos that I've never noticed before, off-the-beaten-track views that I am astonished I've not made a special trip to see. I have jotted down a list of some of those I have come across since I started to write this book. In fact, I could have filled a whole new book with these glimpses of unexpected Wales.

I noted down just a few that I discovered in a recent tour of the Principality. I admired again the way the Clwydian Range—the first Welsh mountains that visitors see as they drive westwards into North Wales—moves in smooth procession to its climax at Moel Famau; I favoured the contrast between the dark clouds over the lake at Tal-y-llyn and, on the same day, sunlight giving rich colour to the dead bracken in the gorge behind Abergwesyn. A strong, exhilarating wind brought thrilling life to the South Pembrokeshire coastline at the magnificent limestone

*ABOVE The original Severn Bridge, gateway to the mysteries of Wales. In 1966, when it opened, it was one of the longest bridges of its kind in the world, with a single span of well over half a mile. M4 traffic between England and Wales is now served by an even longer bridge several miles downstream.*

**BELOW** *Known as 'the eyes of Ruthin', the seven dormer windows of the Myddleton Arms overlook the town's medieval square.*

**RIGHT** *The wave-sculpted Green Bridge of Wales is one of the highlights of the spectacular Pembrokeshire Coast National Park.*

arch known as the Green Bridge of Wales and almost shook the walls of the little medieval chapel of St Govan, nesting like a gull high up in the rocks.

Rain may come a little too often among the Welsh hills, but it brings added beauty to the myriad waterfalls, and certainly to Pistyll Cain, hidden in the woods near Dolgellau. And how pleasant are the patterns made by sheep wandering among the rocks or the Welsh black cattle casting evening shadows in some lonely field lost among the hills. Man-made patterns can be equally attractive. I noted the elegant formation of the rooftops of Montgomery and the startling originality of the windows sprouting from a hotel in the square at Ruthin. Back to natural patterns again: the sunlight filtering down through the branches of the giant wellingtonia on the Long Mountain, near Welshpool, and the gentle glow of the setting sun over the mountains of the Lleyn Peninsula. There is hardly any section of Wales that cannot supply a similar list of delights and surprises for the traveller with eyes to see.

As I drew up that list of the beauties of Wales I had not noticed before, my mind went back over the years to the way I had first learnt to love the Welsh landscape. It struck me that if I recalled the various stages in my discovery of my native land—from my earliest holidays in Gower, on through my first undergraduate adventures in climbing among the hills, to my latest exploration of Wales and its eastern boundaries on the back of my faithful horse, Toby—I would recapture the delight of first discovery and share that delight with the visitor who is exploring Wales for the first time. This book is thus what I am bold enough to christen an autobiographical guidebook.

**LEFT** *Pistyll Cain cascades through wooded glens near Dolgellau, an area notable for former gold workings.*

Against the background of the landscape, I have set portraits of some of the fascinating people I have met on my travels, for what is a landscape without the folk who live in it and whose work sustains it? Whatever qualities, good or bad, others may find in them, Welsh people for me have one great virtue: they are natural talkers. Perhaps talk is the real national industry! It certainly adds immensely to the pleasure of one's walks among the hills.

I remember a farmer on the steep mountain side behind Dinas Mawddwy who was ruefully surveying a high stone wall which had failed to hold in some of his sheep. 'Boy,' he said to me, 'these aren't sheep. They're antelopes in woolly pullovers!'

Then there was that quiet bar in an inn near the Glaslyn, where the locals seemed to know every salmon personally. They told me that John Snagge, of the BBC, had been fishing the stream a few weeks before. 'A very nice gentleman,' they said, 'but he didn't catch a thing.' 'I'm sorry to hear that,' I replied. 'John's a friend of mine.' 'Well, well,' came the chorus, 'if the boys had only known that, they'd have let one up!'

And if the talk fails—which is rare indeed—there is always the singing!

After that, do I see Wales through rose-coloured spectacles as a little Celtic paradise, a sort of escape hatch from the mounting problems of the modern world? The honest answer is 'Yes'. Of course, I am not blind to the ills that now beset Wales, as they do every other part of Britain. Wales, today, is a nation that seems to be struggling to find its soul again. Visitors may not understand the slogans in Welsh they will see here and there on the walls, but they will feel the sense of urgency that put them there. Yet I want to remind myself, in this book, that, as we face our problems, we in Wales have one consoling and inspiring asset: the rare quality of the landscape around us. It will make the solution of our problems worth while.

There is, however, one problem that continues to puzzle most visitors to Wales, especially when they come for the first time. What are they to make of some of our place names? I have seen tourists pull up their cars sharply in front of a signpost not far from my home in west Wales and get out their cameras. The signpost is marked 'Eglwyswrw'. The whole thing becomes simple when you know that, in Welsh orthography, 'w' and 'y' are vowels. The difficulties of Welsh pronunciation have also been exaggerated. 'Dd' approximates to the English 'th', and 'ch' is exactly the same as the 'ch' in the Scottish 'loch'. The 'll' is a little more complicated; the best plan—as in learning all languages—is to get a sympathetic Welshman or Welsh woman to teach you the knack of it.

In recent years, the Welsh forms of place names have rightly been given priority on road signs. Thus Abertawe comes before Swansea, and the River Towy at

## LANGUAGE OF THEIR FATHERS

WELSH IS A CELTIC LANGUAGE which, over the years, has had to struggle to survive. When Wales was officially united with England by Henry VIII in 1536, Welsh was banned from use in the courts and administration. But it persisted in Welsh homes, and acquired a new confidence in 1588 with the publication of the first Welsh Bible, largely the work of the scholar William Morgan.

Welsh was further reinforced by the spread of religious Nonconformism in the 17th and 18th centuries, and a 19th-century cultural revival: the chapels clung stubbornly to Welsh, and the eisteddfod enhanced its prestige. However, from about 1850 onwards, migration patterns began eroding the prevalence of the language, and schools banned its use.

But the tide had already begun to turn by the 1960s. Welsh nationalism was

**BELOW** *A Cardiff bus carries an advertisement for* Pobol y Cwm *(People of the Valley), S4C's Welsh-language soap opera.*

**ABOVE** *Welsh language tuition is compulsory in some primary schools in Wales; here, children enjoy storybooks written in their native language.*

becoming a stronger political force. Some extremists in the Welsh Language Society took to painting over English-language road signs with the corresponding Welsh terms. In 1967 and 1993, Welsh Language Acts restored equal official status in Wales. Bilingual schools proliferated; and in some areas Welsh was made a compulsory subject. More than 400 books are now published in Welsh each year. And in addition to BBC Radio Cymru, there is the television channel S4C, established in 1982, broadcasting Welsh programmes such as the hugely popular soap opera *Pobol y Cwm* and the children's cartoon *SuperTed*. Though destined to remain a minority language, the number of competent Welsh-speakers probably now stands at about 600,000—a quarter of Wales's population.

WELCOME TO WALES · 31

Carmarthen becomes the Afon Tywi at Caerfyrddin. In this book I have sometimes retained an anglicised spelling to help the visitor.

In the old days, as visitors drove happily westwards from England, they never quite knew when they had crossed the magic line of the Welsh border. Nowadays, the Welsh Tourist Board has put up a notice at all the main points of entry: *'Croeso i Gymru!'*—Welcome to Wales.

This is exactly what I hope this book will be.

## LAND OF THE SETTING SUN

I was born more years ago than I care to remember in the industrial town and seaport of Swansea in South Wales. It has since risen to the splendours of city status, but I always see it as the friendly, happily disorganised piece of architectural knitting I knew as a small boy. Swansea may not seem to be the ideal place from which to take the first, faltering steps in that exploration of the Welsh landscape that has been my personal delight throughout my life. My fellow townsman Dylan Thomas once said to me, 'This town has as many layers as an onion and every one can reduce you to tears.'

But Swansea had a secret that it hugged all to itself. To the west, on its very doorstep, lay the enchanting peninsula of Gower, with its limestone cliffs and yellow sands: an astonishing piece of unspoilt country tucked away in the middle of a coalfield. We called it, grandiloquently, 'The Land of the Setting Sun', because when we looked westwards from the top of our house in Walter Road we could see the Mumbles lighthouse flashing against the sunset to mark the gateway to Gower. It was my first glimpse of the strange contrasts and surprises that make up the landscape of Wales.

There were exciting Saturdays when we were taken for a trip on the wonderful train that ran towards the Mumbles pier round the curving bay. Swansea people boasted with pride that it was the oldest working railway in the world. It certainly looked the part. A panting tank engine drew a string of mobile toast racks, which were as packed in summer as a Calcutta tram. We would get out at Oystermouth and sample the Mumbles oysters. Our rich Uncle Arthur would instruct us in the correct way of swallowing what he called 'the delicious bivalve'. I can still recall the fresh, sea-salty smell that enveloped

**BELOW** *The grey sprawl of Swansea, Wales's second city. The author was born here, as was the poet Dylan Thomas, who described it as an 'ugly, lovely town'.*

Pier & Railway Station, Mumbles.

**ABOVE** *Another trainload of weekenders joins the crowd at Mumbles pier in 1905. This stretch of line remained hugely popular during the author's childhood.*

**ABOVE** *Made from seaweed and oatmeal, laver bread is not to everyone's taste. This delicacy, especially popular in South Wales, is best served with bacon.*

us as the oyster man flicked open the shells with a sharp knife at magical speed. Where will you find oysters at a shilling a dozen now? Certainly not at Oystermouth.

But the full glory of Gower dawned on us only when the family took over the little boarding school at Port Eynon for the annual summer holiday. The journey down to Port Eynon seemed almost as exciting as the holiday itself. In the narrow street beside the Grand Theatre in Swansea, we boarded solidly built buses with the splendidly optimistic names of *Pioneer* and *Vanguard*. As a special treat we were allowed to ride on the roof, strapped on among the huge baskets in which the Gower farmers' wives had brought their butter and eggs to market. As an extra safety precaution, we wedged ourselves against the wooden tubs that had carried the laver bread—that strange, black, treaclelike delicacy, made from seaweed, which is the great Gower gastronomic speciality. Unkind critics, surprised by its appearance, have called it 'the only edible cowpat in the world'. They have never tried it fried in bacon fat—delicious! Laver bread is still sold in Swansea market today, and a taste for it is the true hallmark of a Swansea-born man.

The *Vanguard* or the *Pioneer* slowly chugged its way clear of the last suburbs of Swansea and out onto the wide, breezy 'commons' that separate English Gower from the 'Welshery'. Gower had sprung a surprise on us in the very first few miles of our journey. In a small way, we felt we were crossing an international boundary, for south Gower, like south Pembrokeshire, isn't Welsh at all. It has been entirely English for the last 700 years. As the Normans pushed their way westwards along the coast of South Wales, they colonised Gower and south Pembrokeshire with English settlers. In south Pembrokeshire they used Flemish mercenaries as well. To this day you can trace the linguistic boundary in Gower by the wild, uncultivated commons that ring the 'Englishry'.

We always felt we were in a foreign but friendly country when our bus lumbered down the deep, wooded dingle of Park Mill to our first stop at the Gower Inn. We were far too young to go to the bar. Instead, we wandered around among the pony traps and marvelled at the strange dialect that fell from the farmers' lips. Gower speech was still very much alive in those days. If you drank your tea in a large mug, you had it in a 'dobbin', in front of a fire that was sending up not sparks but 'blonkers'. When we asked the name of the little stream that rippled down through the woods beside the inn, we were told: 'Why, boy, 'tis the Killy-willy.' 'Killy-willy' is the expressive word they also use in Somerset for something that wanders all over the place.

The old Gower bus was also a bit of a killy-willy, ready to stop or go out of its way down a lane to oblige a regular customer. And when the bus stopped we looked out for the exciting landmarks such as Pennard Castle, perched on its high rock overlooking a vast waste of sand dunes. We remembered the story of the wicked Lord of Pennard, who had been the cruellest of the Normans to conquer Gower. His evil career came to a sudden end when his stronghold was overwhelmed in a storm of sand, blown from Ireland, so they say, in a single night.

**BELOW** *Pennard Castle overlooks the dune-fringed expanse of Three Cliffs Bay, one of Gower's finest beaches.*

Then the bus obligingly stopped at a gate at the top of the hill out of Park Mill to give us a swift glimpse of Three Cliffs Bay, where the Ilston stream curved round the bright, limestone crags to the golden sands and the sea.

On went the bus, past the rich woods of Penrice and along the slopes of Cefn Bryn, the backbone of Gower, which held the great cromlech of Arthur's Stone on its high summit ridge. We boys half believed the old tale that King Arthur himself had flung it across from the other side of the Loughor Estuary when he found it in his shoe, and that it came down the river to drink in the stillness of Midsummer's Eve.

Then our bus turned south and came at last to the steep hill that dropped down into Port Eynon. We men proudly got out at the top of the hill and walked down to the little cluster of white-walled cottages round the church which formed the village.

There followed golden days, which always seemed to be full of sunshine, as we went out to great adventures on the 'huvvers and scarras'. This was the name given by the old Port Eynon folk to the wide stretch of pools in the limestone rock that appeared at the foot of the cliffs as the tide went down. Here we pushed our nets under the seaweed and ledges and lifted them up triumphantly, full of darting, snapping shrimps and prawns. On one never-to-be-forgotten morning, we caught a lobster, teasing it out of its deep hole in the pool in approved Gower fashion, with a hook known as a 'penny bender'. You can talk as much as you like about the thrill of catching your first salmon. It is as nothing compared with the excitement of seeing your first lobster floating up through the clear, salt water, with his big claws wide apart and his antennae waving. My young brother gave the memorable shout, 'Look, he's not red!' No, indeed: he was a most delicate, deep, mottled blue.

## SMUGGLERS OF CULVER HOLE

Beyond our shrimping pools, the cliffs of South Gower marched away westwards in increasing splendour, holding fascinating mysteries. The first and most puzzling of them is Culver Hole, just beyond Port Eynon Point. When we were very young, Culver Hole was the daring limit of our exploration of the Welsh countryside, to be undertaken only under adult supervision and accompanied by an elaborate basketful of gastronomic rewards for courage and endurance. The grown-ups carefully shepherded the children off the steep path which seemed almost to tumble over the cliff edge. We scrambled gingerly round a corner into a deep cleft in the rock, which ran straight up from the sea to the cliff top. There we rubbed our eyes with surprise.

The whole of the cleft has been sealed by a wall of rough masonry pierced by a series of windows. With difficulty we were hoisted inside, to find a slippery stone stairway leading up into the semidarkness. There were no signs of floors having been built. A rich aroma of rotting seaweed permeated the scene. A honeycomb of rectangular holes covered the inner wall. As far as I can discover, there is nothing quite like Culver Hole on the whole coastline of Britain. Who would have taken the trouble to build a storage construction in such a wild spot? And for what purpose?

When we were young, we had an instant solution to the problem: smugglers! Gower was full of notable smuggling stories. During the Napoleonic Wars the peninsula, like Cornwall, was a hotbed of illicit brandy running. Old Mr Grove, who took us out crabbing, told us the saga of his grandfather's

**ABOVE** *Squeezed into a great gash in the rocks, mysterious Culver Hole is supposed to have served a number of purposes over the centuries: pigeon loft; smugglers' retreat; armoury; brandy store; and stronghold for the old Port Eynon castle.*

famous trick during the Big Run at Port Eynon. The excise men were hot on the trail, and there was only one thing for it. 'They needed the help of the Lord, and the parson understood. They put the brandy barrels under the altar of the church. Those herring-gutted excise men didn't know a thing. 'Twas the true spirit of the Lord, even if it was brandy.'

Secrecy and cunning were the essence of the smuggler's trade. He wouldn't have wasted his time constructing a vast building that could be seen miles out to sea. Perhaps Culver Hole was a stronghold of the wild Lucas family, who controlled West Gower in Tudor times. There is a third possible solution. Could it have been a gigantic medieval pigeon loft, since there is an old English word 'culver' which means pigeon or dove? Culver Hole remains sinister and mysterious and keeps its secrets.

## BURIED BONES

As we got older, we grew—or were allowed to grow—more adventurous. Beyond Culver Hole and the nearby Overton Mere, the Gower coastline steadily increased in splendour and steepness. I would back this five miles of coast against any other stretch of coast anywhere in Wales. Limestone is my favourite rock. It is so clean and glittering, and the turf on the headlands has a special tender, green softness.

We were allowed to march these memorable five miles under the guardianship of two older boys. A pony and trap, complete with anxious parents, would wait for us at the Worms Head Cottage Tea Rooms ('PARTIES CATERED FOR AT SPECIAL RATES. STRAWBERRIES AND CREAM 6D EXTRA').

This splendid walk has hardly changed to this day. As the coastal path goes on towards Rhossili through gorse and heather, it comes to a dizzy catwalk above the waves. Now the cliffs really take over, and at Paviland they drive the path back from the very edge. Here you reach the second mystery of the marvellous five-mile walk. At Yellow Top, easily picked out by the lichen that covers the summit rocks, the cliffs make a particularly exciting plunge into the sea. At the foot of the plunge is the famous bone cave of Goat's Hole, where, back in 1823, the celebrated Dean Buckland startled the scientific world by uncovering human remains stained red and mingled with those of extinct animals such as the mammoth and the woolly rhinoceros.

Buckland thought that the bones were those of a female, and his find was christened 'The Red Lady of Paviland'. He pictured her as a Romano-British

# THE RED LADY OF PAVILAND

LEFT *Goat's Hole, the cave where the Red Lady was found, which can only be reached by a scramble across the rocks.*

RIGHT *William Buckland caused a sensation in 1823 when he found the ancient skeleton in Goat's Hole.*

BELOW RIGHT *Part of the Red Lady's skeleton is now on display in Oxford's Natural History Museum.*

THE COASTAL PATH along the Gower peninsula offers some of the most spectacular views in Wales, out across the sea which, over the millennia, has carved the soft limestone of the coast into a series of caverns and gullies.

The local people have long put these caves to use as dwellings, fortresses and gaols, and in 1823 a spectacular archaeological find by William Buckland in one of these caves, Goat's Hole at Paviland, proved that the area had indeed been inhabited for a very long time. After a daring climb across the rock face with the sea crashing below, Buckland, reader in geology and mineralogy at Oxford University and later Dean of Westminster, entered Goat's Hole and discovered a headless skeleton. Alongside it were an ivory necklace, some pierced animal teeth that had perhaps served as toggles or jewellery, and the bones of animals long since vanished from the region, such as mammoths, woolly rhinos and hyenas. Iron oxide in the earth had turned the bones red, and the skeleton was duly christened the Red Lady of Paviland.

The Lady, variously held to have been a Romano-British priestess, witch or prostitute, caused a sensation in her day. But in the late 20th century, further examination using radiocarbon techniques revealed that the skeleton was in fact that of a young man, who had lived some 26,000 years ago, making this Palaeolithic hunter the earliest-known inhabitant of Wales. Today, his skeleton lies at peace in the Oxford University Museum of Natural History.

priestess. If this was true, what were her remains doing mingled with the bones of long-extinct animals? Horror of horrors: the good Dean's find might even disprove the truth of the biblical flood.

Modern scientific exploration proved the skeleton to be that of a youth who was buried in the cave some 26,000 years ago, and Paviland has now become one of the important sites in British prehistory. Personally, I thought the Red Lady of Paviland might appear at any minute as we scrambled down the steep grass slide towards the traverse into the cave.

Our trusted leaders immediately betrayed their trust. 'Dare you to follow us,' they challenged. 'Done,' I said, and within minutes I found myself balancing gingerly on a series of holds, high above the ravening waves far below. In truth the holds are veritable jug handles, and anyone with a steady head can traverse into Paviland Caves. But this was my first attempt at moving on steep rock, and I felt as if I had conquered Everest. Of course, I promised to say nothing about it to my parents. I could hear the words 'foolhardy adventure' forming in the salty air, and I came thankfully back to the safety of the path.

The coastline today has become a well-known rock-climbing area, but in those days the gulls, kittiwakes and cormorants were the only living things that haunted the cliffs. Cormorants are my favourite sea birds. They clustered on the edge of the rocks, black suited and looking like a group of deacons discussing the sermon after chapel, or—suddenly changing character as they spread their wings out to dry—miniature Count Draculas.

ABOVE *Cormorants, which haunt the cliffs around Wales, are often seen with wings spread like 'miniature Count Draculas'.*

## THE WORM'S GOLD

The cliffs grow in stature all the way from Paviland, past Thurba, to Worms Head. We walked across the sands of Mewslade Bay at low tide, and I delighted in the limestone spires that leapt up from the sand. These rocky excitements reach their climax at Worms Head itself, one of the most remarkable headlands in Great Britain. It really does live up to the name given to it by the Viking raiders as they rowed towards it to plunder and loot in the Bristol Channel. It looks like a great serpent, winding its way out to sea and rearing its head as it makes its final plunge into the western waves. The Worm can even bellow at certain stages of the tide, when strong winds drive the white breakers into the Blow Hole.

The Worm is the guardian of Rhossili Bay, one of the finest stretches of sand on the coast of Wales. As we ended our walk and sat down in triumph to our strawberry tea at Worms Head Cottage, we looked out over the great shining sweep of the beach, backed by the 600-foot-high slope of the Rhossili Downs. Mr Thomas, the café owner—known as Thomas Yes-Yes-Yes because he kindly agreed with everything anybody said—thrilled us with stories of the 'dollar ship' which was wrecked at Rhossili some time in the 17th century. Was it a Spanish galleon or, as some people maintained, one of the ships bearing the dowry of Catherine of Braganza, the bride of King Charles II? There is no proof either way. All we know is that in 1807 the tide uncovered an area of sand rich in Spanish gold coins. There was great local excitement, but the fickle tide soon covered them up again.

# INVADERS OF WALES

THROUGHOUT ITS HISTORY, waves of invaders have left their mark on the culture and landscape of Wales. The first of these were Celts, who crossed from the Continent during the last centuries BC. Although the remains of their hill-forts can still be seen, their greatest legacy was cultural: Welsh people still attribute their flair for eloquence, poetry and music to their Celtic forebears; and the Welsh language itself evolved from an earlier Celtic tongue.

The next invaders were the Romans in the late 1st century AD. From bases at Chester and Caerleon, the Romans controlled the country for 400 years, introducing roads, forts, baths and piped water. When they left Britain in the early 5th century, the power vacuum in Wales was exploited by Irish raiders, some of whom put down roots. Although these Irish settlers were eventually absorbed or expelled, they did spread Christianity.

*LEFT The renovated keep of Abergavenny Castle, first built by Marcher Lords in the wake of the Norman invasion of Wales.*

*BELOW Llywelyn, the last native prince of Wales, loses his head as Edward I looks on. Since this time, English law has prevailed.*

*LEFT Many Welsh people suffered at the hands of Viking raiders, who wielded fearsome weapons such as this remodelled sword.*

*LEFT Found near Abergavenny, this aureus of Roman Emperor Claudius is the earliest Roman coin to have been found in Wales. It dates from AD 51–2.*

In the early 7th century, Anglo-Saxons attacked the Welsh and contained them within what is approximately the modern border with England—a boundary later solidified by the Anglo-Saxon King of Mercia, Offa, who built a long dyke along its length in about 784. In the following century, the Vikings struck at Wales from bases on Ireland and the Isle of Man, but found the country, under the leadership of Rhodri Mawr, a hard nut to crack.

Although Viking raids continued until the late 11th century, it was the impact of the Normans that was to shape the future of Wales. In the wake of their conquest of England in 1066, Norman nobles began to seize land in Wales and build castles. The Welsh resisted and, during the next 200 years, native princes vied with Anglo-Norman kings and nobles for power. The issue was finally settled when Edward I invaded Wales in 1277: he crushed Welsh resistance and imposed English law.

Edward's invasion, however, was not quite the last. Five hundred years later, in 1797, French troops fighting against England were sent to capture Bristol. They landed instead near Fishguard, and, mistaking the red shawls and black hats of local Welsh women for military uniforms, promptly surrendered.

*LEFT The French surrender at Fishguard in 1797, for which local women in their red shawls and black hats take credit.*

However, twenty-six years later, the tide relented and the dollars appeared once again in the sand. A wild gold rush took place, and the whole of Gower descended on Rhossili Sands, staking out claims, digging frantically against the incoming tide and carting away fortunes to the banks at Swansea. The Gower Gold Rush lasted a few hectic weeks, and then the sands closed once more over the 'dollar field'. For ever? Who knows. Any day now the shining dollars may reappear and the Gower Gold Rush will be on again.

We were all for descending immediately to the sands far below to try our luck, until Mr Thomas hinted that there were other, more eerie and sinister stories concerning the sands as evening fell. Was it not the wicked Squire Mansel of Henllys, who had really lured the dollar ship to its wreck? And, on wild winter's nights, do not the wheel marks of his ghostly coach appear on the damp sands as the tide goes out? And what strange thing crawls out of the sea to tap at the windows of the lonely vicarage, built right on the edge of the sands under the steepest part of Rhossili Downs?

Gower lived up to its reputation as the Land of the Setting Sun when we drove back to Port Eynon. A sunset of surpassing power flooded the western sky beyond the Worm. Our steady old pony clip-clopped his way through the darkening, dusty, deserted lanes, while we determined that, one day, we would return, defy Squire Mansel's ghostly coach and the 'nameless horror' of the Old Vicarage and make our fortune from those shining dollars still hidden in the sands.

We never did. Instead, sixty-five years later, I drove along that old south road of Gower and then walked again those magical five miles of cliffs between Port Eynon and the Worm. Had Gower changed beyond all recognition? Had the old charm been overwhelmed by car parks, caravans and crowds?

I think I must admit, straightaway, that it would be unwise to return to Gower at the height of the August holidays. You may not get to some of the beaches at all because of the queues of cars, and Port Eynon and Llangennith have altered beyond recognition from the tranquil, thatched-roofed oases of seclusion I first knew. But once you get out of your car and start to walk—as happens in so many other places today—the old charm comes flooding back. The gulls still cry undisturbed round the cliffs of Paviland. Rhossili Sands are wide enough to take all the crowds and yet retain their mysteries. The oystercatchers call and pipe on the Llanrhidian marshes, and, as I walked across to Worms Head at low tide once again, I couldn't help feeling how lucky I had been to have gone on my first holidays to Gower.

Without my being aware of it for one moment, Gower showed me that a countryside could be beautiful because of what men had done to it over countless years in the past. By a pleasant paradox, it was Gower—that Littlest England beyond Wales—that really gave me my passion for the exploration of Welsh Wales. I have been happily at it ever since.

**ABOVE** *Worms Head, a mile-long limestone spit resembling a basking serpent, or perhaps a dragon, is outlined in dramatic silhouette against the setting sun.*

# CHAPTER TWO

# THE GREAT ESCARPMENT

'WIN A SCHOLARSHIP AND GET A BICYCLE.' This was my parents' inspiring formula, which set me off on the next phase of my exploration of Wales. I duly got my scholarship and ended up in that most sympathetic and understanding of educational establishments, Swansea Grammar School. It was conducted on the sensible principle outlined by the headmaster to my father when I first entered those neo-Gothic portals: 'Dr Thomas, if your boy has got anything in him, we'll get him a scholarship to Oxford—and even to Cambridge. If he's got nothing in him, we'll make his passage through school as pleasant as possible.' This meant that I had plenty of time to ride off exploring on my bicycle!

Gower had been my delight up to the age of eleven. Now I looked at the map and saw marked on it a line of high hills forming a long, impressive barrier about twenty miles north of Swansea. I immediately climbed up 500-foot-high Townhill behind the grammar school and looked away to the north. It was a clear evening. I could see right across the industrial area to the town and up through the mining valleys to where the high summits marched in procession across the northern horizon. These were the Carmarthen Vans—*van*, in Welsh, means 'a high place'. These places were certainly high, reaching over 2,600 feet on the ridges behind the top of the River Tawe. I looked more closely at the map. The Carmarthen Vans were not the only summits I could see. A whole series of lonely tops stretched away eastwards, all with names musical to a Welshman's ear: Fan Gyhirych, Fan Nedd, Fan Llia, Fan Fawr. And peeping up over the eastern rim came the unmistakable flat-topped summits of the Brecon Beacons. They were only a few feet short of that magical number for a mountain—3,000.

And here may I just lament the habit of the Ordnance Survey of printing the height of our hills in metres? I just can't get used to it. Maybe the next generation of mountain walkers will take it all in their stride, but I still get a shock

when I see the proud 2,907-foot summit of Pen-y-Fan in the Brecon Beacons diminished to a mere 900-odd metres. I shall stick to the old system. When the time comes for me to give up walking on the hills, they will have to carry me out feet first.

But, no matter how you measure them, these hills of the Vans and the Beacons form a challenging escarpment, breaking like a great wave to the north. They come as a dramatic surprise to visitors who think that all the noble mountains of Wales lie in Snowdonia.

Our geography master had carefully drilled into us the image of the South Wales coalfield as a giant saucer. The rocks slope steeply to the centre on the south side and rise more gently to the north. 'You'—he pointed to us

**ABOVE** *The gentle procession of summits that form the huge escarpment of the Brecon Beacons is a greater challenge to ramblers than it may seem. Pen-y-Fan, in the distance, is almost 3,000 feet high.*

dramatically—'are living on the southern rim of the saucer.' He made it sound as if, all our lives, we had been engaged in a precarious balancing act. The northern rim, however, sounded even more exciting, with all those high peaks waiting to be conquered.

My brothers and I bicycled north up the Swansea Valley, then still heavily industrialised with steelworks and tin-plate works, and echoing with the sound of colliery hooters. But after fifteen miles, the hills closed in and the valley twisted away round a steep corner. All signs of industry dramatically disappeared. The River Tawe ran pellucid and musical under limestone rocks, for the coal measures—the central rocks of the saucer—had slipped away to the south. We had passed the outcrop of their last layer, to which the old miners gave the expressive name of the Farewell Rock. The bright limestone, which I had grown to feel was my own personal rock in faraway Gower, now reappeared. Among the shining crags rose a strange structure, a sort of Scottish baronial castle with a Welsh accent. This was Craig-y-Nos, the Crag of the Night, once inhabited by none other than Adelina Patti, the greatest operatic singer of the 19th century.

## POWERHOUSE OF BRITAIN

WALES, with its rich mineral reserves, was a powerhouse behind the British Industrial Revolution of the 18th and 19th centuries. Welsh coal helped make steel and raise steam, turn machinery and drive ships and locomotives. Reserves of copper, lead and iron ore were used to build the hardware of the Revolution, while slate from North Wales roofed the new factories and their workers' houses. Welsh ironworks made cannons for the Napoleonic wars and rails for the opening up of the American West.

Yet over the course of the 20th century, the availability of cheaper raw materials from overseas caused a sharp decline in Welsh heavy industry. Steelworks closed down, as did collieries. In 1914 the South Wales coalfield was the largest exporter in the world, but after the First World War, German reparations meant that the defeated nation provided cheap coal which took over many overseas markets; what is more, coal from East Midlands pits was easier, cheaper and safer to

LEFT *Former miners at the Big Pit museum in Blaenavon now act as guides, showing visitors what life in the pits was like.*

BELEFT *Steel making has survived the industrial decline of the 1900s; production at the Port Talbot works, shown here, is thriving.*

mine. As the century progressed coal began to lose favour as a fuel, and was gradually replaced by oil, which was cleaner and cheaper. By the time of the 1984 national coal strike, the once mighty industry had all but disappeared.

We knew all about her when I was a child in Swansea, for she did not die until 1919. As a little boy, I had been held up to wave to her as she drove from the station with a mounted escort to preside at a charity concert. At the end of these concerts, she always came onto the stage to sing 'Home, Sweet Home' to tumultuous applause. They knew how to treat an artiste in those days!

But why had this exotic vocal bird, one of the richest and most worshipped sopranos of all time, nested at last in the wildest part of an obscure Welsh valley on the edge of a coalfield?

The answer was that Patti may have made a fortune out of her singing, but she had had no luck with her love life. At last she decided to settle down with her principal tenor, Signor Nicolini. Lord Swansea, a great admirer of her talents, suggested Craig-y-Nos as the ideal hide-out, a place where she could rest in seclusion when not on tour. Patti married her tenor, who became an enthusiastic trout fisherman in the Tawe in between arias. She built her own theatre, which still exists at Craig-y-Nos; the curtain is painted with a representation of the diva, blue cloak floating in the wind as she drives a chariot in her favourite role of

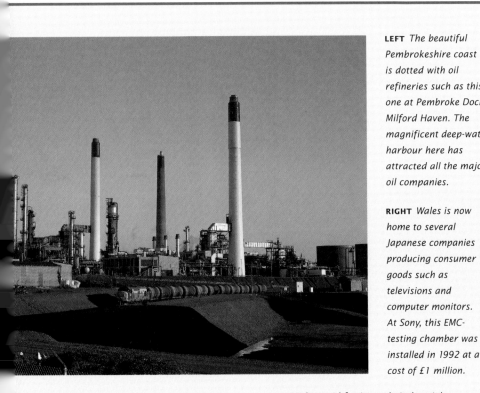

**LEFT** *The beautiful Pembrokeshire coast is dotted with oil refineries such as this one at Pembroke Dock, Milford Haven. The magnificent deep-water harbour here has attracted all the major oil companies.*

**RIGHT** *Wales is now home to several Japanese companies producing consumer goods such as televisions and computer monitors. At Sony, this EMC-testing chamber was installed in 1992 at a cost of £1 million.*

Oil brought new work to southwest Wales, where refineries now ring the beautiful waterway of Milford Haven. But oil spills pose a constant threat to the nearby Pembrokeshire Coast National Park, reminding people perhaps of the price Wales paid for its early industrial prosperity—a huge legacy of pollution.

Many industrial landscapes now provide space for the so-called 'sunrise' industries of aerospace, electronics and computers, with companies such as Sony, Sharp and Orion bringing new jobs. Service industries have boosted female employment, while steel making, which declined in the 1970s, saw a resurgence during the 1990s and now accounts for 19 per cent of manufacturing jobs in Wales.

**LEFT** *Adelina Patti, the greatest opera singer of her time. She was born in Madrid of Italian parents but settled near Swansea, buying the castle Craig-y-Nos.*

**RIGHT** *The theatre at Craig-y-Nos where Adelina Patti entertained her friends. The stage curtain depicts the diva playing the role of Semiramide.*

Semiramide in Rossini's opera of the same name. Craig-y-Nos is a private home but there are occasional performances in the theatre and the hills resound again with the music that Patti loved.

Our thoughts, however, were not on Madame Patti's music as we first bicycled past Craig-y-Nos. We were concerned with music composed by our father, David Vaughan-Thomas, who was a distinguished Welsh musician. Our ambition was to reach the isolated lake of Llyn y Fan Fach which Father had used as a setting for a dramatic cantata. This lonely, wild lake, surrounded by dark cliffs, was the scene of the most celebrated of South Wales folk tales.

## LLYN Y FAN FACH: THE FAIRY LAKE

As boys, Father had told us of the farmer's son who was shepherding his flock near the shores of Llyn y Fan Fach on one still summer's day long, long ago. To his surprise, he saw a maiden of supreme beauty rise from the quiet waters of the lake, accompanied by flocks of animals; she sat on a rock, combing her long tresses with a golden comb. He fell madly in love with her, and could think of no better way to win her affection than by offering her the bread his mother had given him for his lunch. She spurned him:

> *Too hard is your bread,*
> *Not by that I'll be fed.*

Day after day he haunted the lake, and day after day the lady appeared, until, at last, the bread he offered suited her taste. She accepted him in marriage, but made one condition: he was never to strike her three times without cause. Gladly he agreed. They were wed, and the marriage turned out to be marvellously happy and successful. He became the richest farmer for miles around.

But inevitably, and without realising it, he did strike her twice without cause. He struck her a third time when she laughed at a funeral. He tapped her lightly on the shoulder. 'Why do you laugh, wife, at such a moment? This is unseemly.' 'I laugh,' she replied, 'because I know the dead man's troubles are over. But, alas, my husband, our troubles are now beginning. This is the third time you have struck me without cause. I must leave you for ever.'

She rose, went back to the farm and called all the animals together—the magnificent cattle, the noble stallions, the sheep with their fine white wool, the goats and every other animal. She climbed up the steep side of the mountain, followed by her despairing husband and her weeping children. Then, with a last reproachful look, and taking all her flocks with her, she sank into the dark waters of the lake, never more to be seen.

Her husband died of a broken heart, but her sons inherited her magical skills. Legend has it that they became the famous Physicians of Myddfai, the most sought-after doctors of medieval Wales. Their descendants continued the long tradition, and the last of them was Sir John Williams, physician to Queen Victoria.

## A LAND OF LEGENDS

DRAWING ON Celtic mythology and Arthurian romance, Welsh legends and folk tales are among the most fascinating in Europe. Fairies appear frequently in Welsh folklore: tales of mortals marrying fairy women may echo the memory of past invasions and the uniting of two cultures. Fairies are also said to appear before a person's death, and are apparently heard making knocking sounds in mines.

The great storehouse of Welsh legends, however, is the *Mabinogion*, a medieval collection of 12 stories translated into English in 1838 by Lady Charlotte Guest. Mixing Celtic motifs with legendary and semi-historical figures, the stories describe love affairs, jealousy and revenge, as

**RIGHT** *A statue of the legendary Welsh wizard Merlin, a central character in Arthurian romance.*

well as dragon-slaying and a magic cauldron that heals wounds. Some tales are set at the court of King Arthur and include an early version of the search for the Holy Grail.

The lack of historical certainty about Arthur—he may have been a 6th-century Briton or Welshman who fought against the Anglo-Saxons—has helped to encourage the many myths about him, for example that he killed a dragon and received mortal wounds on Mount Snowdon. Another intriguing Arthurian character is Merlin—a sage and magician reputedly born in Carmarthen. Medieval writers describe him as the adviser of Uther Pendragon, father of Arthur. Some add a Christian dimension, linking him with the legend of the Holy Grail. In later tradition, it is Merlin who predicts that Uther's successor will be the person who can draw a sword set in a large stone—a prophecy fulfilled by Arthur.

**RIGHT** *Lady Charlotte Guest, who taught herself Welsh and translated the legends of the* Mabinogion.

**ABOVE** *A well-preserved page from a 14th-century manuscript of the* Mabinogion, *written on vellum with scrupulous care.*

This was the story that had attracted Father to write his musical cantata and which was now exercising an equally powerful fascination on his sons. At any rate, it had landed them in the wild country where the River Tawe rises, ready to tramp over every obstacle to reach the mysterious lake from which the maiden rose on that still summer day in the faraway past.

Looking back on it, I am amazed at the casual way in which we left our bicycles on the side of the mountain road over to Trecastle and gaily set off to tramp across the sort of rough, wild country that must be treated with respect even on sunny summer days. On this particular occasion, mists were forming and then fading round the high tops, which made them seem infinitely mysterious and remote—the right atmosphere for the strange lake to which we were about to march.

Our equipment would have horrified any adventure course leader of today. We had no proper boots, no map and no compass. There was no one on the hills to guide us, and I doubt if anyone in Swansea ever made the journey north to walk on the Vans in those days. The sole preparation for our march through the wilderness was a packet of sandwiches prepared by Mother, which we carried in our jacket pockets.

We looked at the nearest peak looming up through the mist and set off for it. We reached the dark lake of Llyn y Fan Fawr (not to be confused with Lyn y Fan Fach, the fairy lake miles away to the west), then climbed up the steep path to the summit of the Carmarthen Van. From there we followed the edge of the escarpment, with the steep rock slides plunging down to the boggy wastes below, while the mists swirled round us. We felt a little frightened at our own daring. We

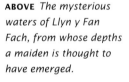

**ABOVE** *The mysterious waters of Llyn y Fan Fach, from whose depths a maiden is thought to have emerged.*

seemed to march for miles, up and down, and then suddenly the mists lifted, and there below us was a dark tarn encircled by strange, layered cliffs of rose-coloured old red sandstone. We clambered carefully down to the water's edge. It didn't seem to matter that the lonely lake had become part of Llanelli's water supply. We looked at the dark surface and secretly hoped that something would stir in the depths.

What did stir, however, was the wind, swirling the mists down and bringing rain. Now we were really frightened. Walking on the Gower cliffs was never like this. We tried to reason things out. We would walk along the foot of the cliff faces and steep slopes until we came back across the big Van lake. If we then followed the stream out of the lake, it would be bound to bring us down to the main Tawe stream. Once there, we could hit the Trecastle road. It was my first lesson in the serious business of walking mountains in safety. I confess that I didn't really enjoy it.

The rain poured down. We were soaked and sodden. Our boots squelched, but the mists lifted occasionally to lure us on. We felt lost and very far from home. Then, at last, the waters of Llyn y Fan Fawr came into sight. We were saved. We got back at last to the Trecastle road and our bicycles. I can still remember the flood of relief that overwhelmed us, and how we got down at last to the Gwyn Arms, where Mrs Rees, who had once served Madame Patti at Craig-y-Nos (the diva was always Madame to Mrs Rees) dried us out before the huge coal fire in the kitchen, while the Welsh hams hung over our heads like gastronomic stalactites.

Perhaps that damp tramp through rain and bog should have quenched all the enthusiasm for mountain exploration that had been stirred by my first view of the great escarpment from the top of Swansea's Guildhall. But somehow, once I was back in the safety of our home, I remembered only the triumph of that walk. After all, we *had* reached the fairy lake and returned soaked but safe. It wasn't long before I was once again bicycling north, but this time with better boots and even a map and compass. I had at least learned something from my first stupidity. The great escarpment had plenty more to offer me.

## LIMESTONE UNDERWORLD

I soon found that there was an underground world in the country round Craig-y-Nos. This whole limestone country is a hollow honeycomb under its rocky surface. Today, the Dan-yr-Ogof show caves are a great tourist attraction, with their underground lakes, glittering stalactites and vast, cathedral-like caverns. As a young man, I felt that I was the only one who dared enter those damp corridors and dripping cracks, hundreds of feet underground.

**BELOW** *Visitors to the great domed chamber of the Dan-yr-Ogof show caves are dwarfed by its proportions.*

I never became a dedicated 'caver'. There seemed so much to see above ground first. Besides, I had no one keen enough to come with me, or experienced enough to initiate me into the complex art of caving. South Wales was not yet on the caving map like Yorkshire, Derbyshire and the Mendips. Years later, members of the South Wales Caving Club showed me exactly how fantastically beautiful is the underground world at the top of the Neath and Swansea valleys. I was equipped with a wet suit, in which I slid down icy water chutes and squeezed through 'letterboxes' and other appropriately named and uncomfortably narrow passages. I often fervently wished myself elsewhere, but I grew to understand the compelling attraction caving can have for the experts.

I came to the business too early. After a short peep, as it were, into these underground excitements, I went back above ground to continue my exploration of the other delights of the great escarpment.

East of the Swansea Valley lay the valley of the Neath, written in Welsh as the Nedd. Again I got a surprise. The Neath Valley, like the Swansea Valley, was industrial in its lower course, but as soon as you came to the Farewell Rock, just north of Glyn Neath, it was farewell to the collieries. Again you entered the clean strange world of limestone; and beyond beckoned the green summits and rose-coloured cliffs of old red sandstone.

The showpiece in the Neath limestone was Porth-yr-Ogof, where the River Mellte flows directly towards the rock and is simply swallowed up in it. When I first saw it, I felt that it was as savage a place as Coleridge's 'deep romantic chasm' in *Kubla Khan*. It's not quite as romantic today since they've built the inevitable car park close at hand and you have only a few yards to walk to see the marvel of Porth-yr-Ogof.

Once the Mellte and the other headwater streams of the Neath reappear after their dive under the limestone, they cut deep, wooded gorges towards the little village of Pont Neath Vaughan. These gorges are filled with the music of constantly falling water. Every little valley has a series of magnificent waterfalls. There may be individual falls in Wales that are higher and grander, but in no area—not even in the justly celebrated Devil's Bridge behind Aberystwyth—will you find such a concentration of delightful falls as in this still unsung moorland at the top of the Vale of Neath.

I find it hard to choose between them. The Middle Clungwyn fall has matchless grace. Sgwd yr Eira—the Fall of Snow—tumbles so far out from its cliff that you can walk behind it. I calculate that you have over a dozen falls to choose from, and the beauty of it is that you have to walk to see every one of them. Maybe this is the only reason why they've preserved their charm.

**BELOW** *A forest path takes walkers behind the waters of Sgwd yr Eira—the Fall of Snow. It is one of many waterfalls that have cut deep, wooded gorges into the Vale of Neath.*

LEFT *The historic town of Brecon on the banks of the Usk, with the snow-capped tops of the Brecon Beacons to the south.*

This is surely true of the whole length of the great escarpment. You can get a general impression of it as you drive up the valley of the Usk from Abergavenny, through the fine old town of Brecon and over to Llandovery in the Tywi Valley. All the way, you see the ramparts of the hills standing in high splendour to the south. And every time I look at them, I feel that somehow they were the mountains of my youth.

## GREAT LITTLE TRAINS

I was born and brought up in the last great days of steam. I still cannot imagine a real train without that most glorious of Victorian artistic creations, the steam engine, at its head, waving its white banner of power as it draws its long line of Great Western Railway coaches over the Brunel-built Landore Viaduct. In Swansea, when I was young, we were all GWR men, although the London, Midland and Scottish crept shamelessly into the town right along the sands of the seafront to Victoria Station.

ABOVE *The coat of arms of the Great Western Railway Company, founded in 1833.*

The GWR's High Street Station had more prestige: from it, the expresses ran all the way to London itself. I even went there myself at last to see the Empire Exhibition at Wembley. I was more impressed, however, by the Severn Tunnel, where the train sank into a deep trench, to be swallowed up by a darkness punctuated only by fires burning in the alcoves along the line to improve the ventilation. I was even more impressed when a portly gentleman in our compartment pulled out his gold hunter watch as we left Wales and entered the tunnel, and then snapped it shut with disgust as we emerged into England. 'Six and a half minutes,' he snorted with disgust. 'Half a minute too long! I'll write to Sir Felix Poole about it.' Sir Felix Poole, General Manager of the GWR! It was as if my portly companion had appealed to Caesar himself!

But then the railways in Wales still had power in the days of my early youth. Buses had penetrated into Gower, and our doctor purred round Swansea, with opulent satisfaction, in the first electric car in Wales. But for us the railway journey was still the crowning excitement of any holiday.

There came a year when the family decided to try fresh fields for the summer vacation, and fixed on Llanwrtyd Wells in mid Wales instead of Gower. There was all the surprise of new country to see as the train left Victoria Station and cleared the old landmarks of Clyne Valley and Pontarddulais to puff its way onwards through the lush, but to us unknown, landscape of the green Tywi Valley.

## THE MIGHTY WELSH DRAGON

VISITORS TO WALES will meet the Welsh dragon—the country's fire-breathing national emblem—almost everywhere they go. Signs bearing its likeness welcome tourists as they cross the border, and it re-appears on all kinds of souvenirs from baseball caps to key rings; it is even available as a fully flameproof soft toy.

Despite its modern-day use as a souvenir motif, the dragon is one of the most ancient symbols in the world. It was introduced to Britain by

the Romans, who used it as a military standard, and both Anglo-Saxons and Welsh adopted the exotic symbol.

Legend tells that the red dragon became the national emblem of Wales when the 5th-century Welsh King Vortigern tried to build a fortress to repel Anglo-Saxon invaders. The wizard Merlin advised him that below the spot he had chosen lay two sleeping beasts—the white dragon of England and the red one of Wales. The King ordered them to be woken, and the animals fought a ferocious battle eventually won by the

**ABOVE** *The coat of arms of King Henry VII featured a red dragon, which he incorporated into the English royal arms.*

red dragon. Merlin interpreted this as a prophecy that the Welsh would one day triumph over the Anglo-Saxons.

The legend was kept alive by the Welsh bards, and could be said to have come true when the Welshman Henry Tudor, who took the red dragon as his badge, ascended the English throne in 1485 and incorporated his emblem into the royal arms. In 1901 the dragon officially became the badge of Wales, and in 1959 a red dragon on a white-over-green background became the national flag that can be seen flying proudly over the land today.

**LEFT** *The red dragon, evocative emblem of Wales, appears on the national flag and is held in affection by Welsh people worldwide.*

At Llandeilo, we had the usual moment of shattering anxiety which always accompanied travel with Father.

He was a charmingly absent-minded man, and at Llandeilo station suddenly discovered he had forgotten to buy the morning paper. He casually got out, strolled down the platform and disappeared from view. The whistle blew, the train moved off. My brothers and I felt utterly lost, abandoned, cast away on a mobile desert island, puffing out into an unknown, dangerous and fatherless future. Then Father reappeared in the corridor, having calmly got in at the last door of the last carriage as the train slowly pulled out of the station.

All our anxieties disappeared as the railway line climbed into the green, lonely hills of mid Wales. We leaned out of the window to watch the engine puffing its clouds of steam as it took us across Cynghordy Viaduct and on into the tunnel under the strange, pointed little peak of the Sugar Loaf. We emerged into the crisp, invigorating moorland air to look out for our boarding house, 'Laswade'. It stood on the wooded slope near the railway line, and the proprietor hoisted a Welsh dragon flag on the flagpole at the bottom of the garden to herald our approach. The train was honoured in those days, for where would the mid Wales spas have been without it?

These remarkable oases of curiously smelling waters still retain traces of their discreet late Victorian and Edwardian gentility, although their full glories have somewhat faded—as have the glories of the railways that created them.

The two 'Wellses' were rather distrustful of each other in the days when we first went there. Llanwrtyd was, perhaps, more Nonconformist, more Welsh, more homely than its rival, Llandrindod. 'Llan-dod' was Church of England (no Church in Wales in those days). The golf course was bigger. The hotels were grander, with cast iron curlicues on the balconies. Llandrindod appealed to the valetudinarians of Birmingham and the Midlands, while visitors to Llanwrtyd remained obstinately Welsh. Both sets of visitors, however, quaffed their waters with long-established ritual and took stately walks to the Pump House where the orchestra played under the palms of the Winter Gardens.

Nowadays—in Llanwrtyd at any rate—some of the sulphur waters run from neglected springs, and no one comes to 'take the chillybeat', as the locals used to say.

At the age of ten, we boys were too young to appreciate the subtle charms of 'taking the waters'. We hankered after Gower and the sea. But the railway journey to Llanwrtyd was another matter. We relished every mile of it, and I am sure it was the foundation of my lifelong fascination with the railway train. Later I came to realise how lucky the railway fan was who had been born in South Wales.

As coal mining developed in the 1800s, the mineral and passenger lines pushed their way up into the maze of narrow and lucrative valleys in the mountains behind Cardiff, Newport and Swansea. The engineers triumphed over formidable natural obstacles. Viaducts—bold, soaring structures which pushed brick and stone to the limit—leapt over every valley. The graceful series at the top of the Taff Valley behind Merthyr still survives, although the sad decline of coal between the wars put paid to so many of them, including the most remarkable of them all, the dizzy cast iron cobweb of Crumlin.

**ABOVE** *A 1930s railway poster, advertising the spa town of Llandrindod Wells to the city folk of Britain.*

## BIG BANG

I must confess that I had a hand in the destruction of one of the most solidly built of the South Wales viaducts, at Llanbradach, behind Caerphilly. My excuse must be that I had just joined the BBC in Wales, and therefore didn't quite know what I was doing. In 1937 I was eager to make my mark as a promising young commentator. The demolition experts proposed to drop all the pillars of the viaduct in one fell stroke. This was to be the most violent explosion in the Valleys since the Chartist riots of 1839.

I persuaded the BBC to bill it in the *Radio Times* under the title 'Big Bang'. The moment came, and I had half of Britain listening. I ransacked the dictionary for florid prose to build up the excitement. Down went the plunger, and a huge chunk of the railway age disappeared into dust before my eyes. I rushed back to the studio in a triumph that lasted barely as long as the explosion.

I was new to the business and hadn't realised one important thing. All the sound engineers between me and the transmitters had to guard themselves against the responsibility of blowing the transmitters off the air. Acting on that great

## THE CHARTIST MOVEMENT

WHILE THE NEWLY INDUSTRIALISED Britain of the 19th century generated vast wealth for a lucky few, the disenfranchised poor—even those with jobs—lived and worked in appalling conditions, suffering hunger and hardship.

In 1838 protest groups published the People's Charter. This was a petition listing six demands, including the vote for all men, payment for MPs and—the only demand of theirs that subsequent history has failed to meet—annual elections. For the next 10 years, Chartism played a prominent role in British political life, but although Chartist pressure helped bring about some economic reform, the six demands were not met. Three times—in 1839, 1842 and 1848—the Charter was presented to Parliament and duly rejected; each time strikes or riots ensued.

One of the worst outbreaks of violence took place in Wales during the 'Newport rising' of November 1839. Over 5,000 miners and ironworkers marched on the town and were met with a hail of gunfire from troops. About 22 protesters were killed, and the insurrection dispersed in disarray. The leaders were condemned to death for treason, though the sentences were later commuted to imprisonment or transportation.

After 1848 Chartism declined. The police, alarmed by revolutionary activities on the Continent, were quick to suppress disturbances. Besides, working conditions had already improved, thanks to more effective laws. Working class activists now turned to Liberal politics or trade unions and Chartism faded away, though its spirit eventually triumphed in later decades.

**LEFT** *In 1839 several thousand angry workers marched on Newport to be met by bullets fired from the Westgate Hotel.*

principle of sound engineers the world over—'It's all right leaving me, boss'—each one turned the tone down a little bit in anticipation of the devastating wave of sound I had forecast as the plunger went in. The result? The Big Bang came out at the other end like the popping of a champagne cork.

Well, perhaps there is something symbolic in this. The railway glories of South Wales didn't exactly end with a bang. They seem to have seeped away almost before we realised what was happening. And—final irony—the great steam engines, the masterpieces of the great railway engineers of the 1930s, were deposed by the diesel monsters and quickly shunted to the graveyard of steam at Barry Dock, only twenty-five miles from the spot where the first steam-drawn train in the world began its triumphant course.

## PIONEERS OF STEAM

Many people still seem to think that George Stephenson's *Rocket* was the world's first practical steam engine, but that honour must go to the creation of a remarkable Cornishman, Richard Trevithick. The place where it all happened was not at the Rainhill trials between Liverpool and Manchester, but on the Pen y Darren tramroad in the Taff Valley, and the important date is not 1829 but 1804.

I recently walked the length of the Pen y Darren tramroad with Richard Keen of the Department of Industry in the National Museum of Wales. Never was a man more aptly named. He has a burning enthusiasm for the remains of the early industrial development of Wales and can extract romance from every broken furnace wall at Blaina and every iron girder lying rusting among the nettles on some neglected coal tip in the Rhondda.

Standing before the monument to the early coal pioneers Robert and Lucy Thomas—a sort of deliciously ornate cast iron umbrella—Richard painted in the background of Trevithick's great adventure. His progressive patron, the ironmaster Samuel Homfray, had placed a bet with his rival, Richard Crawshay, that Trevithick's engine would draw ten tons of iron along the tramway from Pen y Darren to Abercynon. The trial was fixed for February 12, and Merthyr had never seen such an exciting day. The whole of South Wales seemed to have turned up to line the track.

You can still walk along the route of the first train in the world. With Richard Keen, I peered into the dark tunnel where Richard Trevithick had trouble with the smoke stack of his engine. We recaptured the thrill of the seventy people who were brave enough to sit on the trucks and thus become the world's first railway passengers. There is a splendidly emotional account of that first run:

> On the locomotive, stern-faced but hopeful, was Richard Trevithick. His fortunes hung on this venture: the puffing steed might soar with him into immortality. And there stood William Richards, the driver, anxious for the signal; and the Homfrays and Crawshays too…The signal was given, a jet of steam burst forth, the wheels revolved with a hideous clang and slowly the mass moved.

BELOW *A model of the first steam engine to run on rails, designed by Cornishman Richard Trevithick. It was unveiled in 1804, when it hauled 10 tons of iron along a length of tramway in South Wales.*

So the railway age began in this remote industrial valley in South Wales. I have on my desk to this day a spike that held one of the rails. The valley is strangely quiet now. The steam era was fuelled by coal, and who wants South Wales steam coal these days? Yet, as the romance of steam faded in South Wales, it began again in the north. The Great Little Trains started their run into the hearts of every visitor.

The slate industry entered its heyday when the big industrial towns of the Midlands and the North of England began their astonishing mid 19th-century expansion. Slates were needed for the thousands of new Coronation Streets. The quarries of North Wales lay high among wild hills, and this made normal railway construction impossibly costly.

The railway engineers rose to the challenge. They produced a special breed of small engine, little boilerfuls of sheer power. On the Ffestiniog line, you could admire *Taliesin*—the wonderful Fairlie-designed engine which seemed to be facing both ways with equally determined energy—in action. It took the long loads of little wagons round astonishing curves among the crags—so astonishing,

## SNOWDONIA SLATE

DURABLE, VERSATILE and easily quarried, Welsh slate has for centuries found favour with builders. Way back in Roman times, the occupying forces used local slate to roof their garrison at Caernarfon, and in the Middle Ages Edward I incorporated it into his magnificent castles.

In Snowdonia lies a vast seam of slate, in places 1,000 feet thick, derived from ancient deposits of muddy clay or volcanic ash. Systematic exploitation began only in the late 18th century, in the Elidir vicinity. In particular, the English landowner Richard Pennant (later Baron Penrhyn) developed an efficient operation on the Penrhyn estate, with its own tramway, quay and factory near Bangor, and a workers' village, Bethesda. The open-cast quarrying there gouged a 1,100-foot-high amphitheatre into the mountain side. In the Ffestiniog vicinity to the south, by contrast, deep-mining techniques were needed—tunnels and shafts and candlelit caverns.

Production surged during the 19th century, with increased demand for school slates and roof tiles. The peak year was 1898, but a strike at Bethesda in 1900 prompted a three-year lockout. Thousands of slate workers headed for South Wales to become coal miners, and the industry never really recovered.

Today it sustains barely 500 workers, meeting a much-changed demand: plaques and fireplaces; specialist floor tiles; slate fragments for road

building; slate dust for the paint and cosmetics industries. One of the main customers today is the tourist, visiting surviving factories or the Welsh Slate Museum at Llanberis, and riding on narrow-gauge steam trains once reserved for slate slabs and quarry workers.

**LEFT** *A craftsman at the Welsh Slate Museum in Llanberis splits slate with the deft skill of his forebears.*

**ABOVE** *The multi-tiered amphitheatre of Penrhyn Quarry, as depicted by Henry Hawkins in 1832.*

indeed, that they inspired a popular series of tourist postcards, which you can still pick up in North Wales if you are lucky. They show a 'Stiniog train bending round a precipice like a serpent, while the guard in the van at the back shakes hands with the driver of *Taliesin* at the front. At points on this surprising line of Ffestiniog, the postcard didn't seem so far from the truth.

Sadly, the slate industry, like coal mining, declined between the wars. The great quarries fell silent. The quarry men ceased to tramp on cold, damp mornings up the thousands of feet of steep inclines to hang onto the plunging, man-made cliffs. The little lads of fourteen no longer walked to their first day's work slightly embarrassed by the creaking sound of their new corduroys which showed them up as mere beginners. A whole way of life came to an end. The huge crags and caverns that the quarry men had carved in the living rock of the mountains for over 150 years took on a new, strange beauty of their own in the silence that had now returned to the hills.

## RESURRECTION OF STEAM

As the quarries died, so the little trains died with them. I remember walking in the rain in the summer of 1951 through the Porthmadog terminus of the Ffestiniog Railway, among the rusting rails and broken little slate wagons, and lamenting the passing of steam from the hills. I was wrong. The railway enthusiasts now stepped in, those highly practical dreamers from the Midlands and the industrial North who were determined that the Great Little Trains of Wales should continue to run.

I have watched them give their voluntary services at weekends, tackling the rough business of track laying, and in the end carrying the little trains back to where they were born in the quarries behind Blaina and Abergynolwyn. It has been the same on the Welshpool Railway and certainly at Bala, which my friend Mr Barnes seemed to run almost single-handed: he was signalman, guard, ticket-collector and driver all rolled into one. When I saw the sheer pleasure on his face as he gave the 'Right away' to one of his trains, I wondered if the Great Little Trains of Wales were not offering us a new conception of how we should approach our work.

Make no mistake, however. The Great Little Trains are run with complete professional skill and business acumen. It's just that the spirit of those who run them seems so refreshingly different.

**ABOVE** *A replica steam engine, named after David Lloyd George, is serviced at Porthmadog, near the home of its late namesake. The Ffestiniog Railway, which once transported slate from the mountainous quarries of North Wales, is the oldest independent rail company in the world.*

Enjoy the magnificent scenery of the RHEIDOL VALLEY from the miniature trains on British Railways' only narrow gauge passenger line. No visit to Aberystwyth is complete without seeing Devil's Bridge.

**CHEAP DAY TICKETS**
EVERY DAY BY ANY TRAIN
RETURN 2/9 FARE

**SPECIAL CHEAP EVENING TICKETS**
Tuesdays, Wednesdays and Thursdays, 19th July to 25th August
RETURN 2/- FARE

BRITISH RAILWAYS

**LEFT** *An old British Railways poster, advertising the spectacular 11-mile journey from Aberystwyth to Devil's Bridge. This line once served Rheidol Valley's lead mines.*

**BELOW** *Visitors enjoy a ride by steam train on the narrow-gauge Bala Lake Railway, which travels the shores of Wales's largest natural lake.*

**LEFT** *A 1930 monogram of the Brecon and Merthyr Railway Company, which was established to link the hills between Brecon and Dowlais.*

I find it hard to pick my favourite among them. I am naturally drawn to the Talyllyn since I had the honour of opening its new extension, which takes the line up to a dramatic view over the Cadair Idris range. But every company has its own individual character. It reminds me of the day when, as little boys, my brothers and I sat on a seat in Brecon station and puzzled over the inscription 'B & MR' (Brecon and Merthyr Railway). A friendly porter stopped and told us, 'Never forget: B & MR stands for Best and Most Respected.' The Great Little Trains of Wales retain that old-fashioned but touching pride in themselves.

The Ffestiniog and Talyllyn railways stage high-class drama as they twist and turn on the narrow ledges that seem to emphasise the daring of the trains. The Rheidol Valley seems a 19th-century romantic, puffing up to the stunning water-falls of Devil's Bridge. The Llanberis Lake and Bala Lake lines are idyllic as they move beside the still waters. The Welshpool & Llanfair is pastoral among the low, green hills and meadows of the old county of Montgomery.

As for the Snowdon Mountain Railway, let me make a confession. In my youthful, rock-climbing days on the hills, I regarded it as a monstrous device for dumping on the sacred mountain top tourists who were too lazy to make the effort to climb it. I used to anathematise the train from the dizzy foothold on which I was balancing high up on the stern face of Crib-y-Ddysgl, as we heard it panting above the great hollow of Cwm Glas Mawr. We quoted, with a learned fury, Matthew Arnold's lines in 'Empedocles on Etna':

*They are lost in the hollows!*
*They stream up again!*
*What seeks on this mountain*
*The glorified train?*

But how age mellows and experience soothes! I now feel that the Snowdon Mountain train is a glorious train indeed: the only rack railway in Britain and, without question, the most sensational steam-powered ride in these islands.

For many years, this resurrection of steam took place only in North Wales. As a South Walian, I was therefore delighted to be invited to become a director of the Gwili Railway, where a group of enthusiasts are restoring part of the delightful line that once ran from Carmarthen to Pencader through a deep, wooded defile of rare beauty. We can boast that we are the only railway in Wales with a special membership scheme that includes fishing rights.

So the Great Little Trains of Wales puff happily away among the hills, making everybody associated with them happy, too. Can you say that about any other industrial activity?

Let me not forget, however, that the first railway that fascinated me in Wales is still there. The Mid Wales line no longer runs into Swansea, but the trains still rumble over Cynghordy Viaduct and disappear into the Sugar Loaf Tunnel. Only one thing seems to have changed with the passing years: myself!

**ABOVE** *The Snowdon Mountain Railway provides an effortless route to the mist-shrouded summit of Wales's highest mountain.*

# CHAPTER THREE

# CASTLES, ISLANDS AND POETS

MUCH AS I MIGHT HAVE WISHED TO, I couldn't spend all my spare time bicycling up to Llyn y Fan Fach or exploring the Brecon Beacons. After I had taken all the usual examination hurdles, the time arrived to prepare for that scholarship Dr Owen had promised my father should be mine if I worked hard enough. I was entered for a history scholarship at Father's old college, Exeter College, Oxford.

I confess I chose history because it seemed the easiest subject of them all. I am a hopeless mathematician. I nearly blew up the school lab in chemistry—science was clearly not my forte. Over, then, to the arts; and of all the arts subjects, history seemed to me to be the most entertaining—a sort of endless novel, full of marvellous stories and delicious scandals from the past. I threw myself into the study of the subject with enthusiasm. But when I look back on that period, I notice one peculiar thing. I tackled the history of every country but my own. Nobody, in those far-off days, ever suggested that a Welsh schoolboy should first learn the history of Wales.

At the school I went to, we knew all about King Alfred burning the cakes and King Robert the Bruce watching the spider, but no one taught us the names of the early princes of Wales. When I try to sum up my knowledge of Welsh history before I went to the grammar school, I suspect it was about as extensive and as accurate as that of the average English visitor taking his first holiday in Pembrokeshire or Anglesey. We'd heard about St David, for he was our patron saint, but we were a little uncertain about when exactly he'd lived in the misty past—probably at the same time as King Arthur and Merlin. We knew that Edward I had defeated the last native prince of Wales and built many marvellous castles. Then came a complete blank until Henry Tudor marched to Bosworth Field and became the first Welshman to sit on the English throne. Then another blank until a mysterious affair called the Methodist Revival, and David Lloyd George appeared to win the First World War. After which we all fervently sang '*Hen Wlad fy Nhadau*'—'Land of My Fathers'.

From this happy, chaotic ignorance I was delivered by my new history master as we jointly prepared for my scholarship ordeal. He didn't teach me any Welsh history, but he gave me a bit of advice that set me off on the trail of my Celtic past: 'If you want your history to come to life, go to the places where it actually happened.' How vivid the murder of Thomas à Becket becomes when you stand on the very spot in Canterbury Cathedral where Henry II's armed knights struck him down. You feel that you are almost taking part in the trial of Charles I when you look down on the bronze plaque set in the floor of Westminster Hall, under that superb hammerbeam roof.

But where could I go from Swansea to immerse myself physically in the past? Wales, I must admit, hasn't any cathedrals that can compare with the rich splendours

## ST DAVID, PATRON SAINT OF WALES

EVERY YEAR ON MARCH 1, Welsh people celebrate the feast day of St David, their patron saint. Festivities include gala dinners and eisteddfods, and the wearing of leeks and daffodils, traditional Welsh emblems. Some people also dress up in national costume—complete with scarlet shawls, white lace caps and tall, black felt hats for the women. It is unlikely, however, that St David himself would have enjoyed his own feast day: nicknamed the 'Water-Drinker', he was a teetotal vegetarian—indeed his weakness for leeks is said to have inspired their adoption as the national symbol.

St David was probably born in Cardigan in the late 5th or early 6th century. He founded a number of monasteries, including one at Menevia—now St David's. In about 550 he preached at the Synod of Brefi, where, as the legend goes, the ground rose beneath him to form an ideal platform. It was after this that he became primate of Wales and made

Menevia his see. He continued to exert a strong influence on Welsh Christianity until his death at Menevia in 589 or 601—a fact borne out by the existence of more than 50 churches in Wales named after him.

In medieval times, the saint's shrine at St David's Cathedral became an important pilgrimage centre. The cathedral itself dates from the late 1100s and was built on the site of St David's old monastery. Its plain sandstone exterior belies the wealth of decorative features—most notably the ornate nave ceiling—that continue to draw modern pilgrims to its sacred space.

**LEFT** *A Welsh girl wearing national costume and holding daffodils, a tradition of St David's Day.*

**RIGHT** *This ornate page from Hastings Hours (c.1480) shows St David reading the liturgy.*

of Canterbury. Our monasteries—with the exception of Tintern, which is just inside our border—do not rival Fountains or Rievaulx. Cardiff, although it has its fine moments, isn't quite in the same class as Edinburgh when it comes to capital cities. But then, what capital is?

We have one architectural trick, however, that we can play with confidence. When it comes to castles, Wales scoops the kitty. The Principality must be the most 'becastled' part of Britain. Only Northumberland and the Scottish Borders can come near it. My own home town of Swansea had ten fine castles within easy bicycling distance. We even had one in the centre of the town itself.

True, in my youth we couldn't see it properly. The local newspaper had built offices right in the middle of it. The *Cambrian Daily Leader* was Swansea's Liberal standard-bearer, and Lloyd George's star was in the ascendant. So it didn't matter if the presses of progress shook to pieces the ancient walls that were the centuries-old symbols of reaction and repression. Fortunately, Swansea Castle survived both the *Cambrian Daily Leader* and the German Blitz. Like so many other castles in Wales, it was rescued from neglect by the Department of the Environment. We can admire again the elegant arcading with which Bishop Henry de Gower decorated the keep in the early 14th century.

**ABOVE** *The elegant arcading of Swansea's 11th-century castle, situated in the heart of the city.*

I managed to visit most of the castles round Swansea. I thought the most thrilling of them was undoubtedly Carreg Cennen, a breathtaking fortress perched on a limestone crag on the western end of the great escarpment behind Llandeilo. It looked exactly like the castles you see in medieval illuminated manuscripts. To complete its excitements, it has a long passage carved deep in the rock, running from the castle walls to a secret well.

As I prowled among the ruins (and many of them really were ruinous and ivy-covered in those days), I couldn't help wondering why Wales had so many castles. The answer was easy. In spite of its mountains, Wales was always wide open to any determined invader. If you look at the map, you'll see that a whole series of wide valleys—the Usk, the Wye, the Severn and the Dee—lead right into the heart of the hills. Wales has no mountain barrier to compare with the southern uplands of Scotland. All her mountains go the wrong way—a point not lost for a moment on those professional invaders, the Normans.

## NORMAN INVASION

Since my bicycling days, I've always thought that it adds enormously to the pleasure of a visit to a Welsh castle if you know a little bit about how and why it was built. I once came across a very pleasant-looking man who was quietly stroking the stones in the upper ward of Caernarfon Castle. He turned out to be a builder, and he kept murmuring as he touched the stones, 'Beautiful. Beautiful. Lovely workmanship.' Then he looked up at me and said, 'You wouldn't get work like this today even if you paid for it.' And he added wistfully, 'No, there's no overtime in those stones.'

**OPPOSITE** *Carreg Cennen, near Llandeilo, is arguably the most spectacularly situated of Wales's castles, with steep crags on three sides falling 300 feet to the River Cennen at the foot of the ravine.*

Well, when it came to acquiring someone else's land, I'm sure that the Normans never bothered with overtime either. Although 1066 was one of those dates they dinned into us at school, I suppose that in essence it is an English date. The Welsh may even have rejoiced over the death of Harold at Hastings, for he had been a sore trial to them in his day. They shouted too soon. Wales never had its own Battle of Hastings, for William the Conqueror had his hands full with England after that illegal joint-stock promotion, that giant smash-and-grab raid that historians have dignified with the title of the Norman Conquest. But he invited a group of powerful barons who had been his partners in the enterprise to settle along the Welsh border. He gave them special privileges as Marcher Lords and told them, in effect: 'I don't care what you do as long as you keep those damned Welsh quiet.' What the barons naturally did was to seize all the Welsh land they could lay their hands on.

The Norman conquest of Wales was thus a long, drawn-out affair, with those bold, harsh border barons gnawing their way steadily forward along the coastline and up the river valleys of the southern section of the country. The gnawing process lasted nearly 100 years.

## THE MARCHER LORDS

LEFT *Earl Gilbert the Red (after his hair colour) was a 13th-century Marcher Lord who wielded great influence under Henry III.*

FOR MORE THAN 400 YEARS, from the late 11th century, Welsh politics and society were shaped by successive generations of Anglo-Norman barons known as Marcher Lords—because their original estates lay along the Welsh–English 'march', or border.

The first Marcher Lordships were created by William I, who, after his victory over the English in 1066, decided to annex Wales by placing powerful subordinates along the border. Although these first lords—the Earls of Chester, Shrewsbury and Hereford—gained some ground in Wales, it took a new wave of barons to conquer territory in Gwent, Dyfed and elsewhere.

By 1100 Marcher Lords had established themselves in the south of the country, mainly in low-lying fertile areas, leaving the northwest and the more barren hill country to the Welsh. For four centuries, Welsh politics would be dominated by power struggles and alliances between the Lords, the Welsh nobles and the English King. This situation arose because the Lords, being remote from the English court, were virtually independent of the Crown: they built castles, established towns, raised armies and even administered their own system of justice. And some of them increased their power base by marrying into the Welsh aristocracy.

The Marcher Lords more or less kept their power after Edward I's successful invasion of Wales during the late 13th century. They also survived Owain Glyndwr's uprising in the early 15th century and the Wars of the Roses (1455–85), in which the Welsh generally supported the House of Lancaster. But their luck changed with the accession of the Tudor kings: between 1536 and 1543 Henry VIII's Acts of Union joined Wales and England together, abolished the Marcher Lords' privileges and turned their lands into shires.

**RIGHT** *Eleventh-century Chepstow Castle boasts what is thought to be the first stone keep built in Wales.*

**BELOW** *This detail from the Bayeux Tapestry illustrates the building of a motte and bailey in the 11th century.*

Why couldn't the Welsh stop them? Well, the Normans had two military tricks up their sleeves that the Welsh at first found impossible to counter. They were heavily armed horsemen, whose charge, as one chronicler declared, 'could make a hole in the walls of Babylon'. And they could build castles. After the charge of the horsemen had driven the lightly armed Welsh from the field, the leaders immediately organised the building of a castle—or, rather, they threw one up.

I use the words 'throw up' advisedly, for these first castles did not for a moment resemble those marvellous structures of stone towers, battlements and drawbridges that we now admire in Wales from Kidwelly to Caernarfon. They were of the type known as a motte and bailey.

They were easily constructed, too. You simply rounded up a group of reluctant peasants and forced them to dig a circular earthwork and crown it with a high wooden palisade. You piled up a high mound in one corner and put a watchtower on it. If the enemy broke into the bailey, this tower would be the final refuge. Within a week, the motte and bailey could be in business.

In time, the Welsh discovered how to burn them, or to force an entry at the weakest point—the gateway—with a battering ram. The Normans replied by rebuilding the palisade in stone, flanked with towers. Instead of the motte, they constructed the strongest tower of all, the keep. At Chepstow, you can see what is probably the first keep built in South Wales, and at Pembroke the finest: the great round keep of William Marshal, nearly 100 feet high. And very strong and dominating it looks.

The Normans, by the way, called these structures not keeps but donjons. 'Keep' was a word invented by antiquaries in the 16th century. The French word *donjon*, which was applied to the whole building, came to be transferred in English to the lowest of the rooms of the keep, now called the dungeon.

No matter by what name you called it, the keep (or donjon) must have been damnably uncomfortable to live in. As for the sanitary arrangements, they must

# THE CASTLE—A FORMIDABLE STRONGHOLD

WALES HAS MORE CASTLES per square mile than any other country in Europe. When the Normans began to annex the country in the late 11th century they built castles consisting of a motte (a mound surrounded by a ditch and topped by a wooden tower) linked to a bailey (an outer enclosure ringed by a palisade). In times of attack, defenders retreated to the motte, from where they had an all-round field of fire. During the 12th century these castles became more formidable as stone keeps replaced the towers and stone 'curtain' walls enclosed the baileys.

In the Middle Ages, anyone setting out to besiege a stone castle would first announce his intention to do so—and if no surrender was forthcoming, the siege would begin. The gatehouse was the castle's weakest point, and the besieging army would try to force an entry with a battering ram. Alternatively, men would tunnel under the walls and light fires to weaken the foundations, or attempt to scale the

parapets with ladders. Once a route into the interior had been found, the keep would be bombarded with missiles from siege engines—heavy stone-throwing catapults or slings known as trebuchets and mangonels, positioned outside the castle walls.

As methods of attack became more sophisticated, so castles continued to evolve. Round towers were added to curtain walls; ditches were widened into water-filled moats traversed by drawbridges; walls were

*LEFT A late 15th-century manuscript shows attackers besieging a moated castle. The unfortunate medieval soldier, wearing heavy armour and carrying a sword, had to scale the castle walls by ladder.*

built with projecting galleries called machicolations, from which missiles could be dropped on attackers; and gatehouse floors were fitted with 'murder holes' through which boiling oil was poured on besiegers or water on burning gates. Bowmen shot at the invaders through arrow slits in the walls.

In Wales these innovations were found in the castles of Edward I, whose campaign to crush the Welsh in the late 13th century produced an ambitious building programme. His concentric castles had buttressed walls, access to the sea so that they were difficult to starve out, and water defences making tunnelling impossible. In these strongholds the art of defence reached its medieval zenith.

**BELOW** *This gateway at Beaumaris Castle has built-in machicolations— galleries from which missiles were dropped.*

**ABOVE** *Arrow slits (this one is at Conwy Castle) enabled archers to fire at invaders without being too vulnerable to attack themselves.*

**RIGHT** *The trebuchet, a type of siege engine, was used to hurl projectiles such as stone balls or even severed enemy heads over castle walls.*

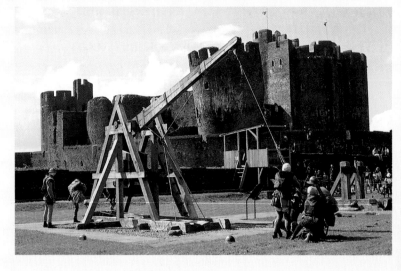

have resembled those of the tower I stayed in at Shibām, a walled city in southern Arabia. Until recently, life here proceeded at a medieval pace.

My host had been lavish in his hospitality when I indicated, as far as I was able with my limited words of Arabic, that I felt the need to make a necessary retirement. The sheik clapped his hands and a servant appeared. He led me up a narrow, winding stairway, until we emerged into the dazzling sunlight of the roof. A row of hunting hawks decorated the battlements, guarded by white-robed retainers. My guide indicated a structure set among the hawks. I entered and looked down. A deep shaft dropped the whole length of the tower to a patch of light at the bottom. As I looked, another servant appeared far below, placed a large bronze bowl at the bottom of the shaft, gave me a friendly wave of encouragement and retired. Clearly, the sanitary arrangements were based on what you might call the long drop system.

The garderobes or privies remained a great problem in castles and walled towns throughout the Middle Ages. Edward I's architect adopted a bold solution when he built the town walls of Conwy. He set up a row of garderobes all along the top of one section of the walls. They still stand there, the highest row of public lavatories in Europe.

## THE CONCENTRIC CASTLE

As the keeps became uncomfortable and the attackers developed more powerful assault weapons, including the great slings of the trebuchet and the mangonel, the stage was set for another advance in the art of defence. So the final phase in the development of the castle is reached.

I wish I could claim that the concentric idea was developed in South Wales. The Welsh can be proud of the fact that the longbow began its remarkable career in Gwent, for how could Crécy and Agincourt have been won without the Welsh bowmen? It was all very well for Henry V to shout, 'On, on, ye noble English', but he relied on his Welsh bowmen to fire into the French knights at machine-gun speed and knock them flat in their armour. To this day, the Society of the Black Hundred, descendants of the Welsh bowmen who fought with the Black Prince at Crécy and Poitiers, hold their annual celebration in the little hilltop town of Llantrisant in the Vale of Glamorgan. I have had the honour of being their guest, and fell before their magnificent hospitality with the speed of the French nobility before their ancestors' arrows.

The concentric castle, however, could defy any Welsh bowman, or any mangonel or trebuchet for that matter. Like all brilliant ideas, the concept was simple in essence. You put one circuit of castle walls inside the other. The inner circuit consisted of higher walls than the outer one and was a sort of giant keep in its own right. If the attackers succeeded in getting over the outer wall at any point, they found themselves in a sort of killing ground between the walls. Surround the whole thing with a series of wide moats and you had the nearest thing to an impregnable castle ever produced in the Middle Ages.

The idea may have come to Europe from the East after the Crusades. The Marcher Lords of South Wales, always in the market for the latest fashion in fortification,

ABOVE *Caerphilly Castle, with its inner and outer walls and huge double moat, occupies over 30 acres and was the first concentric castle to be built in Britain.*

adopted it with enthusiasm. At Caerphilly, young Gilbert de Clare put all his money into it and created a masterpiece of concentric construction, the largest castle of its kind in Wales.

Naturally, I bicycled off to see it in my castle-watching, pre-exam period. I knew Caerphilly in those days only from the name of a cheese—that soft, crumbling delicacy that I used to relish as a boy. It was never made in bulk in Caerphilly itself. The farmers of the Vale of Glamorgan used to bring it to market there, and it was sold as a vital ingredient for the food tin the miners took to work with them. It was supposed to give added strength to the miners' muscles when they worked underground. Like so many other pleasures, it disappeared after the First World War. The mass-produced compound that now calls itself Caerphilly has nothing to do with the town, with Wales or with the original taste.

Although I bought no cheese there, I was overwhelmed by the castle, with its barbican, its inner and outer moats, its gatehouses and the vast platforms that held back the water. No wonder Tennyson exclaimed, when he saw it: 'This isn't a castle. It's a whole ruined town!' I'm always amazed that it's not among the major tourist attractions of Wales. It is a mere seven miles from Cardiff, and the journey across Caerphilly Mountain opens up fine views northwards over the coalfield hills. That may be the snag. The word 'coalfield' frightens people off, although there are no coal pits nearby. Take courage and go to see it.

But why did Gilbert de Clare feel the need to build such a monster when the local Welshmen had been firmly confined to the local hills? For the first time, we must look north to Gwynedd, Anglesey and Snowdonia.

## REFUGE BEYOND THE ROOF OF WALES

The Normans had naturally tried to overrun North Wales as they had the South, and for a short time they met with success. Then the Welsh turned and threw them out. How did the North Walians succeed where the South Walians failed? As a South Walian I must be careful what I say. I am not belittling the courage of the men of Gwynedd for one moment, but they had one advantage denied to Gwent or Dyfed. They had a sure-fire natural refuge to which they could retreat.

The River Conwy runs from south to north, and behind it stand the 3,000-foot mountains of the Carneddau, like a rocky rampart stopping all passage further west. Even today, the road and railway have to tunnel to get past them. In the 18th century, this narrow path between rocks and the sea was a source of horror to the unhappy traveller to Ireland via Holyhead. Coaches had to be dismantled and carried over the crags by sturdy peasants. When I did my walk across the 'Roof of Wales' for the BBC, I ended it by coming down over the rocks of Penmaenmawr. I know exactly how those sturdy peasants felt!

Beyond the mountains, and completely protected by them, lies the fertile island of Anglesey, with its cornfields and black cattle. No wonder they called it Môn, Mam Cymru—Anglesey, the Mother of Wales.

**BELOW** *Anglesey has historically been a safe haven. Its lush pastures, seen here in the foreground, are protected by the Menai Strait (nowadays forded by Thomas Telford's famous bridge) and by the great wall of the Carneddau Range.*

This ultimate refuge, this natural keep, enabled the princes of Gwynedd to maintain their independence in North Wales, and even to extend their rule into parts of the South. The two greatest of them, Llywelyn ap Iorwerth and Llywelyn ap Gruffydd, dominated Wales throughout most of the 13th century. They showed what the Welsh could have achieved if left to develop on their own. This was one of the great periods of Welsh literature, with the monasteries producing their most important chronicles. Meanwhile, the princes lived in considerable splendour in the nobly carved wooden hall in their palace at Aberffraw in Anglesey.

The Llywelyns took a leaf out of the Marcher Lords' book: they, too, built castles. They didn't have the cash to build a series of Caerphillys, but they constructed those romantic towers of Dolbadarn and Dolwyddelan, so beloved by architects and photographers. The most interesting of the Welsh castles, to my mind, is Ewloe, tucked away in a hollow off the main road between Hawarden and Northop in the county of Clwyd. It was built by Llywelyn ap Iorwerth and added to by his grandson Llywelyn ap Gruffydd, the last and, for a few brief years, the most successful of the native princes.

He had his moment of glory when Henry III ruled in England. By the Treaty of Montgomery in 1267, Llywelyn became ruler of nearly the whole of Wales; with his boundaries touching the Clare lands to the south, it was no wonder that Gilbert de Clare hurried on with the building of Caerphilly. Incidentally, Llywelyn ap Gruffydd was the first native prince who actually used the title Prince of Wales. He was unlucky enough to come up against one of the toughest and most competent of the medieval kings of England, Edward I.

## EDWARD I'S STRANGLEHOLD

I admit I don't warm naturally to Edward. He was certainly a great soldier and a brilliant administrator. Perhaps this last quality was the cause of the trouble: he had a bureaucrat's mind. I can picture him at a meeting of his council pursing his lips and muttering, 'We'll have to finish off this Principality of Wales. It's administratively untidy.'

In two brilliantly organised campaigns, he did finish off Wales. He overcame the natural fortress of Gwynedd by sending the fleet of the Cinque Ports to sail up the Menai Strait and cut Anglesey off from Snowdonia. Llywelyn tried to wriggle out of the trap. He crossed the mountains to raise help in the South, but he was caught near Builth in 1282. The court poets cried in their despair during that wintry December:

> O, God, that the sea might engulf the land!
> Why are we left to long-drawn weariness?

Edward I wasted no time in any courtesy towards his fallen opponent. Llywelyn's head was cut off and exhibited on London Bridge, and his body, by tradition, was taken to Abbeycwmhir near Rhayader. A simple monument in the form of a slab of North Wales granite marks the spot.

**ABOVE** *On the site of the ruined abbey at Abbeycwmhir, this granite slab, carved with a Celtic sword, commemorates the death of Llywelyn ap Gruffydd.*

The victor, meanwhile, was working at top speed to grip North Wales in an iron ring of new castles. They went up at an astonishing speed under Edward's brilliant architect, Master James of St George. The Welsh may have had to do the hard and humble labouring jobs, but Master James organised masons, carpenters and craftsmen from all over the kingdom to carry out 'the King's works in North Wales'. This was the most ambitious and concentrated building scheme undertaken in the Middle Ages. No wonder tourists flock to see the results today.

It is impossible to tell which of these masterpieces of military art is the best. Caernarfon has multiangular towers, inspired by the walls of Byzantium and designed for imperial splendours. Beaumaris is the perfect concentric castle, constructed with mathematical precision. Harlech is the very image of the romantic castle. Rhuddlan, together with the Marcher strongholds of Denbigh and Ruthin, must be added to the list. There they stand, still splendid in their ruin, proud and impregnable.

But were they as impregnable as they look? In theory, yes. In practice, some of them were captured—but usually by treachery. No architect could protect his castle

## THE PRINCES OF WALES

WHEN QUEEN ELIZABETH II invested her son Charles with the insignia of the Prince of Wales in 1969, there were some who refused to acknowledge the event. 'No Englishman is Prince of Wales', they said. Theirs was a bitterness that had festered for 700 years since the death of Llywelyn ap Gruffydd, who in 1267 was the first and only native Prince of Wales to be recognised by the English. Fifteen years later, however, his head was touring London on a stake. He became known as Llywelyn the Last.

**RIGHT** *Elizabeth II invests her son and heir Charles with the insignia of the Prince of Wales at Caernarfon Castle in 1969.*

Edward I, Llywelyn's killer, rubbed salt in Welsh wounds by proclaiming his own son Prince of Wales in 1301, despite having promised the Welsh a prince who was 'born in Wales and spoke never a word of English'. If legend is to be believed, however, then Edward kept half his word: his son, the future Edward II, was born in the Eagle Tower of Caernarfon Castle, during a royal visit in 1284.

Since then, the title of the Prince of Wales has been conferred upon most heirs to the English throne. Prince Charles, the current incumbent, has done more to identify himself with the Welsh people than any of his 20 predecessors,

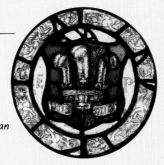

**RIGHT** *The badge and cipher of Edward II, who in 1301 became the first Englishman to be made Prince of Wales.*

many of whom never once set foot in their principality. He studied Welsh at Aberystwyth University, and is active in projects designed to tackle social problems in Wales.

Prince Charles's investiture was one of the great spectacles of the century: set in the romantic splendour of Caernarfon Castle, it drew an estimated 500 million TV viewers world wide. Surprisingly, the modern investiture ceremony dates back only to 1911, when the young Edward VII reluctantly accepted the title (he was unhappy with the 'preposterous rig' he was forced to wear). Prior to this, the investiture was generally a private ceremony performed in Westminster or in Windsor.

against the traitor within. When the Welsh rose in revolt in 1401 under Owain Glyndwr, they captured several of the castles, but only because they were shown the way in by a sympathiser. And during the Glyndwr revolt another 'traitor' appeared before the castle walls: the gun. Gunfire was the sound of doom for all the works of Edward I and Master James of St George. They mouldered away into quiet ruin or, like Carew Castle in Pembrokeshire, had their walls pierced with elegant windows to make them not fortresses but princely dwelling-places.

There was a brief moment during the Civil War when the old gentlemen, like Don Quixote, donned their rusty armour for the last time. But once the guns were brought up, our castles became some of the ruins that Cromwell knocked about a bit.

The first phase of the Civil War came to an end when, in 1646, the Marquess of Worcester was compelled to surrender his castle of Raglan, packed with works of art as well as military supplies, to the forces of Parliament. I followed my history master's precept when I first went to Raglan. I stood on the very spot in the now ruined and roofless great hall where the unhappy marquess had waited at the

## THE QUEST FOR INDEPENDENCE

DESCRIBED IN SHAKESPEARE'S *Henry IV* as 'a great magician', Owain Glyndwr led the last full-scale Welsh uprising against the English and in so doing made himself a national hero.

Born in about 1354, the descendant of Welsh princes, Glyndwr studied in London and served in the English army under Richard II. In 1400 he returned to his estate in Wales, where a neighbouring English noble seized some of his land. Glyndwr launched a raid in reprisal and unwittingly fanned the smouldering embers of Welsh resentment against repressive English rule. Now at the head of a popular uprising, Glyndwr took the castles of Criccieth, Conwy and Harlech.

By 1404 Glyndwr had captured most of Wales. In the same year he set up a parliament at Machynlleth and, declaring himself Prince of Wales, pursued alliances and diplomatic ties with the French, Scots and Irish. Later, he hatched a plan with dissident English nobles to divide England and Wales into three parts. Glyndwr's vision never materialised, however, and

**LEFT** *Owain Glyndwr, the Welsh prince and hero, as depicted by a Victorian artist.*

**ABOVE** *A bronze belt or harness mounting bearing the arms of Owain Glyndwr—four lions rampant.*

by the end of 1408 his English allies had been defeated. Glyndwr himself struggled on as best he could but by 1410 he had become an outlawed fugitive; from 1412 nothing is heard of him, and he is thought to have died in 1416. Despite the failure of Glyndwr's uprising, the obscurity

surrounding his end helped to create the romantic hero of legend. Indeed, the resonance of his name was such that the Welsh nationalist extremists of the 1970s and 80s who burnt down English holiday homes in Wales dubbed themselves Meibion Glyndwr—the 'Sons of Glyndwr'.

**LEFT** *The state quarters of Raglan Castle, a Royalist stronghold in the English Civil War.*

**BELOW** *A 1648 print of Sir Thomas Fairfax in council with the officers of the New Model Army.*

head of his household to make his submission to Sir Thomas Fairfax and the men of the New Model Army. It was Wednesday, August 19, 1647, and the Marquess could see through the windows 'the General and all his officers entering the Outward Court as if a floodgate had been opened!' I could feel, across the long years, all the bitterness of that moment.

A month after that first visit to Raglan, I found myself in another great hall, that of Christ Church, Oxford, sitting for my scholarship examination. The first paper dealt with medieval history. Believe it or not, the third question was: 'Discuss the development of the concentric castle in Western Europe.' I seized my pen and set to with a will. The Marquess of Worcester had not surrendered Raglan in vain. I got my scholarship to Exeter College.

## THE ISLAND SPELL

I fell under the island spell during my first long vacation from Oxford in 1927. A friend had a boat at Solva and proposed that we should spend a month on Ramsey Island off the coast of Pembrokeshire. Those were the days, long before nature reserves and bird sanctuaries, when few people wanted to spend holidays on lonely Welsh islands. In fact, few people knew that Wales had any islands at all. I had to buy a map to find out exactly where Ramsey was.

I picked it up off the St David's Peninsula—that gnarled, sea-battered, rock outcrop of a land, shaved by the sea-salt winds. This is the most westerly part of Wales, its true Land's End. Beyond Ramsey, the map shows a welter of wild rocks named the Bishop and the Clerks, obviously christened after the clergy of the nearby cathedral of St David's, which cowers from the wind in a rocky valley a few miles from the sea's edge.

Old George Owen, the Tudor historian of Pembrokeshire, coined wonderful phrases about the Bishop and the Clerks, which, as he wrote, 'are not without some small choristers who show themselves only at spring tides and calm seas. The Bishop and these his Clerks preach deadly doctrine to their winter audience and are commendable for nothing but their good residence.'

Landscapes that excite you at nineteen never loosen their grip on your mind. For me, Ramsey will always remain the finest island in Wales, simply because it was the first one I really got to know. My friend and I had no idea of the dangers of the surrounding seas, so vividly described by George Owen. This noble whaleback of an island is separated from the mainland by a narrow sound, half dammed by a sinister line of jagged rocks with the ominous title of the Bitches. We got sucked into the race through the sound when it was in full flood. We were in a small yacht with no engine, and I held my breath as the helmsman struggled to keep her straight amid the roaring waters, while our eyes were almost blinded by the spray from the overfalls. The races round the Pembrokeshire islands on bad days have an inhuman savagery about them. We came into the lee of the Bitches half drowned and bailing for our lives. We stayed in the security of Ramsey for a month.

Ramsey in 1927 seemed an enchanted place to me. You are either a natural island lover or you hate them like hell. I am a completely island-crazed man. The waters that you cross to get to islands seem to cleanse you of crowded suburbs, piped music, the whine of jet engines and the birdcages of power lines. I haven't had to live my whole life on a Welsh island, or even stay there through a winter: perhaps then I might change my tune. We are not realists in our dreams. All of us keep at the back of our mind a picture of some place where we can slip out of the mundane world and live the perfect life, where the earthly paradise would be made visible and viable.

On its western side, Ramsey plunges down into the sea in magnificent cliffs. The surrounding waters are littered with the rock fangs of the Bishop and the Clerks. From late August to mid October, the grey seals come onto the hidden beaches to breed in great numbers.

Apart from the seals, the island's most remarkable inhabitant was the man who was then farming it—if taking a half-hearted interest in a singularly independent flock of sheep could be called farming. Mr Edwards came to the island after the First World War. It suited him to claim that he had come to cultivate Ramsey, but what he really wanted to cultivate was birdwatching, seal friendship and the art of telling stories.

**ABOVE** *A passenger ferry crossing Ramsey Sound is careful to avoid a sinister line of rocks known as the Bitches, which disappear at high tide, leaving visible only the swirling waters seen here in the foreground.*

Any farming that did go on seemed to be conducted by Mr Edwards's Welsh assistant, William. To us young men, William seemed fabulously old. He looked like an Old Testament prophet who was partial to a nice drop of beer in between his sessions of sin-denouncing. Mr Edwards, for his part, was a neat man, who seemed country bred and English in the plus fours of the period—until he started to talk! He was the first gifted storyteller I ever met, a genuine artist of the spoken word, for he had nothing to do with writing.

'Why don't you write your memoirs?' we urged him.

'Write things down?' Mr Edwards snorted in disgust. 'Printers' ink kills wit.'

He had something there. The storyteller with a pen or typewriter is a different man from the vocal artist. The vocal storyteller needs a background and he needs time. He is no good on television. The pace there is so fast that he ends up in anecdote and wisecracks. In 1927, Mr Edwards had all the time in the world to deploy his effects, and we had all the time in the world to listen.

## SPEAKING WITH SEALS

The setting was unfailingly right: the kitchen of the old farmhouse on a wet evening, with the cold-nosed farm dogs nuzzling our hands and the firelight playing on William's face as he underlined Mr Edwards's narration with interjections of 'True, very true', like a deacon in chapel counterpointing the preacher. All Mr Edwards's stories needed William's reassuring murmurs. Even at nineteen, we were a little worried about the absolute authenticity of some of them.

For example, there was the story of how Mr Edwards had been cut off from his unit in the great retreat of 1918. He was splashing along through the rain when a staff car drew up. A bemedalled general emerged and asked Mr Edwards what he would say, as a typical Tommy, to raise the spirits of the army. Said Mr Edwards in reply, 'I'd tell them that we have our backs to the wall, but, believing in the justice of our cause, we have no alternative but to fight it out where we stand.' The next day every village along the front was plastered with Haig's famous 'Backs to the Wall' despatch. Inspired by it, the British army ceased its retreat and Europe was saved.

'Ah, what did I want with rewards,' sighed Mr Edwards with the resignation of an unpublished philosopher. 'Like a Welsh Cincinnatus, I have retired to my farm, happy to till the land and speak with the birds and seals. I mean that literally, of course.'

'You mean,' we enquired with astonishment, 'that you can actually understand what the seals are barking about?'

'Certainly. Once you live on an island like this, you get to know their language. As a matter of fact, I've spoken to a group of seals that lie up on the beach under Ynys Cantwr. I drill them—the usual square-bashing. Be there tomorrow and I'll put them through their paces for you.'

We were there the next morning, for this time we felt in our bones that Mr Edwards had gone too far.

The south end of Ramsey breaks down into a huddle of small islands, and the nearest one, Ynys Cantwr—the Singing Isle—protects a little beach under the cliffs of the main island. We crawled cautiously to the edge of the cliffs and looked

ABOVE *A grey, or Atlantic, seal suckles her pup on the Pembrokeshire coast. Grey seals are widespread along the shores of Britain.*

down. Four seals were lying up on the seaweed and stones. They had flopped in through a narrow passage in the rocks. Mr Edwards whispered, 'That's my squad. Stay here and watch me give them their drill.'

He slipped off and worked his way down the cliffs out of sight. The four seals lay basking on the warm rocks, fat, comatose and unmovable. Nothing, not even a cat in front of the fire, looks so totally at peace with the world as a seal asleep on a beach in late summer.

He stood in a splendid military posture and shouted his order: 'Ah…ten…shun!' The seals' heads came up. 'Eyes right!' Every eye swivelled towards him. 'Single file!' The seals scrambled into line. 'Quick march!' Smartly the seals set off towards the sea. 'Right wheel!' The flopping file swung right on command and plunged into the breakers.

We nearly fell over the cliff in our astonishment. Mr Edwards rejoined us. 'Well, what do you think of them, eh? Smart, aren't they? Highly important, I think, for the future. We've got to communicate with our wild friends. When I really get to understand them, just think what we can do together!'

We drifted back through the heather, and the dogs came out from the farm to greet us. We had a vision of Mr Edwards and his trained seals revolutionising the fishing round St David's, or running an underwater messenger service. Anything seemed possible.

'We still do not know the boundaries of knowledge, boys,' said Mr Edwards. 'I am trying to extend them in my humble way.'

'Quite right,' chorused William. 'This time it's even truer than the truth.'

It wasn't until we had spent some days back in the sober atmosphere of St David's on the mainland that we realised what Mr Edwards had done. How stupid we'd been. The solution was obvious.

It wouldn't have mattered what noise Mr Edwards had made when he stepped out from behind that rock. In any case, the seals would have looked up towards the source of danger and then made for the sea. They had to move in single file, since they were forced to go through the narrow rock passage before turning right to reach the safety of the breakers. All that Mr Edwards did was to give the appropriate order before the seals did what came naturally. It was a masterpiece of split-second timing. That was all!

I have always regretted the loss of illusions. How pleasant it would be to go through life believing that somewhere, somehow, there is a man on a Welsh island who can communicate with the grey seal.

In the many years that have passed since I first set foot on Ramsey, I have had the chance of visiting every one of the islands off the Welsh coast, great and small. They all have the authentic island spell upon them. Flat Holm and Steep Holm in the Bristol Channel have cast-iron Victorian cannon lying rusting in their abandoned emplacements among the nesting gulls. Caldey, off Tenby, is permeated with the moving peace of its monastery the day after the tourists leave. Skomer and Skokholm, off the southern tip of St Bride's Bay in Pembrokeshire, are our greatest bird islands. In summer, the kittiwakes and a host of other birds, screaming and fluttering, occupy every cranny in the cliffs. The endearing, parrotlike puffins scuttle into their burrows, while offshore, multitudes of Manx sheerwaters assemble in vast 'rafts' as the evening falls. The air is filled with the constant crying of sea birds, and the sea campions cover the cliffs with russet splendour.

Ten miles further out in the western sea lies Grassholm. In May and June it is one of the most astonishing sights in southern Britain. Over 30,000 pairs of gannets now occupy the top of the island in a white, chattering mass. A cloud of birds circles constantly over the colony. From a distance, Grassholm looks like a white volcano in eruption. As you come near, the great soaring birds fold their wings and plunge down into the sea like white dive-bombers.

Another ten miles out, beyond the gannets in their plunging glory, a stone tower stands on a rock in a waste of wild water. The Smalls lighthouse marks the most westerly and loneliest patch of the land of Wales. Beyond, the ocean stretches unbroken for thousands of miles until you reach America.

## TRAPPED ON BARDSEY

All these are South Wales islands, but I do not forget that North Wales has its islands, too. Without question, the most notable of them is Bardsey, off the very end of the Lleyn Peninsula. Again I must confess to partiality: as with Ramsey in the south, I've

had the luck to live for a time on Bardsey. Let me add that my stay was involuntary. Bardsey Sound is a vicious place, as tough as Jack Sound and Ramsey Sound in Pembrokeshire. The wind blew hard, and no boat would venture across that waste of tumbling white water to take me back to the mainland.

Somehow I didn't mind. Bardsey is a wonderful place to be cut off. When you reach the village of Aberdaron at the end of the Lleyn Peninsula, with its wide beach and surrounding moorlands, you know that you have come to the Ultima Thule of North Wales. But when you go to St Mary's Well, on the actual headland, and look across the turbulent waters of

ABOVE *The wide, rocky beach of Aberdaron, a tiny village at the end of Lleyn Peninsula. The poet R. S. Thomas was parish priest here in the 1960s and 70s.*

the two-and-a-half-mile-wide sound to the humpbacked outline of Bardsey beyond, you know that you have reached an even greater solitude. No wonder that Bardsey was one of the great places of pilgrimage in medieval Wales, the holy island where it was claimed that 20,000 saints lay buried.

Old Thomas Fuller, the antiquarian, in his *Worthies*, published in 1662, had his doubts: 'But where would so many bodies find graves in so petty an island? But I retrench myself, confessing it more facile to find graves in Bardsey for so many saints than saints for so many graves!'

Bardsey supported a vigorous farming community up to the First World War. Lord Newborough, who then owned the island, built the islanders sturdy farmhouses that could stand up to the winter storms. He even appointed the most prominent inhabitant, Love Pritchard, as 'King', complete with crown. Love Pritchard is still remembered in Aberdaron. He was a formidable character, a giant of a man with a legendary appetite. A visitor in 1910 found him sitting down to a surprising meal.

'His Majesty sat in his grandfather's chair eating supper, which consisted entirely of crabs and beer. On one side of the chair was a collection of good-sized crabs among seaweed in a wooden pail; on the other side was an equally big pail of beer. The King was smoking, but every now and then he reached down into the left-hand pail, lifted out a crab, put it on the back of his left hand and brought his right fist down on it with a crash. He took out the insides of the crab, dropped them in the beer and swallowed the lot in one gulp.'

Love Pritchard claimed the support of an influential London physician for his strange diet. The doctor came to Bardsey, saw Love at work on this supper and made his pronouncement: 'Yes, certainly, the best food possible.'

And now no one will come to Bardsey to try this island speciality. Only one man still farms on the island, and the houses are occupied in the summer by bird-watchers and nature lovers. But the tall Celtic crosses still stand guard over the scanty ruins of the old priory, the gulls still nest on the slopes of Bardsey's hill,

**ABOVE** *Love Pritchard, who was crowned 'King' of Bardsey by Lord Newborough, one-time owner of the island.*

**RIGHT** *The heathered hills of Bardsey, 'isle of 20,000 saints', flatten out towards the lighthouse—the last outpost of North Wales.*

and the seals look at you wide-eyed as your small boat comes gently to rest on the shingle of the narrow landing cove. There is still a rare peace on the island of 20,000 saints.

## DYLAN'S WALES

A few years ago, in the mellow sunshine of a still day in early October, I was walking on the gentle hills that overlook the lower valley of the River Tywi between Carmarthen and Llandeilo. Below me, the river ran in graceful, serpentine curves through the meadows and woods that give this part of South Wales such an easy-going, contented look. This part of the Tywi can boast of more than its fair share of snug gentlemen's seats, surrounded by trees. The romantic castle ruins of Dryslwyn and Dynevor seem deliberately placed in positions that would meet the approval of 18th-century amateurs of the picturesque, while the delightful neo-Gothic folly of Paxton's Tower looks down over it all.

The tower was built in 1810 in honour of Lord Nelson by the enormously wealthy Sir William Paxton, of nearby Middleton Hall. We used to go on elaborate picnics to it when we were small, and I still associate Paxton's Tower with hot summer days, cucumber sandwiches, cool lemonade and prizes being offered by a jovial uncle to the boys who made the best attempt at picking out most of the seven counties you were supposed to be able to see from the summit. I was never there on a clear enough day to put the legend to the test.

On this particular October day, when the woods were already touched with autumn gold, I detected what those 18th-century romantics would call 'a pleasing melancholy' in the air, and I remembered that one of those wooded eminences beside the Tywi was Grongar Hill, the title of the once-celebrated poem by John Dyer. Dyer was born near this very spot, and published the effusion in 1726. It looks a bit stilted today:

> *Ever charming, ever new,*
> *When will the landskip tire the view?*

Certainly, the 'landskip' below Paxton's Tower will never tire my view. I walked through the quiet lanes, the only sound the rustle of little birds in the hedges beside me, and another quotation floated into my mind, this time not from old John Dyer but from a far more modern and vibrant poet:

> *A springful of larks in a rolling*
> *Cloud and the roadside bushes brimming with whistling*
> *Blackbirds and the sun of October*
> *Summery*
> *On the hill's shoulder…*

Dylan Thomas's 'Poem in October', of course. I was lucky enough to be born in the same town and to go to the same school as the greatest lyric poet of our time.

**ABOVE** *High on a hill overlooking the village of Llanarthne stands Paxton's Tower. It was built in 1810 by Sir William Paxton as a memorial to Lord Nelson.*

**BELOW** *The great lyric poet Dylan Thomas making a recording at the BBC in 1948. He died five years later after a heavy drinking bout.*

I was slightly older than Dylan, and got to know him better after we had left school, but I had his father as my English master. He was a rather formidable figure, who drilled a love of literature into the skulls of reluctant youth. I owe to him any appreciation I may possess of the odd corners of the English literary world, but the oddest corner of all was undoubtedly Dylan himself. Dylan died young, and I still think of him as the companionable drinker I knew, as the young poet who would unroll a crumpled poem out of his pocket over a pint, not as the 'wild Welsh wizard' of the American tours, and least of all as the officially canonised national monument, high on the list of the tourist attractions of the Principality.

I was intrigued recently to see an advertisement for 'TWO MEMORABLE DAYS IN DYLAN THOMAS COUNTRY'. So Dylan has annexed a country to himself, rather as Thomas Hardy did in Wessex and Sir Walter Scott in the Scottish Borders! Dylan's Wales, however, is a very small, precise area, and until he appeared it was hardly on the main tourist circuit. It doesn't include any of the wild mountain country you might expect. I don't think Dylan ever climbed a mountain willingly in his life. No, Dylan's Wales—the landscapes that really made him a writer and which seem to echo through all his poems and stories—can be clearly divided into three.

At the beginning stands Swansea. Even I, a native son, have already confessed that it is hardly a health resort, although the graceful curve of the bay, cleared of the railway and backed by the high hills, can look oddly beautiful from the Mumbles on a summer's night. But the earnest literary pilgrim can climb the steep hill to Dylan's birthplace, then sit in Cwmdonkin Park, which inspired so many of his early poems.

The second section of Dylan country is that Carmarthenshire landscape of small, chequered fields, little woods and white-walled farms where the Tywi flows down to meet the sea. This is the modest, unspectacular countryside from which his mother's family came. Here lies Fern Hill. The landscape changes imperceptibly to the final part of Dylan country, the coast where the Taf loiters out through its sandbanks to the sea, past the small and ancient township of Laugharne.

**LEFT** *This boathouse on the 'heron-priested shore' of Laugharne was once Thomas's home. Nowadays, the building houses a museum in honour of the poet.*

**RIGHT** *Dylan Thomas wrote a large part of his work in this paper-strewn shed, which has been preserved as it was for visitors.*

**ABOVE** *Laugharne's town hall, with its clock and weather cock, supplied some of the imagery in Thomas's famous play,* Under Milk Wood.

Laugharne, whether it likes it or not, has been permanently labelled as the origin of Llaregyb in *Under Milk Wood*. In truth, Dylan was always fascinated by little, old-fashioned towns by the sea. He lived for some time at New Quay on Cardigan Bay, and Llaregyb clearly has some New Quay elements in it. In the end, however, the Dylan pilgrim and the Dylan tourist all end up at Laugharne. Here is Brown's Hotel, where Dylan drank his warm, Welsh beer. Here is the tiny town hall with its clock, its chiming bell and its weathercock, which supplied so much of the hidden imagery of *Under Milk Wood*. Here life moved at the easy pace that suited Dylan in his last period, for the burgesses of Laugharne quite rightly have no desire to rush their delightful town into the unfriendly future. I have had the pleasure, as Dylan had, of attending the Portreeve's breakfast, the only breakfast I know that ends at 10pm.

Dylan came to live at the Boathouse—his 'house on stilts'—perched on the rocks above the sand flats of the estuary. He worked in the quiet of his 'shed' on the gorse-covered slopes behind it. He called it his 'water and tree room on the cliff'. I remember him scattering his manuscripts on the floor and stubbing endless cigarettes into tin tops on the rough table. Dylan was no slapdash relier on inspiration produced by beer, as many people have supposed, but a dedicated practitioner of his 'craft and sullen art'.

My last image of him is on the balcony of the Boathouse looking out over the 'heron-priested shore' towards the little town of Laugharne. I could almost see him as the Reverend Eli Jenkins. And surely the Reverend's evening prayer in *Under Milk Wood* says everything that should be said in memory of that rare, eloquent and wayward genius who was Dylan Thomas:

> *We are not wholly bad or good*
> *Who live our lives under Milk Wood,*
> *And Thou, I know, wilt be the first*
> *To see our best side, not our worst.*

# CHAPTER FOUR

# THE WILDS OF SNOWDONIA

**ABOVE** *Climber George Abraham wields his camera as a companion scales the sheer face of Gimmer Crag.*

ONE WET AFTERNOON during my second year at the university, I found myself in the library of the Oxford Union. Ostensibly, I had gone there to finish a much-overdue essay on the development of the wool industry in England during the 15th century. Somehow I didn't seem able to concentrate my mind on a succession of obscure Acts of Parliament designed to encourage the weavers of the Cotswolds and the merchants of London. They certainly didn't inspire me. I wandered along the shelves in search of more entertaining reading.

Almost at random I picked up a stout volume entitled *Rock Climbing in the English Lake District,* mainly because the name of the author caught my eye: Owen Glynne Jones. Alongside there was a sort of companion volume, entitled *Rock Climbing in North Wales,* by George and Ashley Abraham. I carried the two weighty volumes down to a comfortable armchair before the library fire and turned the pages. I was immediately carried into a new world.

The date of the first volume was 1897 and the photographs had been taken on a heavy plate camera which must have been carried up the crags with enormous trouble and difficulty. But the photographs were of surpassing quality. The very texture of the rock seemed to stand out on the paper. However, the real surprise was the acrobatics that the climbers were performing on those same rocks. There they were, happily balancing on tiny ledges over dizzy precipices or wedged into damp cracks hundreds of feet up a cliff. I had thought I had been daring indeed when I walked along the edge of the precipices round Llyn y Fan Fach, but clearly that was mere beginner's stuff in the world of mountaineering. Rock climbing was the next step in my adventure into the high hills.

Owen Glynne Jones was obviously the man to follow, for he had been the first Welshman, as far as I then knew, to have made a great name in the small, tight world of rock climbing. He was a London Welshman, whose family had come from the area round Dolgellau. He was a scientist by profession and physically extremely tough and strong. One friend described him as having 'arms like a gorilla', with exceptional strength of grip in his fingers and an astonishing sense of balance. As a result, he had burst like a bombshell into that closed society of dons, civil servants, public school men and comfortably-off heirs to long-established family businesses who were then the guardians of climbing tradition.

He upset the establishment. He made enemies, who were horrified that he had written his book on the rock climbs of the Lakes with photographs taken by the Abraham brothers, professional photographers. 'This,' said the *Alpine Journal*, 'is suspiciously like horseplay on the heights.' He was shortsighted, and some detractors quipped about one of his most daring routes: 'Well, he'd never have climbed it if he could have seen it.' Jones didn't worry about criticism. He declared that his initials, O. G. J., stood for the 'Only Genuine Jones', and went on pushing the climbing technique of the day beyond the accepted limits. Sadly Jones was killed in a climbing accident on the difficult ridges of Dent Blanche in Switzerland.

Naturally, I didn't think of this finale to his career when I resolved, in that comfortable armchair in the Oxford Union, to follow in the footsteps of O. G.—or, at least, in the easiest of them. He had made his first climb on that noble mountain, Cadair Idris. He had conquered the east arête of Cyfrwy, the sharply outlined

ridge that is conspicuous when you look up at the great north wall of Cadair from the Dolgellau side. Most people now start their ascent of Cadair Idris from the car park that the National Parks Authority has constructed just beyond Llyn Gwernan. When I was last there, I was happy to see that they have made a reference to Owen Glynne Jones's first ascent of Cyfrwy on the information panel they have put up near the entrance to the car park.

Jones had been completely ignorant about climbing techniques when he first tackled the arête. His spirits had soared when he first saw it, so in his ordinary suit and with no nails on his shoes he strolled up the mountain by himself and completed what has rightly been called the first serious rock climb in Wales. The momentous date was May Day, 1888.

## IN THE FOOTSTEPS OF O. G. JONES

In 1928, exactly forty years later, accompanied by the same friend with whom I had explored Ramsey Island during my first long vacation at Oxford, I arrived at the foot of Cyfrwy and looked up at the east arête. My climbing apparel was not so very different from the clothes worn by those early pioneers of the 1880s. I didn't quite sport a Norfolk jacket, knickerbockers and hobnailed boots, but I did have an old tweed coat, plus fours and nailed boots—although the nails were the more modern tricounis. On my head was an old trilby, and I kept a faded beret in reserve. We also carried a brand-new climbing rope, thick enough to moor a battleship—although we had no idea how to use it correctly.

My friend and I looked up at what seemed an impossibly steep cliff. Could O. G. Jones actually have wriggled up that crack and balanced out onto that dizzy edge? Well, there was no dodging it—we had to try.

**BELOW** *The author, wearing his faded beret, on the precipitous rock face of Glyder Fach in 1930.*

I'll always remember my first steps onto really steep rock. I moved up thirty-odd feet without daring to look down. The view was certainly hair-raising, even frightening, but in a curious way the fright was enjoyable. You felt that you were treading on air with a strange confidence. I gripped the rock with what I hoped was O. G.-type strength.

We heaved ourselves over the edge and came sprawling onto a strange, level rock platform a third of the way up the cliff, which we discovered afterwards was called the Table. It was one of those dramatic spots you find on great rock races, cut off from the rest of the world and only to be reached by climbers. From this Table of Cyfrwy the high cliffs curved away in a noble semicircle to cradle the dark tarn of Llyn y Gadair. The vast scree slide of the Fox's Path poured down to the little lake almost from the very summit. It was a heart-lifting place.

However, when I turned to look at the route ahead my heart was anything but lifted. A solid wall of rock, genuinely perpendicular, barred the way. It was certainly far, far more perpendicular—if I can use such a phrase—than that rock face I had negotiated many years before to get into the Paviland Caves in Gower. Again we reasoned: if the Only Genuine Jones had conquered it with no nails on his shoes, we ought to be able to do it with our brand-new ropes and tricounis.

And conquer it we did. The holds came to hand, and once again I felt that strange thrill of being a fly on a wall, safe as long as I gripped the rock firmly in O. G. style.

Since that day, Cadair has always seemed a very special mountain to me. It shows a magnificent line of cliffs to the north, and if the central peak above Llyn y Gadair had only been a few hundred feet higher it would have rivalled Snowdon itself for grace. On the south side, the savage hollow that holds Llyn Cau has been carved by ancient glaciers out of the huge bulk of the mountain; it was this that inspired Richard Wilson, the first important Welsh painter, to create one of the first landscapes of real quality to be painted in Britain. Add to this the wild pass that leads up from Tal-y-llyn Lake under beetling crags, and you can see why Cadair is a mountain that holds its admirers in a vicelike grip!

Yet, while I rhapsodise over that first climb on Cadair, I must confess that, as usual, I was thirty years behind the times in the climbing world. While I was following reverently and wobblingly in the footsteps of O. G. Jones, further north, on Snowdon, Sir Jack Longland was leading his historic climb up the forbidding face of Clogwyn Du'r Arddu, marking a new breakthrough in British mountaineering.

Clogwyn Du'r Arddu—the Black Cliff—is savage enough when you look across at it from your comfortable seat in the little mountain train as it puffs up to Clogwyn station. When you clamber down to the dark tarn under the cliff and look up at those smooth rocks plunging down towards you without any obvious hand- or foothold for 400 feet, the Clogwyn looks positively menacing. No wonder a well-known expert of the day printed a since-celebrated warning in the *Climbers' Club Guide*: 'No breach seems either possible or desirable along the whole extent of the west buttress, though there is the faintest of faint hopes for a human fly rather on its left side.'

At Whitsun 1928 the human flies appeared in the persons of Jack Longland and his party. They conquered the west buttress up a series of uncompromisingly steep slabs, now rightly called Longland's Climb. It was the epic of the period, but one incident during the climb called forth growls of stern disapproval from the pundits. At the crux of the climb, the Faith and Friction Slab, A. S. Pigott actually drove in a piton—one of those artificial aids to safety that had already been used in the Alps for a decade. He had done so in flat defiance of the pronouncement of a president of the Alpine Club, who had laid down the law: 'The hand that could drive a piton into English rock could shoot a fox.'

Too late: the new technique had arrived, and after the Second World War there was no stopping the new invasion of the hills by daring young men who didn't worry overmuch about the traditions and rules laid down by the older generation. They weren't dons or civil servants or undergrads from the universities. Joe Brown was a builder from Manchester, who effortlessly won new routes up Clogwyn Du'r Arddu, chain-smoking as he went and with all the latest climbing ironmongery dangling from his belt. The climbing world in Wales was never the same again.

**ABOVE** *Jack Longland, who made his historic ascent of Clogwyn Du'r Arddu in 1928.*

**ABOVE** *Pitons, driven into cracks in the rock, are now essential climbing gear.*

**ABOVE** *Renowned climber Joe Brown, laden with equipment, in action on the cliffs of Castell Helen, on Anglesey.*

**ABOVE** *This vast bowl, or cirque, with its deep black lake, was carved by the glaciers of the Ice Age. It forms part of the Snowdon Horseshoe, Wales's finest mountain walk. Here, the path known as Pyg track can be seen rising towards the cirque's hazardous spine.*

## THE SNOWDON HORSESHOE

Today there has been a rush to the hills. Hardly a crag has been left unclimbed. There are climbing schools and adventure courses where the beginner can be taught the rudiments of the craft. The tourists drive down Llanberis Pass and pull up in the lay-bys to train their binoculars on the parties festooning the lower cliffs with their ropes as they follow their leaders up routes such as the Spectre, described in the *Climbers' Club Guide* as 'Exceptionally severe. Exposed, strenuous and delicate also…The rock is excellent, the steepness awesome.'

It certainly is. I look at those crash-helmeted, ironmongery-hung experts at work on the Spectre and realise how hopelessly out-of-date I am. I restore my mountaineering morale by staying with my friend Chris Briggs at the historic inn of Pen-y-Gwryd, right in the heart of the most romantic and spectacular part of Snowdonia. Behind it, the rugged Glyders rise to over 3,000 feet. A short walk down the road brings you to one of the great views of Wales. As you look up into the vast hollow of Cwm Dyli, with all the high peaks of Snowdon grouped round it, you can trace the finest mountain walk the country has to offer: the Snowdon

Horseshoe. I have done it more times than I can remember, and it is always new, exciting and, at points, breathtaking. I ought to add that it is not for complete newcomers to mountain walking and only for those who are properly equipped.

You begin round the corner from Pen-y-Gwryd at the youth hostel at the top of Llanberis Pass. You climb, and sometimes struggle, up a very steep 3,000 feet to the first summit of Crib Goch—the Red Comb—where you realise at once how apt the name is. Before you lies a surprisingly narrow ridge, with dizzy drops away to the north into Cwm Glas Mawr. An airy scramble takes you over the teeth of the comb and gives you the feeling of treading a rock tightrope raised high in the mountain air. Most people will find the passage of the Crib exhilarating, but I have seen certain anxious climbers painfully negotiating the ridge astride. Whichever way you do it, Crib Goch is thrilling.

You come off the ridge among the celebrated Crib Goch pinnacles, then climb steadily up the rocks of Carnedd Ugain, Snowdon's second summit. From now on, you have the little train for company as you go up the final few hundred feet to the actual highest top.

I wish I could say that Snowdon's summit is a place of awe and inspiration, as it ought to be. Alas, there is a sort of concrete hotel under the very top, crowded with half the world on a fine day in summer. No, no, I do not 'lift up mine eyes to the hills' to see if I can buy Coca-Cola. I hurry away from the desecrated High Place of Wales, down the zigzags that lead to the col of Bwlch y Saethau—the Pass of the Arrows—where, legend says, King Arthur himself met his death by a fatal arrow shot. Then I head up the last and most consoling section of the Snowdon Horseshoe, the summit of Lliwedd. Here peace, serenity and beauty are gloriously restored. Only those who genuinely love the hills come here. The great precipices drop below you; myriad lakes and tarns glitter in the lonely mountain hollows. Then you follow the narrow path that drops with reluctance from the high places to the shores of the dark Llyn Llydaw. Here I always stand for a few moments to admire the perfect grouping of the Snowdon peaks round the Horseshoe. Finally, I swing down the rough road towards the waiting bar of the Pen-y-Gwryd Hotel, which has now been welcoming climbers for over 100 years.

## THE LOCKED BOOK OF PEN-Y-GWRYD

Long ago, in the 1850s and 1860s, distinguished men of letters such as Charles Kingsley and scientists such as Tyndall, Lyall and Huxley had found this inn out and sung its praises. The first wave of rockclimbers in the 1890s made it their headquarters. The famous Locked Book, in which the pioneers described their early explorations and drew careful diagrams, is still reverently preserved here. The Locked Book was instituted to exclude poetic tourist effusions of the type that littered the other Pen-y-Gwryd visitors' books:

> *Been up Snowdon,*
> *A nice ascent.*
> *William Boden,*
> *Burton-on-Trent.*

My heart rather warmed to the gentleman who had stayed for two weeks of constant rain and written of the menu provided:

> *Mutton chop by night*
> *And mutton chop by day,*
> *'Til when you meet a mountain sheep—*
> *You turn the other way!*

The inn fell on rather lean times between the wars, but soon after the Second World War a keen Yorkshire climber, Chris Briggs, took it over and splendidly revived its ancient glories. Here, the team who first climbed Everest came to make final adjustments to their equipment; here the assault of Kangchenjunga, the world's third-highest mountain, was planned. Chris has kept fascinating mementoes of both these famous first ascents behind the bar in the Everest Room. A fragment

**LEFT** *The celebrated Everest team of 1953, who trained in Snowdonia and stayed at the Pen-y-Gwryd Hotel.*

**RIGHT** *The Locked Book at Pen-y-Gwryd celebrates the conquest of Everest by Edmund Hillary and Tenzing Norgay.*

of rock from the highest summit in the world rests in a place of honour in this inn among the Welsh mountains.

Chris tells charming stories about the Sherpas who were invited to Britain after the conquests of Everest and Kangchenjunga, and who, until then, had never left the lonely valleys of Nepal. They had not been impressed by the Savoy Hotel in London: 'In this lamasery,' they exclaimed, 'the abbot does not appear to have his monks in good order.' But Pen-y-Gwryd suited them down to the ground.

Only one thing worried them. Chris came down in the morning to find the bunkhouses and the kitchens full of sheep. The Sherpas had looked out during the night and, as they afterwards explained, had been horrified to see the sheep still scattered over the moonlit hillside. They had spent the rest of the night rounding them up and driving them into Chris's hotel, as a good deed to protect them from the wolves. When they asked Chris what was to be the climbing plan for the day, he proudly pointed to the round of the Horseshoe. 'Oh,' said the Sherpas through their interpreter, 'we did that after we had rounded up the sheep before breakfast!'

So the stories still gather round the climbing inn of Pen-y-Gwryd, and I hope that for many years to come I shall be returning to its welcome after a circuit of the Snowdon Horseshoe—although not, I fear, at the speed of the Sherpas.

## SOJOURN IN ABERYSTWYTH

Oxford bowled me over. For the first time, I found myself living in a city that seemed to have been built strictly with an eye for beauty. Dear old Swansea was warm-hearted, vital, full of the people with whom I had grown up. But not even the most devoted citizen of my native town could claim that Swansea rivalled Oxford when it came to spires and domes and classical façades. Oxford Street, Swansea, was never like this!

Indeed, I think that Oxford gave me a slight inferiority complex in regard to architectural splendours. Those little Welsh towns I knew in my youth were warm, welcoming places, but made no attempt to compete with Bath or York or Ludlow. Of course, there are all sorts of good reasons for this. Fine architecture needs cash, and Wales was never a rich country. What's more, the average Welsh village did not grow up tightly huddled round the church and the manor house. It was a much more scattered affair, with small farmers living on even smaller holdings. The church, with its bell cote in place of a tower or spire, stood apart, and the worship-

pers rode to it on horseback. When the Methodist Revival brought the chapel to challenge the church, the villages gave themselves biblical names after their chapels. One little Carmarthenshire village acquired more biblical glory than it bargained for when it called itself Bethlehem. Its post office was overwhelmed at Christmas time by visitors who clamoured for the Bethlehem postmark on their Christmas cards.

**RIGHT AND ABOVE** *Every year the post office (now closed) in the little village of Bethlehem was inundated with visitors who wanted their Christmas mail stamped with the Bethlehem postmark.*

I think I began to take a more benevolent view of Welsh building when I ceased to expect masterpieces from it and my expectations became humbler and more kindly. I had come down from Oxford after specialising in medieval history—a splendid preparation for the realities of life in the Great Depression of the 1930s. I tried a whole series of jobs, but no one seemed to want an expert on the history of the Second Crusade. At last I managed to creep into the only corner for which Oxford had trained me. I became a very junior keeper of manuscripts and records at the National Library of Wales in Aberystwyth.

No, 'corner' is not the right word to describe this imposing classical building, which looks down from its hill to the curving seafront of the pleasing town at its foot. The library houses a magnificent collection of early Welsh manuscripts and books, built round the nucleus first put together by Sir John Williams, physician to

Queen Victoria and last legendary descendant of the long line of the Physicians of Myddfai, with whose story I had been familiar from the days of my early walks round Llyn y Fan. As I sat at my desk in the library, looking down on the town, I couldn't help thinking how strange it was that, in the long run, Wales owed its library to the magic lady who rose from the lake; even stranger, that the library was in Aberystwyth at all.

As the project for a national library matured, a fierce fight broke out between North and South Wales as to where the building should be placed. This was not the first time that North and South had disagreed. They have done so throughout history, for the great wilderness of Plynlimon that lay between them made cooperation more than difficult in the days before the railway and the motor car. For many years, the National Library floated mid way like Muhammad's coffin, before coming to rest at last near the halfway point, at Aberystwyth, the town of happy compromise.

I looked down on it again from my window and liked what I saw. Aberystwyth as a watering place was the dream child of a robust mid-Victorian railway

## THE GREAT DEPRESSION

THE WORLDWIDE economic slump known as the Great Depression began in America in 1929 with the infamous Wall Street Crash. In Wales, however, decline had already set in, soon after the First World War.

The Welsh economy, based almost entirely on coal and steel, had bloomed over the previous half-century, but the postwar recession hit these industries particularly hard. Demand dropped for both commodities as America and Germany supplied them more cheaply. The miners went on strike repeatedly, but nothing could stop the pit closures.

Rural industries were vulnerable too— prices for milk, corn and livestock dropped after the war, and again in 1929. Consequently, the wool and leather industries suffered, and hundreds of workers were laid off.

Although the British economy began to revive in the mid 1930s, Wales remained depressed. At that time, nearly a third of the Welsh population was unemployed, with the figure rising to almost 50 per

cent in mining areas. There were hunger marches from South Wales to Bristol and London, and demonstrations in Hyde Park.

The government responded by encouraging the poor to move to more prosperous areas of England, such as the Southeast and the Midlands; as a result, nearly half a million people left Wales between the wars. In 1936 the government

**ABOVE** *South Wales miners march to the Trades Union Congress in Bristol in 1931.*

awarded grants to attract industry to the South Wales coalfield, and in 1938 began to set up factories. But state intervention was not enough to dent the unemployment problem: it took another world war, hungry for manpower, to solve that.

ABOVE *The elegant seafront of Aberystwyth, university town and popular seaside resort. Beside the pier stands the imposing Gothic-style building of the University College of Wales, which originally served as a hotel.*

promoter, Thomas Savin. He built a splendidly spiky, Gothic-style hotel on the seafront near the old castle, and proceeded to promote it with offers of special hotel terms for everyone who bought a return train ticket in London. He was the pioneer of the modern package tour. Alas, like all pioneers, he was ahead of his time, and inevitably he went bankrupt. His hotel stood empty until, by a stroke of luck, it was seized on by the Welsh educationalists, who found it ideal for the first college of the embryonic University of Wales in the 1870s. The townsfolk also found it an inspiration. Poor Savin may not have done very well for himself personally, but he had put Aberystwyth on the tourist map. A curve of attractive, bow-windowed houses spread along the seafront in the 1860s and 70s, ending against the shaley cliffs of Constitution Hill. From here, eventually, a romantic funicular railway hauled visitors up to the summit to gaze over the faraway moorlands of Plynlimon and, on a clear day, at Snowdon itself, away to the north across the waters of Cardigan Bay.

The coastline of Wales—as I discovered when I bought my first secondhand motorbike and careered off in a wobbling fashion on weekend voyages of exploration—offers a whole series of modest architectural pleasures. The 19th century did not do too badly when it hit the sea.

The early years saw the creation of Regency Tenby, in South Pembrokeshire, which boasts elegant hotels perched along the cliffs above golden sands and is still encircled by medieval walls. It must have been a delightful place in the 1820s, when it attracted a whole string of fashionable visitors and had the atmosphere of a Jane Austen novel. It still retains its charm, even though it does get a little over-whelmed in the heat of high summer.

Further up, on Cardigan Bay, is the small port of Aberaeron. Again, it has a Regency feel about it, which is not surprising, for Aberaeron was created in 1807 by a local couple, Susannah and Alban Thomas Jones, who had inherited a fortune. Inevitably, the plan has been attributed to John Nash, who was certainly in Wales about this time and, according to one account, was happy to stay there for a period to dodge his creditors in London. Whoever laid it out, Aberaeron retains a quiet charm. There are no outstanding individual buildings, but the whole place is a quiet expression of architectural good manners.

Let me also put in a good word for Llandudno, on the north coast. I like the sweep of hotels ending with the pier, which juts out under the protection of the white limestone cliffs of the Great Orme. The place has a solid look about it, as if the honest 'brass' of Lancashire which built it were still in steady supply. Would that it were!

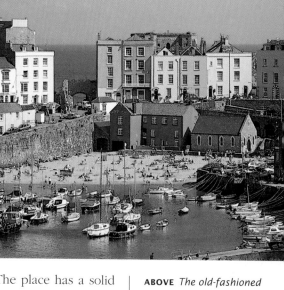

**ABOVE** *The old-fashioned Regency town of Tenby, in the area known as 'Little England beyond Wales', was fortified in the 13th century to keep out the Welsh. It remains anglicised today, drawing summer visitors from across the border in their hordes.*

## PORTMEIRION: A WELSH XANADU

To my mind, the first prize among the seaside fantasies on the coastline of Wales must undoubtedly go to Portmeirion, the creation of that remarkable, if eccentric, genius Sir Clough Williams-Ellis. He was a brilliant architect, but also a pioneer conservationist and a passionate defender of the landscape and architectural heritage of Britain. He was the only man I ever knew to ask for a romantic ruin as a wedding present. After the First World War, he boldly bought a big estate on the estuary of the River Dwyryd in northwest Wales, the perfect place to realise his architectural dream. On the low hills above the winding sandbanks of the Dwyryd, against the thrilling background of the dark mountains of Snowdonia, he placed what looks from the distance like a little Italian town, complete with towers and domes and white-walled houses, transported by Merlin's magic from some hillside on the Appenines. His dream was an instant success. Noël Coward stayed at Portmeirion to write *Blythe Spirit.*

All through his life, Sir Clough Williams-Ellis could not resist improving and adding to his village, re-erecting in Portmeirion buildings that had been under threat elsewhere. He made it, as he said with an infectious chuckle, 'a rest home for fallen buildings'.

I feel that the apotheosis of Portmeirion and its creator came when we celebrated Sir Clough's ninetieth birthday in 1973. The fireworks soared over the mountains as we cheered the last of the great Welsh eccentrics, who walked in his famous yellow stockings and tweed breeches and coat through his carefully planned vistas and elegant colonnades. When he now looks down on it from heaven—which he is surely busily re-planning to give it a more civilised appearance—he must be pleased to see that his Welsh Xanadu will be safe for posterity.

I remember once going round Portmeirion with him and rather wickedly suggesting that there was a gap in his collection of 'fallen buildings'. 'You've not got a single example of the earliest architecture in Wales. Where is your cromlech? Why haven't you got a stone circle?'

Sir Clough laughed. 'Yes, you have a point. But I think I had better have a fake one, not the real thing. In the late 18th century, no Welsh gentleman's estate was complete without one. And I know of some charming fake ones down at Stout Hall in Gower. But a real cromlech—a real circle? Too dangerous, even sinister. I designed Portmeirion as a happy place. Those dark stones from the far-off past are a little—shall I say—too powerful for me.'

## VIBRATING CROMLECHS

I, too, have felt the strange power of the standing stones, the circles and the cromlechs that stand in the lonely places of Wales. They seem to defy us from their lost sites on the mountains, against the sound of the sea; they are even more mysterious when the mist forms and clings round them. We know so little about them. The cromlechs are clearly the stones that formed the burial chambers of ancient barrows; the earth or stones that were once heaped over them have been worn or torn away in the long passage of time. But what deep need drove the builders to drag the great stones into position to make the circles, or to set up great boulders on wild crags and lost moorlands? And what powerful rulers once lay buried under the cromlechs?

Above all, how did they arrive in Wales? Archaeologists suggest that a powerful and mysterious people, who may originally have come from the Mediterranean, spread from peninsula to peninsula along the coast of Western Europe—from northern Spain, through Brittany, across to Cornwall and then into Wales and Ireland. They eventually went further north still, reaching western Scotland and even the remote Orkneys and Shetland. Were they in search of metals? Did they bring a new religion with them? Did they set up their stone circles as astronomical observatories of an extremely sophisticated nature? The plain truth is that we do not know, and this allows us to let our imaginations roam as freely as we wish.

I have vivid memories of my first archaeological tour of Anglesey on my newly acquired motorbike. Naturally, I had read everything I could find on the subject in the National Library: that was one lucky bonus of my sojourn at Aberystwyth. Anglesey has always seemed to me an immeasurably ancient land. It contains the oldest rocks in Wales—the Precambrian—which date back many millions of years, and there are cromlechs and hut circles in profusion.

**ABOVE** *Sir Clough Williams-Ellis, eccentric creator of Portmeirion, seen here sporting his trademark yellow stockings.*

**OPPOSITE** *Portmeirion, Sir Clough's 'rest home for fallen buildings', is an architectural oddity. Endangered buildings from around the world were broken down and rebuilt alongside new structures in an eclectic mix of styles.*

ABOVE *Bryn-celli-ddu—
Mound of the Dark
Grove—was built by
Anglesey's late-Neolithic
inhabitants. Some
people believe the tomb's
stone circle holds
mystical powers; the
author was unconvinced.*

ABOVE *A specimen of
spotted dolomite, a
form of bluestone that
originated in the Preseli
Hills of Wales and was
used in the building
of Stonehenge.*

Probably the finest of the Anglesey chambered tombs is Bryn-celli-ddu—the Mound of the Dark Grove. I was groping my way out from its dark grave passage when I bumped into a tall, gaunt and white-haired man who was just coming in. He seized me by the arm and whispered intently, 'Have you felt them?' 'Felt what?' I said. 'The vibrations, the vibrations,' he almost hissed. 'I'm psychic, and the vibrations are particularly intense—just here.' And he fairly dragged me to the stone that guards the entrance. 'Place your hands here,' he commanded. I duly obeyed; it seemed the wisest thing to do in the circumstances. 'Now,' he insisted with a gleam in his eye, 'you feel them—and I tell you this. They are evil. Powerful and evil!' I hastily agreed, and left Bryn-celli-ddu in a hurry.

Did I feel anything? Truth to tell, not a thing; but I can well understand why some people are almost overwhelmed by the power of the past which still seems to emanate from the ancient stones. When it comes to theories about their meaning, however, I prefer to stay with the archaeologists and to keep my feet firmly on the ground. I was lucky enough, later on, to get to know Professor Glyn Daniel, who showed me one of the most remarkable exhibits from this world of the remote Welsh past. He put into my hand the specimen stone used by the distinguished Welsh geologist Dr H. H. Jones in 1922, to prove beyond doubt that the bluestones that form the inner circle at Stonehenge came from the Preseli Hills in north Pembrokeshire. He discovered that these bluestones were composed of a type of rock that occurs only on the outcrops of Carn Meini on the eastern end of the Preselis.

These remarkable rock formations are not many miles from my present home at Fishguard, and I have often walked among the strange, contorted outcrops on autumn days, when the bracken is dying and covering the whole wild hillside with wine-dark glory. As I follow the sheeptracks round the savage tors on such days, the remote past seems to come very close. I can almost see those men of nearly 5,000 years ago struggling to haul the great stones to their final resting place in the shadow of the great triliths of Stonehenge.

## THE CELTS: CRAFTSMEN AND WARRIORS

We don't know what language those early builders of cromlechs and circles spoke, nor to what race they belonged. We can be certain, however, that they were not Celts. The Celts, the ancestors of the modern Welsh, came much later. They arrived from the Continent in a series of waves, the earliest of which settled in Ireland.

Those early Celts have fascinated whole generations of latter-day Welshmen— including me! For as far as I can trace, my family is pure Welsh on both sides. They never left rural Wales, and therefore—even allowing for the Irish who settled in South Wales in the 5th century, or the occasional Viking raider, or some unprincipled Norman adventurer with no respect for Welsh womanhood—my blood must have descended to me through the long centuries from those first Celts. I therefore made a point, during my Aberystwyth days, of reading what the historians had to say about them. This was quite a lot, it soon appeared, and with far more detail than they could give me about those mysterious cromlech builders.

From Roman writers such as Livy, Pliny, Tacitus and Julius Caesar, we get a vivid picture of an aristocracy of warriors, wielding those great iron swords that gave them easy supremacy over the original bronze-using people of Wales. The great hill-forts they left behind in places such as Oswestry, on the Welsh border, show that Celtic society was in a constant state of turmoil between the great tribal units. The warriors used two-wheeled chariots to take them into battle, as did the Greek heroes in the Homeric epics; and, like the ancient Greeks, they delighted in listening to elaborate praise sung by their household bards as they feasted and drank their mead. The National Museum of Wales at Cardiff contains impressive examples of the massive gold torques, bracelets and brooches they wore with swaggering

## TRUMPETS AND TRINKETS

THE 1ST CENTURY BC saw a flowering of Celtic art across Britain. The designs of that time are usually abstract and curvilinear in form, although occasionally stylised animal forms such as fish, cats, boar, sheep and—more rarely— human faces and figures, make an appearance. The Celts were an artistic people, and used these motifs to decorate everything from personal jewellery and household utensils to weapons. Celtic plaques, shield bosses and swords have all been discovered in Wales, many decorated with a 'triskelion' design of three curved figures (the number three has magical signifiance in Celtic legend), perhaps symbolising arms or legs, radiating from a centre.

But towards the end of the century, and on into the next, Celtic

predominance waned with the arrival of Roman traders followed by an occupying army. Later Celtic metalwork increasingly shows the adoption of the newcomers' techniques: more use of straight lines, and stamped, repeated motifs replacing traditional repoussé work (raised designs hammered out from the underside of the metal). An ornate trumpet brooch dating from the end of the 1st century AD, found in Dyfed, is a fine example of the Roman practice of casting in silver— rather than the bronze traditionally used by the Celts—

**ABOVE** *This trumpet brooch from Dyfed is typically Celtic in design, but was made using Roman metal-working methods.*

then gilding in a mixture of gold dust and mercury. This piece of jewellery was found in what was once the Romano-British town of Moridunum. A large proportion of later Celtic metalwork has been discovered near old Roman forts and these objects, with their amalgam of Roman and Celtic styles, provide compelling evidence of a culture in transition.

**BELOW** *A Celtic bronze plaque, found at Llyn Cerrig Bach in 1943, bears a triskelion motif of three 'arms'.*

pride, for the Celts were craftsmen who delighted in curves. Nothing about the Celts—from their fields and houses to their ornaments, their fortifications and even their verses—ever seems to have been constructed in hard, straight lines. They left that sort of thing to the Romans, and perhaps that was the reason why the Romans conquered them. The Romans were certainly a people who thought in straight lines, which took them directly to the point. They clapped Wales into a straitjacket of military roads and forts which lasted for over 300 years—rather longer than the British Raj in India.

I got my first vivid impression of the contrast between the conqueror and the conquered when I got on my motorbike to visit the remains of the Roman town of Caerwent down in southeast Wales not far from the Bristol Channel. Only a week before, I had been up in North Wales looking at some of the British settlements of pre-Roman times. I had climbed up over 1,000 feet to the old fort of Tre'r Ceiri, high on the graceful mountains they call the Rivals.

Tre'r Ceiri—the 'Town of the Giants'—has a splendid setting, with a panorama of sea and mountains at its feet. The original settlement was built before the Romans arrived; the huts are therefore round, and the defences wriggle in curves

**BELOW** *The ruins of Tre'r Ceiri fort on the Lleyn Peninsula, where Celtic curves do battle with Roman angles.*

across the hilltop. However, once the Romans had set up their fort at nearby Caernarfon, the villagers of Tre'r Ceiri, up on their mist-wrapped hill, felt that they ought to follow the new fashion. You can still see the places where they made obvious and rather pathetic attempts to straighten out some of their main buildings. But the Celtic curves always seem to be struggling to get out from beneath those Roman straight lines.

I saw how straight those lines could be a week later when I visited Caerwent. Its Latin name was Venta Silurum—'market town of the Silures'. It was not a military centre, but rather a civilian town where the legionaries who had served their term in the great military camp of Caerleon could retire and settle. The town was forced to equip itself with walls in the stormy days when, at long last, the power of Rome started to crumble. The walls were, naturally, sternly straight. Even when bastions were added later, they were rectangular. To the end, the Romans would not admit the Celtic curve.

## MYSTIQUE OF THE DRUIDS

There was one group of Celts, however, that continued to fascinate the Romans, as indeed it has intrigued many Welsh and non-Welsh people, too, up to our own day. The druids have been a smash hit with the romantically minded for the last 200 years. My own family was, as it were, infiltrated by druidical dreams, for my maternal grandfather was a firm believer in the infinite wisdom of those far-off Celtic seers; so much so that he insisted that the inscription on his gravestone should be carved in a curious, angular script called *Coelbren y Beirdd*, which was supposed to be the actual method of writing on oak trees used by the druids. As a result, I have almost to stand on my head to decipher it when I pay my annual tribute to his memory.

Of course, he got his image of the druids from the great 18th-century antiquaries like Stukeley, who, although they were remarkable pioneers, made one fatal assumption that has bedevilled our history right up to our own day. They associated the druids with stone circles, especially Stonehenge. There is not the slightest evidence that the druids were ever linked with stone circles. All the evidence stresses that the druids placed their shrines in the depths of the woods and sacred groves. But Stonehenge, with its mighty triliths, made an ideal setting for druidical mystique. My grandfather was convinced that every stone circle and cromlech within range of his home at Pontarddulais, outside Swansea, was the scene of strange ceremonies staged by the druids, all white-robed and white-bearded, with splendid golden torques round their necks. The Latin writers had talked of these noble figures also presiding over human sacrifices. My grandfather brushed these stories aside, or excused them with the enlightened comment, 'No doubt all the people they sacrificed were English.'

**ABOVE** *The title page of William Stukeley's book,* The History of the Religion and Temples of the Druids. *The illustration represents the modern stereotype of the white-bearded druid associated with stone circles.*

# FESTIVITIES OF THE EISTEDDFOD

**LEFT** *Children perform a 'flower dance' for the Archdruid and his entourage at the 1998 National Eisteddfod.*

**BELOW** *Edward Williams, 18th-century creator of the Gorsedd of Bards. He became known as the 'Cambrian Shakespeare'.*

CELEBRATIONS OF WELSHNESS reach a spectacular climax every August at the week-long National Eisteddfod. An extravaganza of literature, poetry, music, song and dance, Wales's most important cultural gathering is conducted solely in the Welsh language. Its attractions include competitions, concerts, art and craft exhibitions, and rock and pop shows. The festival is held in a different place each year, alternating between the north and south of the country.

Following centuries-old tradition, hundreds of smaller eisteddfods take place in towns and villages throughout Wales. They evolved from ancient bardic tournaments in which apprentice poets and musicians competed for a seat of honour in a noble's household. However, since it was first held in 1861, no occasion has carried such emotional appeal as the National, which draws up to 200,000 people to enjoy its dazzling pageantry.

At the heart of the ceremonies is the Gorsedd of Bards, or Bardic Circle, invented by the 18th-century Glamorgan stonemason Edward Williams. As well as writers, musicians and artists, the Gorsedd embraces many other champions of Welsh culture and language—including TV stars, rugby players and opera singers. Highlights of the Eisteddfod are the 'crowning' and the 'chairing' of the Bard, when members of the Gorsedd assemble on stage in colourful robes to hear their elected leader, the Archdruid, reveal the results of the poetry competition.

While the National is pledged to sustaining Welsh consciousness, the International Musical Eisteddfod is devoted to the cause of world harmony. Established soon after the Second World War, and held every year since at Llangollen, it is an occasion for nations to celebrate 'togetherness'. Singers, dancers, orchestras and choirs from more than 40 countries converge on this small town in North Wales to take part in competitive events open to both amateurs and professionals. For six days in July, Llangollen is overtaken by a frenzy of music, poetry and colour, culminating in a Saturday evening concert, when winners of the week's four major choral competitions vie for the title 'Choir of the World'.

**LEFT** *Each year this trophy is awarded to the 'Choir of the World' at the International Musical Eisteddfod.*

**LEFT** *The original poster advertising the first International Musical Eisteddfod, which was held in Llangollen in 1947.*

**RIGHT** *Choirs gather outside the Royal International Pavillion at Llangollen in 1996.*

His druidical obsession was reinforced by his study of the works of a remarkable Welshman, Edward Williams—'Iolo Morganwg'—who transported Stukeley's druids back to Wales. Iolo was a brilliant poet in his own right, but preferred to pass off his poems as the work of the medieval bards. He it was who held the first meeting of the Bards of the Isle of Britain in a circle of small stones which he arranged on Primrose Hill in London. Out of his overheated imagination he created the Gorsedd of white-robed bards who grace the National Eisteddfod every year and who are also responsible for scattering fake druidical circles outside every town in Wales.

In defiance of scholarly research, one such circle stands in the gardens immediately opposite the National Museum of Wales in Cardiff—appropriately enough in the shadow of the statue of that druidical spellbinder David Lloyd George.

When I was young, I used to chuckle at the white-robed procession of bards—some with their trousers peeping from underneath their 'nightgowns'—as they straggled uncertainly onto the Eisteddfod platform. Nowadays I cast a kinder eye on their proceedings. Wales possesses precious few chances for ceremonial rituals. The end of Welsh independence, long ago in the 13th century, means that Wales has no indigenous orders to match the Order of the Garter or the ancient orders of Scotland. Nations need a little ceremonial to make their past vivid to their present. It no longer worries me that the Gorsedd of Bards had its origin in Iolo Morganwg's romantic druidical dreams. It has given Wales a much-needed ritual, based not on wealth or military power but on homage to the arts. Let me confess that I have joined the Gorsedd myself and am proud to travel with my fellow bards in white-robed glory to the Eisteddfod field.

The Gorsedd is a delightful—even a necessary—fiction, but is there any genuine survival from that remote past, from the world of the real druids that so entranced my grandfather? Well, I have a theory—which will probably be shot down by the experts—which takes us leaping across 2,000 years to the last place where you would expect to find traces of the druids: the Welsh chapel.

## THE METHODIST REVIVAL

In the 18th century, the Methodist Revival shook Wales like an emotional earthquake. There were dissenters aplenty in Wales before the Revival, but it was the Methodist preachers who really persuaded the Welsh peasantry to desert the Church of England in droves. The ground had been prepared beforehand by an important change in Welsh society. When the Tudors came to the English throne, something like a job-rush to London occurred among the Welsh gentry. This very understandable move to the centre of power continued under the Stuarts, and by the mid 18th century the aristocracy of Wales had become almost completely anglicised. 'Speak no Welsh,' wrote one Welsh squire to his son at Oxford, 'to any that can speak English, no, not to your bedfellows, that thereby you may attain and freely speak the English tongue perfectly.'

The Welsh aristocracy certainly succeeded in following the squire's advice. The peasantry remained Welsh-speaking, and a great gulf opened between the classes.

**ABOVE** *In 1588 a Welsh translation of the Bible was printed in London. Armed with this weapon, Welsh preachers were able to convert the peasantry of rural Wales, sparking the Methodist revival of the 18th century.*

Into this gulf stepped the fiery Welsh Methodist preachers, armed with a weapon inadvertently supplied to them by the Tudors: a translation of the Bible into Welsh, which was as poetic, as singing and as mind-possessing as the English Authorised Version. Naturally, they swept the country.

Their first chapels, built in the face of fierce opposition from the squirearchy, were simple affairs, as had been those of their predecessors, the earlier dissenters. Those that still remain are moving in their whitewashed simplicity. As the century progressed, the builders gained in confidence and enterprise. In the 1900s, their chapels blossomed into columns and even spires.

The Welsh chapel has not had much architectural acclaim. In my own brash youth, I was loud in my disapproval:

> *Swift through the dark flies the 5.49,*
> *Past Slough and past Didcot and derelict mine,*
> *Past pubs and Lucanias and adverts for ales*
> *Till the backsides of chapels cry 'Welcome to Wales!'*

Now that we are only too familiar with the horrors of modern concrete-slab architecture, however, the 'front sides', if not the 'backsides', of Welsh chapels seem far more sympathetic to the eye. Within, I never found them other than architecturally exciting, with the elegant curve of the gallery and the organ pipes rising like rockets of thrilling sound behind the altarlike pulpit.

**LEFT** *Gwrhyd chapel in West Glamorgan. Although Welsh chapels can hardly lay claims to architectural splendour, their humble outward appearance often belies a lively interior.*

**RIGHT** *An ornate ceiling arches over the pulpit and gallery of Gwydyr Uchaf chapel in Conwy.*

The preacher rose to the full splendour of his position in the architecture of the chapel as he came to the climax of his sermon, producing those mysterious cadences in his voice, those ever-rising cascades of orchestrated sentences known as the *hwyl* (pronounced as nearly as possible in English by running together the two words 'who-ill'). In the hands of an expert practitioner, the *hwyl* could be a moving experience. As the voice of the preacher rose, fell, and then climbed again, ever higher and higher, his words became a compelling chant loaded with mesmeric power, which carried the whole congregation into a new world of religious ecstasy.

I had an uncle who was a connoisseur of the *hwyl*. He would follow the great preachers from chapel to chapel, carrying a tuning-fork. When one of the last of the great exponents of the *hwyl*, the Reverend Philip Jones, reached the height of his peroration, my uncle excitedly struck his tuning fork and shouted, 'Top C, by God! Well done, Philip *bach*!'

Now where did this remarkable exercise in vocal hypnotism come from? It surely has nothing to do with the logical, organised procedure of the orthodox church service. I maintain that it is pre-Christian. It must come from the dark recesses of folk memory, which carries us back to the incantations of the druids in their sacred groves of Anglesey. I am sure that Professor Glyn Daniel will shake his head in disapproval, but, in my imagination, I see the preacher in the *hwyl* uniting cromlech and chapel through the severing mists of 2,000 years of the strange history of wild Wales.

# 'EVERY VALLEY SHALL BE EXALTED'

AS I SAT AMONG THE BOOKS in the tranquil recesses of the National Library of Wales in the closing months of 1933, I began to feel restless. Aberystwyth had been kind to me. It had introduced me to the world of Welsh poetry and legend, to mysterious and mystic Wales. But I knew in my heart that I was not a genuine scholar. I did not have the patience and devotion to hunt through the fifty-odd versions of Master Blegywryd's treatise on *The Laws of Hywel Dda,* or to unravel the complexities of the genealogy of the Vaughans of Golden Grove. Instead, I idly glanced through the Appointments Vacant column of the *Western Mail,* on a morning when I should have been cataloguing the papers of the Ocean Colliery Group.

An advertisement for an administrative assistant to the South Wales Council of Social Service caught my eye. The job involved travelling through the mining valleys, giving grants to clubs for the unemployed. In the 1930s, the Great Depression struck South Wales with stunning force. Almost overnight, the Rhondda and the other valleys changed from the Black Klondike into the problem area of Britain. Long queues of unemployed men stood outside the dole offices. The great wheels of the winding gear of the pit shafts were as inactive as the men who once worked them. Whole communities that had once throbbed with a strange, tough, yet vital life became dead and listless.

The unemployed clubs were clearly no complete cure for the woes of the South Wales coalfield, but at least they offered a little hope to those who had suddenly become hopeless. I applied by post, and got the job. I deserted the quiet groves of the Aberystwyth Library, and for the next three years chugged my way in the rain through the steep streets of Maerdy, Ferndale, Treorchy and Treherbert.

When you first hit it, the landscape of the Valleys comes as an architectural shock. The two Rhondda Valleys, the Fawr (or 'big') and the Fach ('small'), narrow steadily as they bite deeper into the hills. The valley floors become crowded with a wonderful mix-up of chapels and welfare halls, pubs, shops and billiard saloons, all fighting for space with the tall winding gear and surface buildings of the collieries. The long lines of terraced houses crawl like stone caterpillars over the lower slopes, while the waste from the pits is carried 1,000 feet up the hillside on aerial ropeways, or even perched precariously on the mountain tops. So precariously, indeed, that in the nearby valley of the Taff in 1966 the tip base gave way, and the vile sludge that had accumulated over the long years of exploitation slid tragically downhill through the mists to overwhelm the unsuspecting schoolchildren of Aberfan. The architecture of the Valleys holds grim memories for those who live with it.

I think I had been half prepared for my first view of the Rhondda by my delving into the Ocean Colliery papers. I had spent weeks tracing the story of the sinking of the company's first shaft at Cwmparc—and what a drama that was! The setting was the Rhondda Fawr Valley, which, in 1864, still retained the lonely beauty that had

## HYWEL DDA, THE LAWGIVER

THROUGH INHERITANCE, marriage and, some claim, assassination, King Hywel ap Cadell (c. 887–950) brought a new political unity to Wales in the 10th century by extending his rule to cover almost the whole country.

The epithet *Dda* (the Good), given to him long after his death, probably reflects impressive achievement rather than a saintly character. In his 40-year reign Hywel Dda protected his territories from marauding Norsemen and remained on good terms with the English, submitting to their rule and appearing regularly at the courts of four Saxon kings. He was the first Welsh ruler to issue his own coinage, a silver penny minted at Chester. And, most importantly, he is credited with revising and codifying Welsh law.

Tradition has it that during Lent in the year 930 Hywel summoned six wise men from each of the three main districts of Wales to his hunting lodge at Ty Gwyn ar Dav (now Whitland in Carmarthenshire). Six weeks later the laws were

proclaimed, with a curse upon anyone who dared break them. Though not egalitarian by modern standards, the laws nonetheless contained degrees of compassion and common sense that were unusual in Europe until much later. They recognised divorce by common consent, for example, describing detailed arrangements for the division of belongings: 'Of the bedding, the husband shall have all the bedclothes which are beneath; the wife those which are above.'

Since Welsh law continued to evolve, and the earliest extant

**RIGHT** *This 13th-century Welsh law book contains the laws of Hywel Dda in Latin text. It is the only known illustrated law book of that time.*

**BELOW** *Although Hywel Dda submitted to English rule, he was sufficiently independent to mint his own silver pennies.*

versions of *The Laws of Hywel Dda* are 13th-century manuscripts, it is difficult to identify with certainty those laws that date to Hywel's time. But for his work in unifying the diverse legal customs of Wales alone, Hywel deserves to be called *Dda*.

delighted the traveller Benjamin Heath Malkin fifty years before. As he wrote, in his florid style, 'The stream fertilises the valley with its pure, translucent waters…The contrast of the meadows, rich and verdant, with mountains the most wild and romantic, surrounding them on every side, is in the highest degree picturesque.'

## STRIKING BLACK GOLD

Into this lost solitude there suddenly erupted all the steam-driven paraphernalia of Victorian industrialism, inspired by the restless energy of David Davies, one of the most remarkable of the early pioneers of the coalfield. He was a self-made man, if ever there was one. He had been born at Llandinam in mid Wales, and had made his way by the shrewd use of money he had acquired by his own hard work, becoming the leading railway contractor in Wales. You can see the sort of man he was from his statue on the roadside at Llandinam. There he stands, sturdy and resolute, with the plans of his latest enterprise in his hand, almost defying the world to stop his onward march to success.

He did defy the world in his venture at Cwmparc. In his self-confident way, he put his own money at risk to sink his pits 700 feet down towards the rich seams that he was sure lay underneath his property. But by 1866 there was a dramatic tension all over the valley. The coal had not been struck. David Davies was almost at the end of his financial resources. He had poured £30,000 down his mine shafts, and there was still no sign of the lucrative Rhondda number three seam. Davies called the men together. He told them frankly, 'Boys, I'm sorry, I cannot go on here any longer. There's some grand coal here, and I believe we are close to it. But I can't go on.' He paid out the wages, and when the final pay packet was handed over added, 'That leaves exactly half-a-crown in my pocket.'

'We'll have that, too,' one man shouted. David Davies shrugged his shoulders. 'Take it,' he said, and tossed him his last half-crown.

But, as always happens in film epics, the men had been impressed by Davies's courage. They decided to give him one week's work for free. The master had gone off to supervise the construction of the unfinished Whitland–Tenby railway, convinced that he had lost his hard-earned fortune. Bankruptcy stared him in the face. Then on March 9, 1866, William Thomas, the railway foreman, suddenly saw an excited figure making its way along the embankments and brandishing a piece of paper. It was David Davies, with a telegram. 'William, I'll not take £40,000 for this piece of paper. They've struck the seam at Cwmparc!'

Moses striking water from the rock in the wilderness did not produce a more spectacular result. From the seams of the Rhondda flowed the vast wealth of the Davies family, but at the same time every other valley seemed to be taking off, too. The black gold poured from the valleys to the ports of Newport and Cardiff, and the David Davies drama began its final act.

All of Davies's coal had to go down to Cardiff docks over the land of the 3rd Marquess of Bute; to the fury of Davies, the Bute interests charged him a pretty penny on every load of coal he sent down to Cardiff. A battle was inevitable, and the contestants were sharply contrasted.

**ABOVE** *The Welsh entrepreneur David Davies made his fortune after discovering coal at Cwmparc in the Rhondda Valley.*

**OPPOSITE** *As coal production boomed in the 19th century, the green valley of the Rhondda became scarred with ranks of terraced housing.*

RIGHT *WIth its romantic turrets rising out of the trees, Castell Coch, built in the 1870s, resembles a medieval castle.*

ABOVE *John Patrick, 3rd Marquess of Bute, seen here in the robes of Rector of St Andrew's University, Scotland.*

ABOVE *The ornate ceiling of the drawing room at Castell Coch is extravagantly decorated with butterflies and birds of paradise.*

## A MAN OF MANY TALENTS

The Marquess was also a remarkable man in his way. He was, without question, one of the most gifted of our Victorian noblemen—an authority on Coptic Church symbolism, a leading investigator of psychic phenomena and the translator of Turgenev. The coal of the Rhondda and the adjacent valleys was also making him one of the richest men in Britain. His money naturally led him into the delights of building: as Ruskin had now made the Gothic style respectable, the Marquess demanded towers, battlements and all the architectural bric-a-brac of the Middle Ages—anything, one feels, to shut off the view of Victorian Cardiff. He got them in full measure with the help of his architect, William Burges. Together they converted Cardiff Castle into a Roman fort, and then gaily stuck a pseudo-Gothic architectural fantasy on the west wall. Then they looked around for new ruins to conquer.

They found what they were looking for at Taff's Well, some five miles north of Cardiff. Here, the River Taff breaks through a line of high limestone cliffs in a narrow gorge. The coalfield and its industry are out of sight, and the hills are steep, wooded and charming.

Perched on a crag near the gorge were the ruins of Castell Coch, the Red Castle, built by one of the Welsh princes or by an invading Norman baron to pen the Welsh back into their hills. There are few written records of the castle's history, and this made Burges's task all the more delightful. He and his patron could give full reign to their antiquarian enthusiasm. In 1875 they cleared the site, and at last there arose a romantic, turreted reconstruction, which looks for all the world like the castles depicted on old hock labels. There was even a drawbridge that really worked—so well, indeed, that it once tipped half a Sunday-school outing into the dry moat.

As the Marquess gazed with pride at his new castle, he could not fail to notice how closely the site resembled the slopes of the Rhine, the Mosel and the Loire. Clearly, there was only one thing wanting to make the picture perfect: a vineyard at the castle gate. When you have the Bute millions behind you, it is possible to order a vineyard as the rest of us order a new car. The Marquess made his decision, and Britain's biggest vineyard of modern times grew on the hillside.

The wines of Castell Coch actually came on the market—perhaps the first British-made wines to do so for 450 years, since the Dissolution of the Monasteries ruined the old monkish vineyards. *Punch* was pleased to be witty at the expense of the Marquess's first offering. It declared that it took four men to drink one bottle: two to hold the victim down, and one to pour it down his throat. This was unfair. The wine soon proved acceptable, and the vineyard would be there to this day but for a succession of damp summers just before the First World War.

The Castell Coch vineyard site looks perfect for the job on a sunny day in early summer. You can imagine the grapes ripening happily, and the Welsh *vignerons* singing—in four-part harmony of course—as they tended the vines before going to choir practice in the nearby chapel. But, alas, such days were rare. As one old Welsh countryman once reminded me, 'Never forget that Welsh weather is teetotal!'

The vineyard has gone, but Castell Coch and the reconstructed Cardiff Castle remain to delight the modern visitor. The Marquess and his successors gave one final legacy to the capital city of Wales when they bequeathed to it the site of the civic centre at Cathays Park, in the shadow of the castle. Here arose, in the early days of the 20th century, a choice collection of white-columned buildings, equipped with splendidly florid statuary and neo-classical decoration, aligned with careful elegance along tree-lined avenues. Here were clustered the law courts, the City Hall, the National Museum of Wales and the University College. At the far end, one open space remained, reserved—so the rumour ran—for the Welsh Parliament of the future. Cardiff civic centre may look like a Welsh rehearsal for

**BELOW** *The National Museum of Wales stands in Cathays Park, which was bequeathed to the nation by the Bute family. In front of the museum is a statue of a local MP who fell in the First World War.*

Lutyens's New Delhi, but it gave Cardiff the air of a worthy capital city long before it gained the title.

While the Marquess of Bute was busy raising his Gothic towers in Cardiff and at Castell Coch, his formidable rival was also occupying himself with construction—but of a radically different sort. David Davies had come to a bold solution to his exporting problems. He decided that there was only one thing to do: he would bypass both the Bute interests and Cardiff docks. He would drive a new railway out of the impasse of the Rhondda, pouring his money into tunnels, deep cuttings and high viaducts. Eight miles down channel from Cardiff, he would build a brand-new port at Barry, equipped with the most modern coal-loading machinery in the world. He carried out his plan with ruthless energy and efficiency.

## BARRY: THE GRAVEYARD OF STEAM

I followed the fight as I sat in my quiet room in the National Library of Wales. The papers of the Ocean Colliery became as exciting to me as a Balzac novel. Here were the secret geological reports, the quiet transaction to acquire the land before

## AN ASSEMBLY FOR WALES

ALMOST 600 YEARS after the last Welsh parliament was held, cheering crowds lined the streets of Cardiff in May 1999 to welcome the Queen, who had come to Wales's capital city to open the new National Assembly. And whereas the 1405 parliament, convened by Owain Glyndwr, had sought to sever Wales from the control of the English monarch, this time around the Queen's presence was a symbol of the ties that still link the principality to the rest of Britain.

The enthusiasm of the crowds belied the fact that only half the electorate had voted in favour of the Assembly in a 1997 referendum, and a mere 46 per cent of the 2 million Welsh voters had turned out for the Assembly elections. Despite a trend towards devolved politics in Britain, many Welsh people were unconvinced of the benefits of this constitutional shake-up, and First Secretary Alun Michael admitted that the Assembly would have to work hard to 'convince people' of its value.

On July 1 the responsibilities of the Secretary of State for Wales (also Alun Michael) passed to the National Assembly: it has no capacity to raise taxes or pass legislation, but is responsible for spending a treasury grant, and has powers over education, health and transport. Its first meeting

**ABOVE** *A computer-generated image of the new Welsh Assembly building* (right); *the underground debating chambers will be visible to the public from ground level.*

was to discuss the issue of BSE, or Mad Cow Disease—a subject close to the hearts of the Welsh farming community.

prices skyrocketed, the diplomatic letters nobbling MPs to support the scheme, the spies counting the wagons rolling over the Bute lines and in the end the Act of Parliament that embodied the triumph of David Davies. No wonder a second statue of him, complete with plans, stands at the gates of Barry Dock.

What irony in the present fate of the docks he created! In 1913 South Wales reached its export peak, with the ships of the world queuing up in the roadsteads of Cardiff, Newport and Barry. Welsh steam coal was the oil of the period. By the end of the First World War, all that was altered. Oil was cutting savage swaths into the market. The age of steam was coming to an end, and with it the glories of the Rhondda and Barry Dock. Today, the sidings at Barry form a dumping ground for the old steam locomotives of British Rail. Barry has become the graveyard of steam. I wouldn't be surprised if David Davies shudders on his stone pedestal.

I shuddered a little, too, as I left my study of the Ocean papers to pay my first visit to the unemployed club at Ton Pentre. Now, curiously enough, it wasn't the actual appearance of the Valleys that shook me. The landscape has a strange attraction, a dark, unexpected, dramatic power. Today, when so many of the pits have been closed, the tips have been levelled and grassed and the forests have advanced over the bare mountain tops, you can find again traces of the sylvan beauty that delighted the old traveller, Malkin, nearly 200 years ago.

**ABOVE** *Barry Dock in 1895 was a bustling port, shipping coal from Wales to the rest of the world.*

To savour the change that has now come over the coalfield, you should begin your drive at Port Talbot and follow the Afan Valley as it cuts deep into the hills. Not one of its old collieries is working today, and the Forestry Commission is busy reclothing the hillsides. You pass the little village of Pontrhydyfen, perched on a rock in the middle of the gorgelike vale. Its railway viaducts give it a visual excitement. Along the parapet of one of them my father toddled as a boy of four, to the horror of his parents. In the shadow of the same viaduct, Richard Burton was born as Richard Jenkins. Like everyone else who has been born in the Valleys, he was always proud to return to his birthplace.

The Afan twists and turns into the mountains. Beyond Blaengwynfi, the road climbs dramatically, before emerging onto the high mountain plateau. The pine trees are now growing tall, but the view is still splendidly extensive over almost the whole of South Wales. The unmistakable flat-topped summits of the Brecon Beacons rise far off in the north. At your feet lies the deep trench of the Rhondda Fawr Valley, crowded with a sea of terraced houses in which the chapels and welfare halls float like black icebergs. It is one of the most exciting viewpoints in the Principality.

Alas, things become very much more mundane as you drop down 1,500 feet along the zigzag road that lands you in Treorchy. Every time I drive it today, my mind goes back over forty years, for this was the way I first entered the Rhondda on my motorbike. The Ocean papers had prepared me for the physical appearance of the area, but not for the deep anxiety that now possessed it. The old David Davies confidence was gone. No one was now rushing to make his fortune in a great, booming mining camp. Everyone who could was struggling to get out.

**LEFT** *Welsh sporting hero Tommy Farr fought the legendary Joe Louis in 1937 for the world heavyweight boxing title, but lost to the American fighter.*

**RIGHT** *Miners in the Rhondda Valley gather round the radio after their shift to await the result of the Tommy Farr/Joe Louis heavyweight title fight.*

One old miner, whose father had been one of the men to whom David Davies had tossed his last half-crown in 1866, put it to me: 'There are only three ways of getting out of this place, Mr Thomas. You can box your way out. You can play your way out. And you can sing your way out!'

## GREAT WAVES OF SONG

**BELOW** *Rugby is a hugely popular sport in Wales; here, Cardiff (in blue and black) take on Abertillery in 1999.*

Boxing was still one of the excitements of the Valleys when I first came to them. The chapels may have disapproved, but the great boxers were still local heroes. Little Jimmy Wilde, the Tylorstown Terror, the greatest flyweight in the world, still showed you his Lonsdale Belt with pride, and Tommy Farr was on his way to challenge Joe Louis himself.

As for playing yourself out, naturally, you turned to rugby. Rugby had spread up the Valleys from the big coastal towns, where the first clubs had received their impetus from public-school, middle-class England. But the game was transformed when it got into the hills. The local rugby teams played as if they were exacting vengeance at last for the defeat of Owain Glyndwr. The fervour and splendour of modern Welsh rugby as displayed in the national shrine of Cardiff's Millennium Stadium have their roots in the small clubs, which were backed by the pride of the whole local community.

I remember watching a rugby match against a visiting English team on a ground that had been carved out of the mountainside by the local surveyor. He had given the left touchline an imperceptible slope to the south, which was worth a certain first try to the local team. If there was also a strong wind from the west blowing against the backside of Salem chapel, which stood just behind the goalposts, the conversion was in the bag as well. On this occasion, however—to the consternation of the local crowd—the English scored first. The stentorian voice of a spectator behind me rallied the ranks with the immortal shout: 'Rub their faces in the dirt, boys, *bach*—but in a sporting manner, of course!'

That was the key to it. Even the roughest game was conducted in a sporting manner. Then, once the game was over, everyone adjourned to the pub for singing. Welsh rugby and singing are inseparable. The great waves of song that break from the crowd as Wales establish a lead in an international must terrify the visiting team as surely as the chants of the druids terrified the Roman legions as they prepared to cross the Menai Strait into Anglesey in AD 61.

The Male Voice Party shared with the rugby team the devoted loyalty of the community. I presume the tradition of part singing came from the chapel, and the chapel singing may have been based on something far more ancient. Giraldus Cambrensis, the Norman–Welsh writer of the 12th century, noted that even in his day the Welsh were much given to singing in harmony. In modern times, Wales is the only nation that has raised a monument to a choir conductor.

In 1872 and again in 1873, Griffith Rhys Jones, known by his bardic name of Caradog, led his great choir to victory in the choral competition at the Crystal

## GERALD OF WALES, THE GREAT CHRONICLER

THE MEDIEVAL SCHOLAR and cleric Gerald of Wales, also known as Giraldus Cambrensis and Gerald de Barri, was born in about 1146 at Manorbier Castle, a fortress on the Pembrokeshire coast. Gerald's parents were the Welsh Princess Angharad and a Norman baron, William de Barri.

Gerald was a cosmopolitan character: after growing up in Pembrokeshire he went to Paris to study at the Sorbonne, and later returned there to teach. In 1175 he became Archdeacon of Brecon, but his lifelong ambition was to succeed to the bishopric of St David's and make it independent of English control. His nationalist zeal, however, meant that he was continually passed over for the role.

As a loyal churchman, at the beginning of Lent in 1188 Gerald embarked on a six-week tour of Wales with Archbishop Baldwin of Canterbury to recruit troops for the Crusades. The Welsh had a

fierce military reputation and soon 3,000 men had signed up, much to the dismay of their wives. During the journey Gerald amassed material for two books which he wrote (in Latin) on his return: the *Itinerarium Cambriae* or *Journey Through Wales* (1191),

and the *Descriptio Cambriae* or *Description of Wales* (1194), two travel journals giving a topographical and historical account of the country. Gerald enthused about the landscape, and painted a vivid portrait of the contemporary Welshman, describing him as musical, witty, skilled at storytelling and religious, as well as frugal in his diet, which consisted mainly of meat, oats, milk, butter and cheese. He also had an eye for other fascinating details of everyday life, such as the page-boy hairstyle that was sported by both men and women, and the great care that the people took of their teeth. The *Itinerarium* and the *Descriptio* have left modern-day readers with an enchanting picture of life in Wales in the 12th century.

**LEFT** *Gerald of Wales is depicted at work on his* Descriptio Cambriae *in this 12th-century manuscript.*

# THE LONG ROAD TO MARKET

HIKE ALONG an obscure valley lane, or drive along a single-track roadway over the Cambrian Mountains, and you might be following one of the great old drovers' roads of Wales.

Dating back at least to Norman times, these roads stretched eastwards from Wales towards the lucrative markets of England. What colourful cavalcades these roads carried! Countless sheep; gaggles of geese, their feet protected by a coating of tar and sand; pigs parading in leather-soled woollen bootees; even—from the 18th century—troops of turkeys. Above all, herds of hardy Welsh black cattle, or 'Welsh runts'.

The pattern varied little over the centuries. A licensed drover bought his cattle at summer fairs. At staging posts such as Tregaron or Llandovery they were shod, herded into groups 300- or 400-strong, and sent on their way. They were supervised by a dozen jobbing drovers, several of them mounted on ponies, while corgis yapped underfoot, keeping order. The procession travelled for two or three weeks, stopping overnight at farms for board and pasture, and covering perhaps 16 miles every day (except on Sundays, when droving was forbidden).

Dangers lay in wait: mist over marshes; stampedes; cattle rustlers and robbers. But it was worth the risk. The cattle would quickly

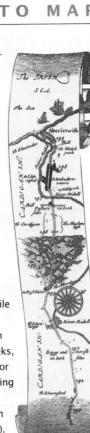

fatten again in the Kent or East Anglia pastures, and fetch good money at the autumn cattle fairs.

Master drovers often performed other crucial tasks, too. They might deliver mail and even settle accounts on behalf of clients—prompting the formation of several Welsh banks in the 18th and 19th centuries. And they would bring English commodities and trends back to Wales—cloth and salt, plants, and, of course, English news and popular tunes. Their effect on Welsh culture, therefore, went well beyond that of mere livestock exporters.

The drovers' roads faced competition in the mid-18th century from a new network of 'turnpike' roads, but many drovers couldn't or wouldn't pay the tolls. What finally effaced the drovers' roads was the arrival of the railways, which began to transport the animals a century later.

ABOVE *Alfred Worthington's painting* Llanbadarn Church *(c. 1880) depicts drovers resting outside the Black Lion pub.*

RIGHT *A pair of Welsh drovers pose for the camera in a rare photograph dating from the late 1800s.*

BELOW *An old drovers' bridge crosses the Tryweryn stream in Migneint, a bleak area of wet moorland.*

LEFT *The Llandovery Bank was founded for drovers in 1799 by David Jones. His notes depicted a black bull, and the bank was known locally as 'The Bank of the Black Ox'.*

Palace. The Valleys were convinced that Caradog had shown the world that Wales was in truth the land of song. They immortalised him in bronze, forever waving his baton in the square at Aberdare.

Great singers, too, have come from the South Wales coalfield, and the little village of Cilfynydd, outside Pontypridd, has the distinction of having produced two opera stars, Sir Geraint Evans and Stuart Burrows. Perhaps opera was the natural line for them to follow, for life in the Valleys can sometimes have an operatic intensity that seems to be crying out for some Verdi or Puccini to set it to music—whether tragic or light.

I look back on the turbulent history of that century or more since David Davies sunk his pit at Cwmparc—over that almost epic story of fortunes won and lost, of strikes, explosions, fiery political speeches and devoted lives lived in the anguish of unemployment—and I count myself privileged to have shared in it in a small way for a few years. Until you have seen the Valleys, you cannot understand modern Wales.

## THE ROOF OF WALES

When I returned from the war and lived in London, I cherished one ambition about Wales. Was it possible to tramp Wales from end to end keeping entirely to the mountains? I was approaching my fiftieth birthday. If I was going to walk the south–north mountain route, it was now or never. I persuaded the BBC to let me tramp what I christened the 'Roof of Wales' to celebrate my fiftieth birthday in 1958.

I got out the map and decided that I would follow the dividing line between the rivers that flowed east or southeast and those that flowed west or southwest. I had to start at the point where the mountains come closest to the sea in the south: clearly, this is at Port Talbot, and I made a symbolic beginning at the gates of the giant Abbey Steelworks in Margam. Then my route went over the high hills of the Glamorgan coalfield, and what a surprise it was to find that the crowded valleys and their mines were almost invisible, lost in the deep slots in the landscape carved by the Rhondda, the Afan and the Taff. The next day took me onto the great escarpment. I followed the skyline in a wonderful steeplechase over those familiar summits of my youth, coming down from the prow of the Carmarthen Vans to my night's rest at Trecastle.

The third day was a bit of an epic. I had to get up at dawn to clear the Eppynt moorlands before the guns opened fire, for most of the Eppynt is now an artillery training range. I wonder what the old drovers would have said if they could have seen their favourite inn, the Drovers Arms, standing lonely and deserted on its high ridge, with the red flag of danger flying near what is left of the bar!

From the Eppynt, I plunged into the vast and then almost trackless wilderness of the Green Desert of Wales, finding my night's rest at the farm of Nant-yr-Hwch.

The fourth day saw me tackling the toughest part of the wilderness. I passed the great black bog where the Tywi rises; then, relying on my compass, I cast myself adrift on the waves of green ridges, which flow away without a tree or any sign to walkers that they are on the correct route. My compass reading was good.

**RIGHT** *The sun sinks low behind the shores of Bala Lake, tinting sky and water in lurid shades.*

I struck the lonely Teifi Pools and the even more lonely lakes of Llyn Du, where the terns were breeding in clamorous white clouds. I contoured the deep trench of the Ystwyth Valley, and came at last, after what seemed to me to be thirty miles of the toughest walking I had yet done, to the café at Eisteddfa Gurig, nearly 1,000 feet up on the side of Plynlimon.

After that, I almost took Plynlimon in my stride. I came down off the summit, past the tarns of Bugeilyn—the Lake of the Shepherd—and Glaslyn, to the abandoned lead-mining centre of Dylife. All its glory has gone. Even the church, where one of the chief investors, John Bright of 'free trade' fame, used to lead the prayers (always for more profit, declared his enemies), has gone to ruin. Only the Star Inn testified to the wealth that once came from this wild corner of the Welsh hills.

I paused to admire the spectacular waterfall of the Ffrwd Fawr, which must be one of the least known of the great falls of Wales. Then I cleared the boggy moor of Trannon, with only the grouse protesting as I walked.

The sixth day was, again, one of the tough ones. I marched up and down towards the north, over moorlands where few people stray. As I dropped down through tangled heather to little Llyn Coch-hwyad, I got my first sign that I would, barring accidents, complete my conquest of the Roof of Wales. The jagged peaks of the North were rising before me: the Arans, the Arenigs and Snowdonia itself, all familiar friends. It was a day of clarity and sun. I felt exhilarated as I almost flew up the grassy tongue that separates the precipices of Aran Fawddwy from those of Aran Benllyn, then went happily down in the rays of the setting sun to Llanuwchllyn, by the breeze-blown waters of Bala Lake.

The last three days would take me over the highest mountains of the Roof of Wales, but now I was travelling on well-known paths, and I had walked myself fighting fit. In two days I cleared the Arenigs, then made my way up through the tangled country by Blaenau Ffestiniog to my old haunt at Penygwryd. So I came to the last day. I went over Glyder Fach and Tryfan, down to Llyn Ogwen. Then it was up the last climb of my nine days to the summit of Carnedd Llywelyn. I paused at the cairn and looked to the south. It seemed a long, long way to my starting point far away in Margam, but I was glad I had come the whole distance on my own feet.

I turned and followed the high ridge of the Carneddau to come down at last over the crags of Penmaenmawr to the sea, where I was greeted by a handshake from the mayor, the cheers of the crowd and the joyous welcome of the local brass band.

Twenty years later, the madness fell upon me again. The BBC suggested that I repeat the walk to celebrate my seventieth birthday. Buoyed up by a feeling that I wanted to test my chances of survival before I became an official geriatric, I covered the route once again. I even added some extra mileage to its rough 220-odd miles of twists and turns across the mountains.

Unluckily, a mist caught me in the middle of the Green Desert, just beyond the Teifi Pools. Proudly I took out my new Swedish compass, and stupidly, without reading the instructions—my Swedish is not fluent!—I decided that the white end of the needle pointed north and the dark end south. They didn't. And I tramped eastwards through the mists for mile after boggy mile, until the thin veils parted and I found myself looking down on a vast lake where, according to my map,

## WALES'S PRECIOUS FLOCK

**LEFT** *The green hills of North Wales, dotted with hundreds of sheep—the cornerstone of Welsh country life.*

**RIGHT** *At the Merioneth Country Show, sheep farmers demonstrate their shearing skills.*

All Welsh Lamb identified by the Guild of Welsh Lamb Suppliers logo is fully traceable to the farm of origin.

## Welsh Lamb
### Naturally Sweet
CIG OEN CYMREIG · CYNNYRCH CEFN GWLAD CYMRU

**ABOVE** *Ewe's-milk cheese is once again being made by traditional methods on Welsh farms.*

**LEFT** *Welsh lamb, bred on lush, verdant pastures, is renowned for its sweet taste and tenderness.*

SHEEP REARING HAS FORMED the bedrock of country life in Wales for more than 1,000 years. The Welsh wool industry—the oldest in Europe—depended for its success on the hardy Welsh mountain sheep, a small breed renowned for its high-quality, lightweight white fleece. The fleece was used to make cloth as well as knitted items, and by the end of the 18th century Wales was supplying a huge export market.

The Industrial Revolution brought power looms to the Teifi Valley in Cardiganshire, enabling the manufacture of large quantities of flannel shirts and underwear for the growing mining communities of southeast Wales. The Teifi mills continued to prosper during the First World War, meeting the need for vast supplies of blankets and uniforms.

But since the 1920s wool and cloth production—the traditional source of rural prosperity—have been in decline, with only a handful of mills surviving. Production today is aimed largely at the tourist market. For example, the Museum of the Welsh Woollen Industry at Dre-fach Felindre near Lampeter (*see page 154*) sells clothes made of extra-strong flannel and a soft, lightweight fabric called saxony. Fashions on sale here include farmers' shirts and flannel shawls, traditionally passed from mother to daughter. And at Tregwynt Mill in Haverfordwest, a range of knitted designs is made into cosy woollen blankets.

As for meat, in recent decades Welsh sheep farmers have found it hard to compete on the world stage. While Wales's hilly terrain and fertile, well-watered soil make for lamb of incomparable flavour, the smallness and remoteness of many farms, and the low price of sheep, mean that the farms are often uneconomical. But with government aid, farmers are responding vigorously by promoting Welsh lamb as a brand with connotations of open countryside and a healthy environment, and encouraging the marketing of new cuts of lamb to appeal to smaller families. And the manufacture of tangy ewe's-milk cheese, established in Wales in the 17th century, has been revived on some farms.

**LEFT** *At Tregwynt Mill wool is knitted into patterned blankets such as the 'madder' design shown here.*

no lake could ever be. To my horror, I realised that I was looking down on the headwaters of the Claerwen Reservoir, a good six miles clear of my route.

I looked at my watch. I had two hours to hit the mountain road down into Cwmystwyth before darkness fell; I grimly set myself to the task. Just as I had given up hope and was floundering in the dark, I saw a light in the far distance. It was a car moving along the road. Joyfully, I set off towards it, and gave a shout of triumph as I felt the surface safely beneath my feet. Round the corner, I came across what looked like a vast army camp. It was the police, complete with radios and tracker dogs, who were preparing to set off into the night to trace the lost wanderer.

The shame of it! Here was I, the man who claimed to know the Welsh mountains like the back of his hand and who was always advising beginners to equip themselves properly, misreading the compass like the veriest tyro. The police kindly forgave me, but I had received a shock—and a lesson. The Welsh mountains cannot be trifled with. They can still surprise even the most experienced walker of their lonely recesses.

I got another shock, too, on that second traverse of the Roof of Wales. In the twenty years that had passed between my two walks, the landscape itself had undergone a change. The Forestry Commission had taken over vast tracts of the moorlands, and the sheep had retreated before the pines. I was saddened to see farms where I had once been welcomed, and where the peat fires had burned on the hearth for hundreds of years, now ruined and abandoned.

Perhaps I lament too much, or have no real right to lament. The population needs new reservoirs, and where else can the water come from except from drowned valleys among the hills? And is the small hill farm now an economic proposition?

I must comfort myself with the thought that there are still great areas of the Welsh hills where the sheep reign supreme. The hill farmers still send their lambs for sale at the markets of scores of small country towns. They still take a glass in the local after the excitements of the bidding and argue learnedly over which breed makes the most successful cross with the sturdy, enduring Welsh Mountain ewe.

I know I shall still hear, as I walk the hills in spring, that most evocative of all mountain sounds: the far-off bleating of the lambs on a distant hillside, with the heart-lifting song of the lark as a country counterpoint.

## KILVERT'S COUNTRY

By a strange piece of ironic luck, I discovered the delightful part of the Welsh borderland we are now proud to call Kilvert's Country when I was at least 5,000 miles away from it. In 1947 it fell to my lot to report the partition of India for the BBC. I found myself in the middle of a nightmare. The communal massacres had begun, and I had to report them in the torrid heat of August in the Punjab. Despair and death were all around me as I came back to my darkened hotel in Lahore after a day of misery spent following the poor refugees tramping through the dust of the Grand Trunk Road.

On a table in the hall of the hotel, I came across a small pile of books left behind by an English official who had just flown back home. Among the usual

**LEFT** *Robert Francis Kilvert, a country clergyman whose diary gives an evocative and charming picture of life in 19th-century Wales.*

**RIGHT** *The beautiful Wye Valley area is known as 'Kilvert Country' and is a place of literary pilgrimage for fans of the Victorian diarist.*

**ABOVE** *This volume of Kilvert's diary covers the period from June 11 to July 17, 1870, when he was curate at Clyro in Radnorshire.*

detective novels was a small, blue-covered book, entitled *Kilvert's Diary, 1870–1879*. I took it to bed with me and started to read. Suddenly I was carried away, far from the surrounding anguish, to another world—a world of Victorian certainty and order, of a serene countryside of rare, unspoilt beauty, inhabited by men and women whose life was governed by the rhythm of the seasons. Squire and clergyman, farmer and labourer, shopkeeper and wheelwright, all had their appointed place and were reasonably happy in it. Round them lay the water meadows of the Wye, the moorlands of the Black Mountains of Monmouthshire and the rich, ploughed fields of red earth that make elegant patterns against the woods. The diarist had a brilliant pen. William Plomer, who edited the diaries, justifiably compared him to Dorothy Wordsworth in his power to describe landscape and weather. And he had a novelist's gift for creating characters. I carried the book with me for the rest of my Indian journey, and it kept me sane amid the madness.

Who was Kilvert, and where did he come from? Well, he turned out to be a Church of England clergyman, who had been born at Hardenhuish near Chippenham, the second son of the rector of the parish. He went to Wadham College, Oxford, and then followed his father into the Church. In 1865, he became a curate at Clyro in Radnorshire, in the valley of the Wye, and remained there for seven happy years. He was eventually presented with the living of St Harmon's, also in Radnorshire. He died at a comparatively early age and is buried in the beautiful churchyard of Bredwardine, on the Wye, just over the Welsh border in Herefordshire.

On the face of it, his was a quiet, uneventful life, passed in country places far from busy towns and the centre of affairs. But the diarist's vivid style, along with his evident love for his fellow human beings and his interest in everything they did, make you feel that you yourself are with him every moment of the day. You are impressed to learn that on October 25, 1870, four guns killed 700 rabbits in one afternoon at Maesllwch Castle. Your eyes see, with Kilvert's, the beauty of the morning of September 20 in the same year, 'the sky a cloudless, deep, wonderful blue and the mountains so light blue as to be almost white.' You sit down with the diarist alongside old John Jones, the stone-breaker, on the roadside near Pentwyn: 'He told me how he had once been cured of his deafness for a time by pouring hot eel oil into his ear, and again by sticking into his ear an "eltern" (elder twig), and wearing it there night and day. The effect of the eel oil at first was, he said, to make his head and brains feel full of crawling creatures.'

Your heart goes out to Kilvert after his interview with Mr Thomas, of Llan Thomas, where he had gone to confess his love for the delightful Daisy Thomas, aged nineteen. Mr Thomas, her father, met him with the enquiry, 'Have you got the living of Glasbury?' Regretfully, Kilvert had to confess that he had no prospect of it. 'Then,' said Mr Thomas, with a Victorian father's authority, 'I cannot allow you to be engaged.' Kilvert went sadly away. He adds a touching note: 'On this day when I proposed for the girl who will I trust one day be my wife, I had only one sovereign in the world and I owed that.'

The temptation to go on quoting from Kilvert is irresistible, but it is even more attractive to remember the diary and walk in Kilvert's footsteps. He himself was a tremendous walker, and covered a great part of the countryside on foot. Many of the places to which he walked are comparatively unchanged, and you can almost see them as he saw them. Not long ago, I walked on the open, rolling moorland of Llanbedr Hill and came across the lonely *cwm* among the bracken where Kilvert met the Solitary—otherwise the Reverend John Price, Master of Arts of Cambridge University and Vicar of Llanbedr Painscastle, who had abandoned the world to live in holy poverty in a rough hut lost among the hills, a sort of shack crammed with books, broken furniture and litter of all sorts. The Solitary had a saintlike quality about him which profoundly moved Kilvert, and I almost felt it myself across the passing years as I walked in that green, unvisited wilderness.

I came back through Rhos-goch; here still stands the mill where the miller—as reported by Kilvert—used to sleep in the mill trough and hear the fairies come in at night and dance to sweet music on the mill floor. And not so many yards up the road is the little chapel, of which Kilvert, as a churchman, rather disapproved: he could not believe that it held 200 people every Sunday evening.

By now, I think you can sense the compelling charm the diary holds for Kilvert addicts—and I am one of that happy band. We take the diary with us wherever we go. We can see the very room in Clyro where Kilvert sat at his desk writing an entry for Friday, March 4, 1870: 'A wild stormy night.' Kilvert had been across to the Swan Inn (now renamed the Baskerville Arms) in the afternoon, and gossiped about the repairs going on at Clyro Court. He could see the Swan from his window, and he quickly seized his pen to note: 'The Volunteers in full march in Clyro at 8pm, band playing and the drum shakes my windows as they march past into the Swan yard.' I bet that Kilvert's windows were not the only things that shook later that evening, as the Volunteers hit the Swan bar!

Inns played a central part in the village life of those days, but perhaps teetotalism had already begun its all-conquering march across Wales. As Kilvert crossed the border at the fine old half-timbered inn at Rhydspence, he noticed that 'the English inn was still ablaze with light and noisy with the song of revellers, but the Welsh inn was dark and still'.

Of course, some of the places that Kilvert knew 'ablaze with light' have now become dark and still with the passage of time. Hay Castle, where Kilvert admired Daisy Thomas's grace at an archery contest, has been damaged by fire, and the little town of Hay-on-Wye, by a strange turn of fortune, has become almost the capital of the secondhand-book trade. The country houses where Kilvert was entertained by the richer county families remain, but the rich, confident squires who once owned them have long since departed.

Kilvert was fascinated by the strange figure of Father Ignatius (J. L. Lyne), who endeavoured to revive monasticism in the Church of England. In 1869 he founded a new monastery in the lonely valley of Llanthony, in the Black Mountains of Monmouthshire. Kilvert climbed over the high pass from Hay to see the first monks at work on the wild hillside, cultivating the land and working on the foundations of the monastery. But Kilvert was too fond of life, too human, to approve of the monks cutting themselves off totally from the world. A 'morbid, unnatural life', he called it, and could not help turning back to note the natural beauty of the setting in this lovely valley.

The trip to Llanthony and over the pass to Hay provides one of the most delightful expeditions in the footsteps of Robert Francis Kilvert. The last time I was there, I walked up from the south, following the deep, romantically wooded valley of the Honddu past Cwmyoy church. I don't think Kilvert came as far, but nobody could pass Cwmyoy without having a good look at the church. Subsidence on the mountain behind it, back in the Middle Ages, has twisted tower, chancel and nave in three directions. The effect is extraordinary. When you walk up towards the altar, you feel that you are trying to keep your feet on a ship at sea.

You reach firmer ground, and are also firmly into Kilvert Country, a few miles further on, when you come to the ruins of the old Llanthony Abbey, nestling among whose graceful arches is a small hotel. Poor Kilvert found the ruins overrun with tourists. He particularly hated the leader, who was busy orating about the history of the abbey, and let fly with one of the few outbursts of temper in the diary.

BELOW *Welsh cobs doze in front of the peaceful ruins of Llanthony Abbey, which has over the years suffered the ravages of border strife.*

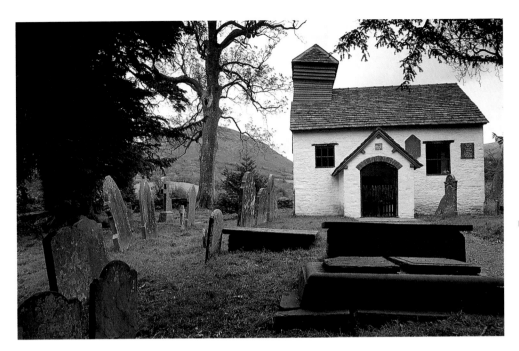

He wrote: 'If there is one thing more hateful than another, it is being told what to admire and having objects pointed out to one with a stick.'

I felt a little guilty when I first read that entry, for I tend to pour out information about Welsh historic sites and beauty spots to all and sundry, although I don't think I point at them with a stick. Well, perhaps Kilvert can be excused, because the tourists had arrived at the abbey a few minutes before him and had ordered a large lunch. The diarist and his companion had to spend an hour reading that powerful organ of public opinion, the *Hereford Times*, while they waited impatiently to be fed.

He was back to his old good humour, however, at the top of the valley a few miles further on. He delighted in the chapel at Capel-y-ffin: 'the old chapel, short, stout and boxy with its little bell turret (the whole building reminded one of an owl), the quiet peaceful chapelyard shaded by the seven great solemn yews…'

The little chapel is still there, exactly as Kilvert describes it. Behind it, the road winds up over Gospel Pass towards the Wye Valley and Hay. It has been tarred, and you can now drive a car over it. At the summit of the pass, you get a magnificent view. All round you are the great hills of the Black Mountains, before you the lush valley of the Wye and, beyond, the lonely moorlands of central Wales. You pick up the curves of the river and remember how Kilvert once described it: 'The western light shimmered down the broad reach of the Wye and the river flowed softly by, rippling and lapping gently upon the grey shingle beds.'

I know that when I stand on that Gospel Pass summit I have a slight twinge of envy for the man who could evoke the countryside with such brilliance of phrase. Any commentator would give his eyeteeth to reproduce in speech what Kilvert did so effortlessly with his pen. But then all envy disappears as I look back to the view and remember how Kilvert has repeopled it for us with the vigorous ghosts of the people of the past. I give a private word of heartfelt thanks to the kindly diarist, who, in his pages written over 100 years ago, has given me the freedom of Kilvert's Country.

# CHAPTER SIX

# WALES FROM THE SADDLE

THAT FIRST TRAMP OVER THE ROOF OF WALES had begun a tradition that I cherished all through the 1960s. Hywel Davies of BBC Wales and I would meet some time in January for a leisurely lunch. Then we would clear the glasses aside, spread the maps out on the table and dream up a new way of travelling through the Cambrian countryside. We both agreed—and in this listeners seemed to support us—that we should never travel by car; you cannot see wild Wales through a windscreen. Our journeys had to have some sense of physical challenge about them.

Thus I have sailed round the coast of Wales by lifeboat, jogged over the now-abandoned railways of mid Wales, ridden the whole length of the eastern border on a bicycle and marched around the country in the footsteps of George Borrow.

This exercise became an important part of my life. It was my annual escape from the great slab world that is slowly closing in on us all. I know I can never master the technique of living happily in our air-conditioned, mass-produced and mass-controlled society. The huge office slabs and middle-aged skyscrapers that now float like antiseptic icebergs above the old, warm chaos of our cities frighten me stiff. I know that I could never be a natural slab man. I am happier living in the cracks in between.

Wales has never been viable slab country, and rural Wales is one of the few surviving 'cracks' on a large scale in these islands. I made a beeline for it whenever I could during the sixties, and I regarded Hywel's office as my private Davies Escape Apparatus. I feel a sense of loss that this Welshman of creative vision is no longer there waiting for me.

When we met for our usual planning lunch in 1960—and how long ago that date already seems—Hywel gave me the smile of a man who has already solved all your problems before you even put them to him.

'There's one obvious means of progress,' he said, 'which we've neglected, and which we ought to have thought of at the very beginning. You must ride!'

'But we've always agreed that a car is right out,' I protested.

'I wasn't thinking about a car. I'm talking about a horse.'

I shuddered with horror at the thought, for, although I was now past fifty, I must confess that the horse and I had never met socially. I don't think I had ever ridden one in my life. Of course, I had seen plenty of them around, for in the Swansea of my early youth the motor car and the bus were not yet supreme. I was born just at the tail end of man's dependence on horse muscle for transport and power. Groceries were still delivered in horse-drawn vans and dustcarts still lumbered through the streets.

Milk floats, too, had their patient horses attached, but they always seemed to me to have a rather resigned look about them—with one splendid exception. This was Mr Samuel's cob, Blodwen. Mr Samuel was our milkman, an artist at pouring milk into the milk jug in the splendidly unhygienic manner of the pre-bottling era. Horses were his passion, and Blodwen his special pride. She was dock-tailed and dappled, and high-stepped along Calvert Terrace as if she were on her way to a dance. The brightly polished milk churn swayed and glistened in the cart

## GEORGE BORROW'S WALES

GEORGE BORROW, an English writer and linguist, was a wanderer all his life. His father was an army captain, and the family accompanied him on his postings around Britain. In 1816 the Borrows settled in Norwich, where the 13-year-old George attended school.

It was at this time that the child's remarkable gift for languages became apparent; he taught himself Spanish and Italian, and learnt Romany from a local encampment of Gypsies whom he befriended. By the age of 18 he could speak 12 languages, including Welsh, which he learnt by reading a translation of *Paradise Lost*.

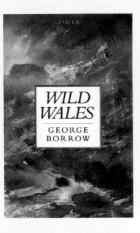

Despite his talents, however, Borrow had difficulty finding work, and spent many years tramping around Europe until, in 1833, he was employed by the British and Foreign Bible Society to translate the good book into Chinese and other languages.

In 1840 Borrow married, and his wife and stepdaughter accompanied him on his first trip to Wales in 1854. Borrow got out of the train at the border so that he might enter Wales on foot—and carried on walking across the country for the next three and a half months. His chance meetings with the 'real Welsh' in taverns or on the road were recorded in a daily journal which formed the basis for his book *Wild Wales*, published in 1862. His choice of title reflects the appeal for him and his readers of Wales's wildernesses, which have changed little since Borrow's time. Indeed, his classic travel guide is still in print and used by travellers almost 150 years after he wrote it.

**ABOVE** *H. W. Philips's portrait of the 40-year-old George Borrow, painted in 1843, shows a striking, silver-haired man.*

**LEFT** *Borrow's* Wild Wales *is an account of his journey through the country and his encounters with the Welsh in the 1850s.*

behind. Its sides were ornamented with the proud boast, 'Purest Gower Milk Alone Sold', and Mr Samuel dispensed the creamy liquid as if he were handing you your winnings on the pools.

Blodwen, he told us, was a show horse. On some days she would appear decorated with rosettes, and Mr Samuel would call out as he arrived with the milk, 'Whoa, Blodwen, *fach*, let the boys look at you. Feast your eyes on these trophies, lads; they are a sign of triumph. Blodwen has been Highly Commended in the Gower Show for the second time running.'

Blodwen was my first intimation that the horse could be a thing of beauty, but I never dared to climb into the milk cart and ride behind the bold, snorting monster.

## TIKA THE PATIENT

And so my early days passed happily but horselessly away. At university, mountaineering gave me the thrill of adventure, and for years I saw the horse only as a foreshortened object far away down the valley at the foot of some great precipice soaring out of the peat bogs of North Wales or Skye. But then came

## WELSH COCKNEYS: LONDON'S DAIRYMEN

CATTLE, LIKE SHEEP, have long been important to Wales. For centuries they were used as currency for settling payments, and were the measure of a prince's wealth. From Norman times until the 19th century, drovers marched their cattle to the lucrative markets of London, where the hardiness of the Welsh black was well known.

With the population boom of the Industrial Revolution in the late 18th century, there was a growing thirst for milk in the cities of England. The old drovers' roads had established well-trodden links with London, and many farmers—in Cardiganshire in particular—responded to the demand, leaving their homes to settle throughout the English

capital. They became pioneers of the London dairy trade, housing their cattle in great cow sheds within the city and grazing them when possible.

The London Welsh developed tight-knit communities, and preserved many of their own traditions. Chapel soon became the hub of their social scene: meals were provided, young people learned Welsh and regular eisteddfods were held.

But with the Milk and Dairies Act of 1922, which encouraged pasteurisation, processing plants increased in number. This development, coupled with the arrival of faster forms of transport, meant that milk could be imported fresh from the countryside; the Welsh dairymen, no longer needed, returned home.

Their descendants, however, remain in London, while in Cardiganshire, to this day, it is not uncommon to hear villagers speak with a hint of a Cockney accent.

**LEFT** *Welsh dairymen, such as these outside their shop in Bermondsey, were once a common sight on the streets of London.*

Hywel's persuasive proposition, and a second horse entered my life. I met that most understanding of animals, the sturdy Welsh cob they called Tika.

Hywel had arranged with Biddy and Dick Williams which horses we would ride. Biddy had been brought up in the showjumping world, but now she and Dick were living at the quiet farm of Dollynwydd, three miles outside Builth Wells in mid Wales, where she then had a popular pony-trekking centre, and also bred horses and ponies.

The Duhonw stream runs down through the fields of the farm. Behind rise the bracken-covered slopes of the Eppynt moorlands. Seventeen horses, ponies and young foals grazed in the valley meadows along the river. On hot days, they stood twitching their flanks against the flies under the tall trees that lined the banks, or clattered slowly through the shallows to frighten the swift-moving trout. When dawn came in late August, the young foals ran among the huge mushrooms that carpet the fields overnight. It was in this idyllic landscape that I was introduced to dear old Tika.

There she stood, white-coated and saddled, with a look of gentle tolerance in her eye, as if to say, 'Ah, well, here comes another one!'

'You'll like her,' said Biddy. 'She's as quiet as a lamb.' In truth, calmness was the keynote of everything about old Tika: she was the classic embodiment of that great principle in physics, the conservation of energy. She never moved unless she had to and then only as far as was necessary. When she did move, unkind spectators in Builth Wells attributed it to the fact that she had heard someone shout 'Milko'.

For Tika had a mysterious episode in her past when she had served a sentence between the shafts of a milk cart somewhere in Weybridge. This might account for the gentle resignation she exhibited when asked to stop anywhere. She was obviously waiting for orders to move on to the next house. I never hurt her feelings by mentioning this trait. She was back among the winds and high bridlepaths of her native land again.

As for her pedigree—well, it seems it had fallen by the wayside during her English exile. I like to think that she had some distinguished blood in her, for sometimes she looked like a duchess who had seen better days. Perhaps she could trace her lineage back to one of those legendary horses that always seem to be the starting point of the breeds of the British Isles. In the case of the Welsh cob, we have the splendidly named Trotting Comet, born in the wilds of Cardiganshire around 1836. If a Welsh cob can trace herself back to Trotting Comet, she enters the Debrett of the cob world.

The origin of the Welsh cob is, however, wrapped in mystery. Some insist that it springs from an animal vaguely described as 'the old Welsh cart-horse'; patriots like to believe that this horse could be descended from one of Owain Glyndwr's chargers. But even they do not claim that this animal possessed the splendid trotting gait that is now such a feature of the breed. It is more likely that the Welsh cob is an Anglo-Welsh promotion: a cross between the English trotting horses of

**ABOVE** *The author (centre), on Tika, sets off on his ride from St David's to Point of Air with Biddy Williams and Rowland Lucas, his producer.*

**RIGHT** *St David's is Britain's smallest city, but it boasts a magnificent cathedral; it was from here that the author set out on his horseback ride across Wales.*

the early 19th century and the sturdy ponies belonging to the Welsh drovers. No matter: for the last 100 years Wales has been the principal breeding centre, and the Welsh cob has the speed and action of an English trotter combined with the toughness and stamina of the Welsh pony. You can use her for riding, on the roads or in a pony trap. She is the ideal general-purpose horse; and she can jump, as well.

All of which I discovered as I set out in 1960 to ride through Wales on the back of that unassuming descendant of Trotting Comet, Tika the patient.

## FROM CATHEDRAL TO COLLIERY

Perhaps 'ride' is a slight exaggeration. I was carried gently through Wales by Tika as if I were a piece of rare Nantgarw china. She never galloped, and she never jumped. The most complicated horsey manoeuvre we performed together was the trot—and that was enough for me. Once I was launched on that strange voyage on horseback from the most southwesterly point of Wales to the most northeasterly—in other words, from St David's Head in South Wales to Point of Air at the mouth of the Dee Estuary in the North—I got the hang of it. I succeeded in riding around 200 miles, over very wild country, without falling off Tika's back. I admit I never went faster than a canter, and I never jumped, but I did a good thirty miles a day, or maybe slightly less.

I have happy memories of that ride through Wales with Tika. We started from the west door of St David's Cathedral, and the clatter of our hooves through the quiet streets of Britain's smallest city brought two sleepy-eyed little boys in pyjamas to an upstairs window. They stood on their beds to look out as our cavalcade went by.

'Ooh, look at that white horse,' the younger one called.

'That's not a horse, it's a pony,' said the older boy. 'Can't you see it's last?'

**RIGHT** *A mountain road now winds its way across the Berwyns, a rugged landscape of purple heather and rocky gullies.*

**BELOW** *The seal of Henry II, whose army was famously defeated by the mountains' treacherous terrain.*

Of course she was. Dear old Tika knew she had a rank beginner on her back and took constant care to see that I travelled at a gentlemanly pace every step of the way. Our route took us from St David's along the coast of northern Pembrokeshire, then over the Preseli Hills to the upper valley of the Teifi. From Tregaron we struck across the wild moorlands south of Plynlimon, a section that gave me, as it were, my baptism of fire. I learned hurriedly how to get a horse through boggy ground and how to nurse the strength of my faithful steed through a long, long day over rough ground. Or, rather, I should say Tika taught me how to do it. She knew by instinct how to tread warily when the earth turned soggy, and she certainly took care to rest whenever possible. After the boggy moorlands, our trot through mid Wales felt almost like relaxation.

Then we took our courage in both hands. We rode over the high track across the eastern section of the Berwyn Mountains, and which is still called Ffordd y Saeson—the English Road. Nearly 800 years before our journey, that colourful and tempestuous Plantagenet, Henry II, had led a powerful army over this very route to crush Owain Gwynedd, who was then the chief Welsh prince of North Wales. The Welsh had harassed him in the thick woods of the Ceiriog Valley, but Henry boldly led his long train of armoured knights, with their squires, their followers and their cumbersome baggage, up onto the open mountain, among the bogs and bracken of the Berwyns. Suddenly, the heavens opened. The whole army foundered among the damp bogs. North Wales was saved.

Believe it or not, no sooner were we out on those bare slopes of Ffordd y Saeson than, once again, the heavens promptly opened. In the drenching downpour that followed, I realised exactly why Henry's knights had hurriedly chucked in their hands and staggered off home!

**RIGHT** *Moel Famau is topped by a monument to George III; the planned 150-foot-tall pyramid was never finished, and the structure was damaged in a storm in 1860.*

Naturally, I have walked on many occasions through mountain rainstorms. You can hardly explore the mountains of Wales without an occasional soaking. On foot, you are always moving, personally fighting the storm. On horseback, the rain has you at its mercy. Woe betide you if you haven't armoured yourself against it from top to toe. There you are, stuck in the saddle, jogging grimly along, while the rain remorselessly searches out the weak chinks in your armour.

All miseries eventually come to an end. The next day, we rode out of the valley of the Dee over the moorlands behind the Horseshoe Pass. Then, in a grand finale, we traversed that green switchback of a mountain range that guards the Vale of Clwyd and reaches its highest point on Moel Famau, where we unsaddled for a moment alongside the strange, squat memorial to poor George III. It was built in 1810 to commemorate fifty years of his reign. Not long afterwards, he went mad, and just over fifty years later his memorial was half ruined in a gale.

Carefully, we trotted down the gentler slopes at the end of the range, then on to Point of Ayr, our journey's end. We had begun at the gates of a cathedral. We ended alongside a colliery. I don't know if there was anything symbolic in that. Tika, at any rate, had traversed every step of the way patiently. I swung out of the saddle and unashamedly kissed her on the nose.

## ADVENTURES ON TOBY

It was twenty years later when Teleri Bevan of BBC Wales suggested, as she had about my walk over the Roof of Wales, that it was high time I repeated my ride. Alas, good old Tika had passed away some time earlier. She went into happy retirement with the Roberts family at Towyn, and appeared in glory at all the local fêtes, drawing a trap in which the children delighted to ride. It is strange how your affections grow round animals. I was happy that Tika lasted to a ripe old age—but then I never really knew her age.

There had been other changes in the horse world. Pony trekking had become big business in rural Wales, and there seemed to be centres scattered all through the wilder parts of the Principality. So it was now possible to plan a route that would take us from centre to centre; there was no need for us to repeat our 1960 arrangements, when we got Dick Williams to lay depots of fodder ahead. One thing was vitally necessary, however. I had to find a successor to dear Tika. And this is how a third horse came into my life.

His name was Toby. He was a cob, of course, but he was black instead of white, or rather black with a white blaze on his nose. He lived with Libby and Alden Holden at their trekking centre at Goytre, near Port Talbot in South Wales. On first sight, Goytre seems a surprising place to run a trekking centre, since the huge steelworks of Port Talbot are only a mile or so away. But Libby and Alden had the vision to realise that the little valley of Goytre has a twist in it that shuts out the industrial world completely. All round are the hills and the woods of the Margam Forest—lovely trekking country and wonderful avenues of escape for the workers in industry.

**ABOVE** *The author cements his friendship with Toby with the aid of Polo mints.*

When Libby Holden introduced me to Toby, I stroked his nose with what I hoped was a professional air and felt in my pocket for a lump of sugar. I had noticed that you can always tell a keen horseman at breakfast in an English hotel: he always steals the lump sugar to ingratiate himself with the next horse he meets.

But Toby was different. Libby advised me: 'Not sugar. Give him Polo mints. He's mad about them.' Indeed he was. My journey through Wales on Toby's back was accompanied by the sound of him happily munching his way through tube after tube of Polos. I was rash enough to mention Toby's gastronomic preference during the first of my daily progress reports on the air. From Crickhowell on, even the shepherds and hikers on the lonely hills seemed to have a tube of Polos ready to greet him. Mile after mile, we munched our way through Wales.

I stroked Toby's nose again. We would get along fine. He was tough, sturdy and steady. What more could I want? Libby said firmly, 'He wouldn't let you down, for all the Polo mints in the world.' Nor did he, although I discovered later on that he had a secret in his life. In the summer, Toby was a model trekker, utterly composed and reliable. In the winter, Libby took him out hunting, and he changed character completely. As soon as he heard the sound of a hunting horn, Toby pricked up his ears and was off like a bird over hedges and ditches and stone walls, to take his place at the very head of the hunt. 'Don't worry,' said Libby, 'no one will be blowing a hunting horn in the open air throughout the length and breadth of Wales.' Toby gave a reassuring munch. All that now remained was to plan our route.

This time, we decided to break new ground: we would ride up through the eastern counties of Wales. Every day brought a memorable delight. We started at

Vaynor church, behind Merthyr Tydfil, where the moorlands roll northwards to the Brecon Beacons. I remember that first day mainly for the perils of riding through the mists—there were deep quarries somewhere behind the grey, swirling, damp curtains of vapour. Our reward was our dramatic emergence high above Llangattock to a breathtaking view out over the Usk Valley to the dark mass of the Black Mountains.

The next day, we descended into that green valley and crossed the river at the bridge in Crickhowell. The church clock struck eight, and I waved rather condescendingly to the few people stirring in the streets. There's no question that you do tend to feel superior in the saddle. I have a theory that you can understand the Middle Ages only if you've ridden a horse. You look down on the hat-touching peasant below you as you trot proudly towards your castle. Orders were obeyed in those days because they quite obviously came from above. Where would the feudal system have been without the horse?

I came back to reality as we climbed steeply out of Crickhowell, for Toby didn't exactly look like a knight's charger. This was just as well, for I'm sure that no

## WILDLIFE OF THE BEACONS

THE FORK-TAILED OUTLINE of a red kite, gliding effortlessly on thermal currents over the upland moors before returning to nest in the oak woods of the valleys, is an awe-inspiring sight for the naturalist exploring the mountains of Brecon Beacons National Park. The peregrine falcon, kestrel and merlin all inhabit the area too, but the kite is king of the air, and its appearance adds a touch of swashbuckling drama to a day in the hills. The welcome return of this magnificent bird, which has spread slowly south into the Beacons from its mid Wales stronghold, is undoubtedly the most encouraging wildlife story of these hills.

At first sight, however, the wildlife potential of the national park may seem unpromising. Vast areas of open, rolling moorland sweep up to the steep escarpments of Fforest Fawr, the Black Mountains and the Beacons themselves, while conifer plantations creep insidiously up the valleys.

But this apparently barren landscape is actually a very rich habitat, and while the birds of prey may be the only wildlife to catch the eye, there is much else here besides. Broad-leaved woodlands are home to the woodpecker, nuthatch and tree-creeper, which are joined in summer by that elegant migrant, the pied flycatcher. Even those

**ABOVE** *Polecats were once killed for their fur, but trapping has declined in recent years and numbers have increased.*

**ABOVE** *The red kite is often to be seen soaring over hills and crags of the Brecon Beacons on rising air; its ruddy coloration and forked tail make it unmistakable.*

**BELOW** *The golden, sun-like blooms of the globe flower brighten up the deep ravines of the limestone country in the southern Brecon Beacons.*

knight's charger could have negotiated the country that lay ahead. We came into the valley of the Grwyne Fawr, which cuts in behind the shapely 2,000-foot peak of the Sugar Loaf. The Grwyne Fawr is a horseman's or walker's valley. There is no road for a car on the spectacular pass that climbs over the noble ridge guarding the valley of the Wye; nor was there any trace of wheels on the path that ran in the warm sun along the foot of the magnificent old red sandstone escarpment, taking us towards our night's stopping place at the Tregoyd Riding Centre on the slopes behind Glasbury. The thud of hooves on the soft turf, the white sheep racing away before us, a warm breeze bending the grass and the gleam of the Wye winding far below through the woods: this was the way one could ride to the world's end.

The third day took me through well-known and well-loved ground, up past the Begwyns into Kilvert Country. We actually passed the hollow on Llanbedr Hill where the Solitary had his hut. Then, on to lonely and superb riding country where no one seems to come, down to the grassy pass above Glascwm.

Here I got a surprise. My first mentor in the riding world, Biddy Williams, was waiting for me, with her eight-year-old daughter Kate. Away we went at a canter,

dark, alien conifers give shelter to two rare little killers—the polecat and the pine marten, both of which are enjoying something of a comeback after many years of persecution.

The fascinating flora of the national park includes rare and delicate arctic and alpine plants, which have tenaciously maintained a foothold in the cliffs here since the Ice Age. The Beacons represent the southernmost limit for many of these species, including mossy and purple saxifrage, roseroot and northern bedstraw.

The limestone country around Ystradfellte is also rich in interesting plants, including damp-loving ferns such as green spleenwort and brittle bladder. Bright yellow globe flowers also thrive here, while the underwater-hunting dipper and curtseying grey wagtail haunt the rapids below spectacular waterfalls.

**LEFT** *Pen-y-Fan* (left) *and Corn Du are the two highest points of the Brecon Beacons; the wooded valleys below provide a habitat for various bird species.*

**RIGHT** *The dipper is a remarkable bird which uses its wings to swim down to the riverbed, and walks underwater against the current looking for food.*

across the inviting grassy tracks that seem to lead for mile after mile to the distant north. We crossed the main road to Llandrindod and rode on into the green wilderness, following the edge of Radnor Forest, which lifted us high over the whole of the old county of Radnorshire. Steep *cwms* plunged away to our right, but at last we came out onto the flat moor that forms the actual top of the mountain. At over 2,000 feet, Radnor Forest was the highest summit I had reached on horseback.

As we unsaddled for a brief rest, we tried to think whether there was any mountain top in Wales that could not be reached either by horse or by its modern equivalent, the motorbike. We decided that there were only two. There is Crib Goch, of course: no one is ever likely to ride anything along that knife-edge. Should we include the actual summit of Glyder Fach, that strange tumble of giant flat rocks? We ruled it out, since you can ride to within 100 feet of the rock tumble. Snowdon and Cadair Idris were not included, for tourists used to ride to their summit cairns by pony all through the 19th century. That leaves one summit, which must surely remain inviolate. No horse or motorbike will ever reach the summit of the peerless 3,000-foot rock pyramid of Tryfan, which guards the Ogwen Pass.

I'll not forget the fourth day of our journey in a hurry. Again, we were in lonely, unfrequented country, and my two guides, keen hunting folk, led me up via unmarked tracks and lost lanes onto the bracken-covered Beacon Hill. We were working our way down a steep slope, towards a little stream which wanders down to join the River Teme, when, in a clearing in the bracken, we came across a dog fox sunning himself and totally at peace with the world. My guides couldn't resist it. They let out the traditional hunting halloo. It was fatal. The fox sprang up and was away, but so was Toby. A ditch lay in front of us. Toby jumped it like a coiled spring unleashed, and I found myself riding an earthquake. The inevitable happened. I sailed quietly through the air and thumped to rest amid some conveniently placed clumps of heather. Toby stopped immediately, moved, I am convinced, by a sense of remorse. The fox also stopped on the horizon, sensing that no hounds were after him. He gave us what seemed almost a contemptuous grin and slipped quietly out of sight.

After that, I rode very carefully indeed to Beguildy on the Welsh border, over the bridge and up to the Anchor Inn on the Kerry Hills, just inside England. I slid off Toby's back with extra caution, for they keep a pet fox in the yard. Toby didn't even look at him. I'm sure he felt a little penitent at his slip from grace, and was vowing never to let me down again.

The fifth day took us along the Kerry Hills. Then came a steady drop down into the upper valley of the Severn. These green hills of Kerry seem to mark the end of the riding country that stretches almost unbroken from the Usk to the Severn. For a brief moment, we left the higher hills and trotted through a country of little hills and winding dales, of lanes lined with golden laburnum and of clear streams running down from the distant high hills far to the west. At the end of the day, we unsaddled at the Llanrhaeadr ym Mochnant Trekking Centre

**BELOW** *The author's peaceful trek on his trusty steed turned into a hair-raising chase when the hunting pony spotted a fox.*

and went to sleep lulled by the soft sound of the finest waterfall in Wales, Pistyll Rhaeadr.

## FORDING THE DEE

I slept uneasily. Ahead of us, the next day, lay our sternest test. Once again, we had to cross the high, dark barrier of the Berwyn range, but this time by a pass even higher than the Ffordd y Saeson we had crossed twenty years before. Our track climbed upwards to the strange stone of Maen Gwynedd, which once marked the southern limit of the old Principality of Gwynedd. Then it was across under the dark summit of Cadair Fronwen to the pass over the main range. Here, high above the valley of the Dee and in sight of every one of the great hills of North Wales, we changed guides. I now put myself in the care of two first-class horsewomen, Rosemary Dunnage and Vida Caswell. Coming swiftly towards us, dropping long veils of heavy rain over the Arans and obliterating the silver shield of Bala Lake, was the inevitable Berwyn storm. Henry II was avenging himself once again. Huddled against the driving showers, we led our horses through the boggy patches. Horses' hooves make horrible sucking sounds, and one seems helpless as they thrash about and almost claw their way to firmer ground.

**ABOVE** *Pistyll Rhaeadr is the tallest waterfall in Britain, with a drop of 240 feet, passing half way through a rock arch.*

Relief came at last. The bogs ended, the rain ceased and the comforting sun came out. We rode safely down to the valley of the Dee, a little west of Corwen at the old mansion of Hendwr. I said to myself, 'Safe at last. There can't be anything worse ahead.' I was wrong.

Near Hendwr is the spot where the Roman road once forded the river. To my horror, my guides now casually proposed that we should use it. 'The old Romans thought nothing of it,' they said.

I don't know about the Romans, but now, nearly 1,800 years later, I trembled on the bank, as the Roman legionaries of Suetonius Paulinus had trembled on the edge of the Menai Strait when they saw the British warriors, urged on by the druids waiting to oppose them.

I followed the two girls down the bank and into the shallows. They struck out boldly into the stream, but suddenly I felt my gallant steed resist. Horses hate anything uncertain under their feet, and he had seen nothing like the Dee in flood. Neither had I, for that matter. The water, to my inexperienced eye, seemed to be running like a mill race. Toby started to splash, almost stamp, in the water. 'Come on, come on,' I muttered, but the girls shouted, 'Keep his head up, he's going to roll.' I tugged vigorously at the reins, but still the splashing went on.

Luckily, the girls came plunging back, grabbed Toby's reins and fairly towed us both out into the midstream. Once you are launched onto the ford, there is nothing you can do except pray your horse is not going to lose his footing, and resign yourself to the chill water filling your boots and soaking your breeches.

I kept on talking, my horse kept on plunging forwards, and—to my heartfelt cry of 'Thank God'—we scrambled up onto the safety of the other bank. Since then, whenever I see a film of the US cavalry splashing at high speed across the Rio Grande, I take my hat off to those celluloid heroes.

So to our final day: over the Hiraethog moors and past bleak Llyn Aled and the bright waterfall where the river tumbles towards the lower ground. Menna MacBain had brought her regular trekkers out to escort us over the last few miles. We rode in triumph through Llansannan, then out towards journey's end at the village of Llanfair Talhaiarn. The whole place seemed to have turned out to greet us.

Llanfair Talhaiarn has an extraordinarily steep hill, dropping down into the centre of the village as you come to it from the south. Halfway down stood a pleasant, white-walled house, its garden glorious with flowers. At the gate I saw a little group, with a dear but obviously very old lady in the centre. She held a beautiful bouquet of her garden's flowers in her hand. The procession pulled up, or rather braked with difficulty on that steep hill.

I guided Toby carefully across the slope. Her son and daughter-in-law gently helped the old lady to lift up the bouquet. Fatal move! Toby had realised that the last few minutes of his long journey had come. Obviously the bouquet was a tribute to him: the biggest Polo mint in the world. He took a grateful gulp, and the bouquet disappeared.

I am sure that the old lady didn't mind. Like the rest of us, she was simply saluting Toby, and saying 'Thank you' on my behalf for all the miles of pleasure he had given me across the green hills of Wild Wales.

## 'WE'LL KEEP A WELCOME'

There comes a time in everybody's life when you want to return home permanently; when you feel the overwhelming need to settle at last among your own folk, in a place where you can grow mellow and, as Voltaire advised, 'cultivate your garden', a quiet corner from which you can still make happy forays into the big world.

I have always maintained that the perfect recipe for settled contentment is a room with a view over the sea, with mountains in the background and a trout stream round the corner. I was lucky enough to discover the one spot in Wales where all three delights come happily together. Needless to say, it lies in the delectable old county of Pembrokeshire.

Pembrokeshire, in some ways, is the perfect mirror of Welsh history. South Pembrokeshire has been completely English since the 12th century. Using the winding waters of Milford Haven as their secret point of entry, the tough Anglo-Norman barons steadily drove the Welsh out from the southern half of the county, obliterating even the old place names and substituting Broad Havens and St Florences for the old Eglwyswrws or Llanychaers! Castles are everywhere, and even the churches of this Little England beyond Wales look as if the vicars were ready in a moment to don their armour and defy the Welsh raiders from the top of their battlemented towers.

The clear-cut line of demarcation between the races is known as the Landsker. North of the Landsker, the Welsh still refer to the folk south of the line as the 'Down Belows'. I have settled in the Welsh-speaking part, up above. I had already known its charms for fifteen years, and I was lucky enough to find a house on the coast at Ceibwr, a romantic and secluded creek north of the ancient borough of Newport in Pembrokeshire. The view was magnificent. The great cliffs run north to the high prow of Cemaes Head, with its 500 feet of dramatically twisted rock. The seals breed in the innumerable caves, and I flattered myself that I could always lure one old bull seal to appear for me if I played on my tin whistle. I noticed he preferred Welsh folk songs—as all good Welsh seals should.

The Pembrokeshire Path runs along the edge of the sea, across the little flower-bright acre of land—salty from sea spray in the winter—that they call the Patchyn Glas, the Green Patch. I later sold the land back to my good neighbour, Mr James, all except the Patchyn Glas and the edge of the Ceibwr stream. I have a strange feeling of pride in owning a small part of the surface of Wales. When I depart, I shall leave it to the National Trust. It will be the only memorial I shall want.

Let me hasten to say that I have no intention of departing for many, many years to come. I have now settled, with my wife Charlotte, in the small town of Fishguard. Our house stands at the end of a little row of elegant Regency villas which once belonged to the retired sea captains, who were the chief product of the coastline of Cardigan Bay for over a hundred years.

**BELOW** *In 1982 the author and his wife Charlotte donated a little piece of their Wales to the National Trust.*

**BELOW** *Lower Town, Fishguard, boasts a picturesque harbour dotted with sailing boats and fronted by fishermen's cottages.*

Our own house, a friendly, rambling affair overlooking the small harbour of Lower Town, once belonged to Sir Evan Jones, a great civil engineer who constructed docks and breakwaters all over the Empire and then retired to his native Fishguard to build his last great breakwater: 'He built it in the wrong place,' the local experts will hint to you in the bar of the Ship Inn in Lower Town.

Sir Evan made no mistake, however, in the house he built—or rather reconstructed—at the end of Tower Hill. It has a splendidly Edwardian interior: teak panelled, with Art Nouveau copper fireplaces and an entrance hall with staircases going in all directions. The whole affair is Edwardian, and reminds me that, by birth, I am an Edwardian, too.

My small boat swings gently against the quay wall below, inviting me in summer to put to sea and trail my line after mackerel off Strumble Head. From my garden, I can look north towards the pointed cone that marks the western end of Carningli in the Preseli Hills. These enchanted moorlands, covered with standing stones and ancient circles, lure me to walk on the autumn days when the heather and bracken are wine-dark on the high slopes.

I can walk there in the spring, too, and not meet a living soul; only a lark springing from under my feet or a fox vanishing among the dark rock faces. However, as often as not, I find myself drawn to the actual summit of Carningli, among the tumbled walls of the old Iron Age fort, where, according to pious legend, the good St Brynach levitated himself for meditation.

## ST BRYNACH'S CUCKOO

If I ever need a patron saint to watch over me in my hide-out in Fishguard, I think I'll adopt kindly old St Brynach. He was an Irishman who settled at Nevern, not so far north of us. You can still see his church set among the dark yews and rich in Early Christian inscriptions from the Dark Ages. I picture him living happily in his modest cell, always ready to perform a miracle or two to oblige a friend, and always preaching to the birds. They may have been the only ones willing to listen to his two-hour sermons in Welsh.

The cuckoo was particularly attracted to St Brynach—so much so that it always came first to Nevern and Pembrokeshire on March 7, St Brynach's Day. In later years, the parish priest never began Mass until the cuckoo arrived to perch on top of the marvellously carved St Brynach's Cross in the churchyard, where it would sing its twin notes.

One year, the bird did not appear. Anxiously, the priest and his congregation waited in the storm and the rain. At last, at dusk, the poor bird fluttered onto the cross. He was bedraggled and exhausted from fighting the violent head winds for hundreds of miles on his long journey from the south. But for generations, his family had had the honour of starting Mass on St Brynach's Day in the saint's own church. He could not let them down. He gave every ounce of his remaining strength to keep faith. He sang his first two notes—and then dropped dead.

As old George Owen, the Tudor historian, quietly adds, 'This religious tale … you may either believe or not without peril of damnation.'

LEFT *The promontory known as Dinas Island culminates in cliffs at Dinas Head. From here there are wonderful views up the coast.*

BELOW *The author spent his final days in Fishguard, a tiny corner of his beloved Wales, where he befriended a seagull that he christened Nelson.*

As I write those last words, a tap comes on my windowpane. I go out onto the terrace to find my own version of St Brynach's cuckoo waiting for me. This is the bold seagull, Nelson, who seems to have adopted us and comes every lunchtime for me to feed him by hand. Then he soars away in effortless flight, up over the harbour and the plunging cliffs of Dinas Head. My eye follows him, then travels on over the high places of the Preseli Hills beyond. And my thoughts move further on still, out over all the hills and valleys of the Principality that I have been describing in this book, and which I have been bold enough to call my Wales. I have a sudden premonition that old George Owen, if he had ever seen this book, might again have commented, with a chuckle, 'This tale you may believe or not, without peril of...'. But no! I am certain that the landscape of Wales really is as splendid as I have maintained it is. Not all of it, I regret to say, for many Welshmen themselves treat the legacy of beauty we have received from the past as if it can be easily exploited for the profit of the present. They ignore the condemnation of the future.

However, once you have seen the infant River Cothi tumbling past the ancestral oaks in its deep gorge, while the kites soar and whistle overhead, and once you have climbed the sharp ridges of the Arans to look down on the mirror pool where the Dovey rises, then you will willingly accept the secret theme of this book, the hidden text of this somewhat light-hearted sermon: 'May you go out and see, and after seeing, help defend the rare but fragile beauty of Wild Wales.' ■

# HIGHLIGHTS

*The best that Wales has to offer*

**ABOVE** *The huge Neolithic cromlech of Pentre Ifan in the Preseli Hills (see page 157) is the finest in Britain.*

**LEFT** *The spa water at Llandrindod Wells (see page 144) can be taken at this spring in Rock Park.*

**BELOW** *Love spoons, carved by young men as love tokens, can be seen at the Museum of Welsh Life (see page 147).*

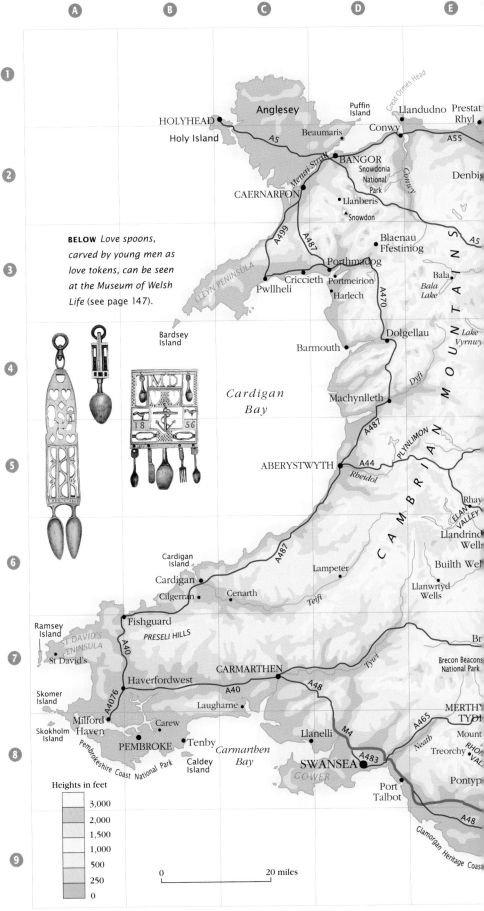

**ABOVE** *Dazzling Rhossili Bay (see page 160) marks the western end of Gower and is one of the highlights of the peninsula.*

Heights in feet

3,000
2,000
1,500
1,000
500
250
0

0          20 miles

ABOVE *The late 17th-century mansion Erddig Hall (see page 148) houses a fascinating collection of contents depicting life above and below stairs.*

BELOW *A 1964 ticket from the station at the tongue-twisting town of Llanfairpwllgwyngyll-gogerychwyrndrobwllllantysili-ogogogoch (see page 158).*

LEFT *A tapestry by Elizabeth Cramp depicts the capture of French soldiers in the invasion of Fishguard (see page 143).*

BELOW *The new Severn Bridge, built in 1996, makes for a dramatic entry into Wales for those arriving by car.*

# CONTENTS

## ABOUT THIS SECTION

NOW that Wynford Vaughan-Thomas's text has shown Wales in all its glorious variety, the following sections help to pick out some of the sights and sites, towns and villages, famous person-alities and festivals that you will want to know about when planning your own days out.

For example, pages 150–52 give details of many of the best-known Welsh castles, while between pages 157 and 163 is a quick guide to some of the national parks, beauty spots, long-distance paths and other outdoor attractions to be enjoyed. There is also a selection of festivals and events, although it is always wise to check nearer the time for detailed information with the relevant Tourist Information Centres, whose addresses and phone numbers are given on page 169. These centres can advise on opening times, entry fees, and so on.

# CITIES, TOWNS AND VILLAGES

### Abergavenny/Y Fenni F7

Abergavenny makes an excellent base for exploring the Black Mountains, the Monmouthshire and Brecon Canal and the industrial heritage of the Valleys. In the town, the ruins of Abergavenny's Norman castle contain a Regency hunting lodge housing the Abergavenny Museum. Just outside town is the dramatically shaped mountain known as the Skirrid, which was almost split in half by a huge landslip in the Middle Ages. The contrastingly smooth-topped Sugar Loaf mountain is one of the area's best-known viewpoints.

### Aberystwyth D5

Tall Victorian guesthouses stretch along Aberystwyth's seaside promenade towards the remains of a castle built by Edward I

and a 19th-century Gothic building that was the original site of the University of Wales. The main campus lies inland on Penglais Hill, close to the National Library of Wales. A Victorian cliff railway (*left*) ascends Constitution Hill, where a camera obscura gives wide views over Cardigan Bay and out towards the mountains of North Wales.

### Bala/Y Bala E3

During the 18th century the wool trade brought prosperity to the town, whose inhabitants were known for their piety and Nonconformist principles. A statue of Thomas Charles, one of the great Nonconformist preachers of his day, stands outside the Welsh Presbyterian Church. Today Bala is a pleasant resort, with the adjacent Bala Lake (Llyn Tegid) offering sailing and windsurfing; the Bala Lake Railway runs along its east side.

### Bangor D2

This university city by the Menai Strait originated in the early 6th century AD as a monastic settlement and has been a bishopric since 546. The town grew in the 19th century as a centre for the slate industry, and the arrival of the university in 1884 gave its fortunes a further boost. Displays at the Bangor Museum and Art Gallery include

16th-century Welsh furniture, local textiles and axes from a Neolithic axe 'factory' at Penmaenmawr. The ornate Victorian pier gives fine views of the island of Anglesey.

### Brecon/Aberhonddu E7

The summits of the Brecon Beacons soar above this market town—known in medieval times as Brecknock—whose web of narrow streets is lined with Georgian façades. The town square, known as the Bulwark, has at one end a statue of Arthur, Duke of Wellington by a local sculptor, and the Brecknock Museum and Art Gallery (*see entry on page 147*) at the other. Within the spacious 13th-century cathedral is a rare stone cresset with 30 hollows for holding torches.

### Caernarfon C2

The castle (*see entry on page 150*) built by Edward I dominates the centre of this coastal town and former slate port, and forms one of the walls that enclose Caernarfon on three sides. A maritime museum beside Victoria Dock tells the town's story, while Segontium Roman Museum (*see entry on page 152*) lies a short walk to the south of the town.

### Cardiff/Caerdydd F9

At the beginning of the 20th century the Welsh capital was the world's leading coal port. But trade slumped in the 1930s, and Cardiff fell victim to bombing during the Second World War. Now the docks have been saved from total dereliction by a huge regeneration project known as Cardiff Bay; the Millennium Waterfront area within the bay

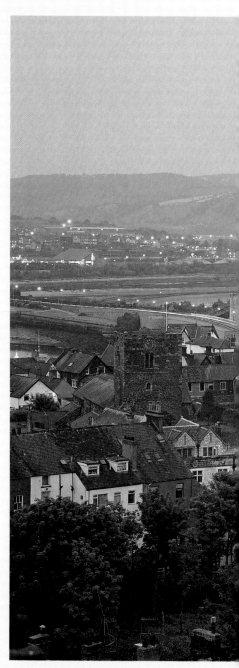

will include the Welsh National Assembly building and provide retail and leisure facilities. Bute Avenue links the bay to the city centre and the Millennium Stadium, the new rugby ground. Bute Park and the grounds of Cardiff Castle (*see entry on page 150*) provide a swath of greenery near the city centre. To the east, in the area known as Cathays Park, the National Museum and Gallery.

**LEFT** *Fascinated onlookers watch a group of street performers in front of the Pierhead Building, a major landmark of Cardiff Bay.*

**ABOVE** *Conwy is one of the highlights of the north Welsh coast, with its magnificent 13th-century castle and superb setting on the Conwy estuary backed by forested hills.*

of the Wye Valley gorge. The town still has many Georgian and Victorian buildings, one of which houses the Chepstow Museum containing exhibits on local life.

### Conwy D2

A garrison town grew up here alongside Edward I's immense castle (*see entry on page 151*), and the town walls with their 22 towers have survived almost intact to make this the most impressive fortified town in Wales (*pictured left*). The rampart walk gives superb views over the rooftops to the Conwy estuary. Next to the castle is a pedestrians-only suspension bridge designed by Thomas Telford in 1826, itself crenellated. The 14th-century Aberconwy House is the oldest house in Conwy—and, some claim, Wales; while Plas Mawr is an outstanding example of an Elizabethan town house, strikingly adorned with plasterwork. You can also visit Ty Bach, said to be the smallest house in Britain at just eight feet four inches tall by six feet wide.

### Denbigh/Dinbych E2

Denbigh was built complete with hilltop castle (*see entry on page 151*) as a defensive town in the late 13th century. Much of the medieval town wall survives around the historic core, which includes an unusual row of arcaded buildings along the High Street. In 1563 the Earl of Leicester acquired the castle and later began building a church nearby; he never finished this project, getting as far as erecting a single wall and arches, today known as Leicester's Folly.

### Dolgellau D4

Nestling at the foot of Cadair Idris, much of Dolgellau was built during the 19th century to provide a base for the Victorian sightseeing public, with their newly acquired taste for romantic wild scenery. The town, built mostly of dark grey granite and slate, still serves as the main base for exploring the surrounding mountainous terrain. Eldon Square forms the attractive central marketplace and focus of the town.

### Fishguard/Abergwaun B7

This attractive little town of three main streets perches on a headland; below it lies Lower Town, a cluster of cottages where the film version of Dylan Thomas's *Under Milk Wood* was shot in 1971. The harbour is much used by pleasure boats. Inside the Royal Oak Inn is a musket taken from a French prisoner following an ill-fated invasion attempt on the town in 1797 (*see feature on page 38*). Today

Cardiff (*see entry on page 147*) and the City Hall, built in 1901–4, form part of an imposing group of civic buildings.

### Carmarthen/Caerfyrddin C7

'When Merlin's oak shall tumble down, So will fall Carmarthen town' prophesied the wizard Merlin (*see entry on page 166*) of his home town Carmarthen. The stump of the tree in question is displayed in St Peter's Civic Hall,

but this lively market town still stands. The Carmarthen Heritage Centre by the River Tywi traces the town's history from its Roman origins to its days as a busy 19th-century river port.

### Chepstow/Cas-Gwent G8

This old border town is the southern gateway to the Wye Valley, and the majestic castle (*see entry on page 150*) and elegant Regency suspension bridge give superb views

# CITIES, TOWNS AND VILLAGES (CONTINUED)

Fishguard is best known as a ferry port for Ireland, with services from nearby Goodwick sailing to Rosslare.

## Hay-on-Wye/Y Gelli F6
As well as being a good base for walking in the Black Mountains, this little hillside border town above the River Wye harbours one of the world's largest concentrations of second-hand bookshops (*see feature below*).

## Lampeter/Llanbedr Pont Steffan D6
St David's University College, a branch of the University of Wales, was founded in this market town in the Teifi Valley in 1822 and is one of the oldest and smallest of Britain's universities. The students help to create a lively atmosphere in town, which has pubs and cafés aplenty.

## Laugharne/Talacharn C7
Writer Dylan Thomas spent the last four years of his life at the Boathouse in this Taf estuary village, thought to be the model for Llaregyb in his play *Under Milk Wood*. The Boathouse and the writing shed are preserved much as they were in Thomas's lifetime, and he and his wife Caitlin are buried in the churchyard. Close by is the 13th-century Laugharne Castle, which was enlarged into a residence in Elizabethan times but fell into ruin after the Civil War.

## Llandrindod Wells/Llandrindod E6
This yellow-and-red-brick town of spacious streets, turreted hotels and fancifully gabled villas is a jewel in the green mid Wales landscape. In Victorian times the arrival of the railway helped Llandrindod Wells to develop as Wales's premier spa resort, bringing well-to-do visitors to take the supposedly health-giving waters; one spring still gushes in Rock Park near the restored pump room, and a wealth of architectural detail from the early 20th century survives intact. To the east is Cefnllys Castle, a finely sited Iron Age hill-fort above a loop of the River Ithon, while at Disserth to the south is St Cewydd's Church, which

## HAY-ON-WYE: A TOWN BUILT ON BOOKS

**ABOVE** *Outside the castle at Hay-on-Wye, bibliophiles browse through shelves laden with books.*

**LEFT** *The little town of Hay-on-Wye, surrounded by wooded hills, is a bookshop-lover's paradise.*

THE LITTLE WELSH BORDER TOWN of Hay-on-Wye, set among mountains and nestling on the banks of the River Wye, is a pretty, bustling place with a maze of narrow streets and alleyways lined with attractive pubs and shops. But Hay is unlike other small market towns in the Wye Valley, since almost all of its shops are dedicated to books, and almost all the shoppers and drinkers are bibliophiles. Hay is a leading centre of the secondhand book trade and boasts over 40 shops where you can pick up anything from rare first editions to cheap, modern paperbacks.

The town's first secondhand bookshop was opened in 1961 by a local eccentric named Richard Booth, who claims the fictitious title of 'King of Hay'. Booth later bought the semi ruined 13th-century castle which dominates the town centre, and filled that with hundreds of volumes too. Today, almost every building here is a bookstore, from the old fire station to the former cinema. Since Booth opened his first outlet, Hay has undergone a book-led mini economic boom—the stores are a huge tourist attraction, and the town is also now internationally famous for its

Festival of Literature which takes place in the last week of May every year.

The festival was founded in 1988 on the strength of Hay's bibliographic reputation by the late Norman Florence and his wife Rhoda Lewis, and is now run by their son Peter. Most festival events—author signings, talks and readings—take place in marquees in the grounds of the local school, but the local Methodist chapel holds concerts, and in 1999, less traditionally, a Mongolian tent known as a yurt hosted storytelling for both children and grown-ups alike.

**ABOVE** *Llandudno's Victorian pier, wood-decked, iron-railed and topped off with a fine pavilion, is the town's star attraction. Built in 1850, it was blown down by a storm 25 years later and rebuilt.*

escaped the Victorian zeal for restoration and retains its 17th-century box pews and ancient roof timbers.

## Llandudno D1

An elegant curve of hotels lines North Shore in this quintessentially Victorian resort—Wales's largest—where donkey rides and Punch and Judy shows take place against the backdrop of an ornate 19th-century pier. In the summer, the pier has a fairground, an aquarium, ice-cream sellers and candy-floss stalls and other typical seaside delights. Boat trips depart from Llandudno and skirt Great Ormes Head (*see page 160*). Llandudno Museum charts local history, while the striking Oriel Mostyn Gallery is a leading venue for changing exhibitions of contemporary visual arts.

## Llangollen F3

Every July the town hosts the International Musical Eisteddfod (*see feature on page 98*), based at the Royal International Pavilion, which is open all year for concerts, films, crafts displays and exhibitions. Across the River Dee from the Llangollen Railway, horse-drawn narrow-boat trips take visitors across Thomas Telford's aqueduct, a precipitous 126 feet above the River Dee. Telford also engineered the Horseshoe Falls,

by which the Dee feeds the canal. Above the town, the medieval ruins of Castell Dinas Bran command a superior view across the valley.

## Monmouth/Trefynwy G7

A fortified 13th-century bridge spans the River Monnow near its confluence with the Wye here at Monmouth. The Shire Hall, which has a statue of Henry V on its front, faces onto Agincourt Square (*below*),

named after the monarch's victorious battle of 1415 against the French. Henry is said to have been born in Monmouth Castle, of which only ruins now survive. In the square is a statue of Charles Rolls—engineer, aviator and co-founder of the Rolls-Royce company—depicting him holding a model aeroplane. A vast collection of Admiral Nelson memorabilia, assembled by Rolls's mother, Lady Llangattock, is displayed in the Nelson Museum.

## Montgomery/Trefaldwyn F5

Founded in the 1220s, the tiny town of Montgomery preserves its original medieval layout, with castle ruins looming from a craggy hill. During the 18th century many buildings along the aptly named Broad Street were rebuilt or re-fronted to give the town's main thoroughfare an impressively unified Georgian appearance; the Town Hall, built in 1748, completes the picture.

## Newport/Casnewydd F8

Following the opening of the Monmouthshire and Brecon Canal in 1796, Newport grew rapidly as a port for shipping iron, steel, coal and tin plate from the eastern mining valleys. An interpretative centre beside the canal's flight of locks explains the story of the port, and further local-history displays can be found in the Newport Museum and Art Gallery (*see entry on page 147*). The Transporter Bridge of 1906, one of only six remaining in the world, conveys passengers and vehicles by gondola high above the River Usk. To the east is Penhow Castle, dating from the 12th century and the oldest inhabited castle in Wales.

## Portmeirion D3

Set on the coast of Snowdonia, this Italianate holiday village, comprising an eclectic collection of buildings, some of which were brought to the site and reconstructed, was the creation of architect Clough Williams-Ellis, who christened it his 'home for fallen buildings'. Through Portmeirion Williams-Ellis attempted to demonstrate the ways in which architecture could enhance scenery. The result is a dreamy, colour-washed assemblage of buildings clustered round landscaped gardens. The village features a bell tower, a town hall, a dome and all manner of surprise vistas and visual effects. The village was used as the set for the 1960s television series *The Prisoner*.

## Presteigne/Llanandras F6

This quietly attractive, old-fashioned border town boasts an array of timber-framed buildings including the Radnorshire Arms, once the home of Christopher Hatton, Elizabeth I's favourite courtier. From the 16th century until 1970 the County Assizes were held in the town, and the Judge's Lodging is now a museum.

## St David's/Tyddewi A7

The tiny cathedral city of St David's, said to have been founded by the saint himself,

# CITIES, TOWNS AND VILLAGES (CONTINUED)

is scarcely more than a village in size. Although the smallest city in Britain, its cathedral is the largest in Wales. St David's offers good walking and climbing, and there is sea life on display in the Oceanarium. (*See also feature on St David, page 59, and entry on cathedral, page 152.*)

## Swansea/Abertawe D8

Swansea, the unofficial capital of southwest Wales and the country's second city, was a cradle of industry in former times, with local coal being used to smelt copper. The copper trade began to wane in the early 1900s and Swansea faced serious economic decline. Heavily bombed in the Second World War, the city is now enjoying something of a resurgence, led by a regeneration project that has transformed the derelict dock area into a Maritime Quarter including a marina and waterfront village. The city is home to the Maritime and Industrial Museum (*see entry on page 156*) and the Dylan Thomas Centre, the national literature centre for Wales. Swansea Museum, opened in 1841, is the oldest museum in Wales and still maintains a Victorian atmosphere. Its wide-ranging displays include social history and Swansea pottery. The Egypt Centre, at the University, boasts Britain's largest collection of ancient Egyptian artefacts outside the British Museum. Plantasia, housed in a glass pyramid, is a hothouse garden with exotic plants, insects and reptiles. On the west side of Swansea Bay, the lively and picturesque resort of Mumbles stretches towards Mumbles Head.

## Tenby/Dinbych-y-pysgod B8

Narrow Victorian and Georgian houses in pastel pinks, greens and blues crowd round Tenby harbour, from where boat trips depart to Caldey Island (*see feature on page 153*). There is sheltered swimming along the mile-long sandy beach, and Regency terraces testify to the town's popularity since the early 19th century as a base for sea bathing; Tenby is still the leading resort along the Pembrokeshire coast. The 13th-century town wall is largely intact, its west gate known as the Five Arches. Within a maze of narrow medieval streets, the Tudor Merchant's House (*see entry on page 149*) recalls life in 16th-century Tenby. The Tenby Museum and Art Gallery includes local history and paintings by the Tenby-born artist Augustus John and his sister Gwen John (*see entries on page 165*). St Catherine's Island, topped by a 19th-century fortress, can be reached at low tide.

## THE TREORCHY MALE CHOIR

T REORCHY IS A SMALL TOWN, in the larger of the two Rhondda Valleys, whose name is synonymous with choral music at its most sublime. Awarding the Treorchy Male Choir with the first prize at the 1952 National Eisteddfod, the chief judge said: 'If there is singing like this in heaven, I am eager to get there quickly.'

The male choir of Treorky (as it was spelt) achieved its first victory in 1883, when a group of 25 men won an eisteddfod competition at the town's Red Cow Hotel. Treorky was one of several great miners' choirs formed around that time in the South Wales coalfields, when song offered a blessed release from the grim life of the pits and gave expression to the men's sense of solidarity and pride in their work. Within 12 years Treorky had been summoned to Windsor to sing for Queen Victoria.

**ABOVE** *The Treorchy Male Choir lines up with resident conductor Andrew Badham and accompanist Rhiannon Williams.*

After the disruption caused by the two world wars, the Treorchy Male Choir was re-formed under the baton of John 'Haydn' Davies. Since then it has won numerous International Eisteddfod competitions and achieved renown from California to Sydney. Alongside its traditional repertoire, the choir has collaborated with international celebrities such as Ella Fitzgerald, Tom Jones and Sir Harry Secombe, and produced some 50 records.

Male choirs like Treorchy make up about a third of Wales's 300 choirs. Female choirs are fewer, and are heavily outnumbered by mixed choirs and choral societies, which continue to inspire a matchless fervour in singers and audience alike.

## Treorchy/Treorchi E8
*See feature above.*

## Welshpool/Trallwng F4
The 'Welsh' prefix was added to this Powys market town's name in 1835 to distinguish it

from the English town Poole in Dorset. At its heart, a Victorian town hall presides over attractive 16th- and 17th-century town houses. The Powysland Museum charts the history of Powys, including an exhibition on the Black Death, which wiped out half its population.

# MUSEUMS AND GALLERIES

### Brecknock Museum and Art Gallery
Brecon E7

This museum, occupying the town's former Shire Hall, re-creates the drama of a 19th-century assize court with life-size figures and sound effects. Other displays include an 8th-century log boat from Llangorse Lake; a Victorian school room; and changing exhibitions by contemporary Welsh artists. In the entrance hall stands *The Death of Tewdrig*, a striking sculpture by Brecon-born Victorian artist John Evan Thomas.

### Castell Henllys near Newport F8

This Celtic settlement re-created on an Iron Age site evokes life over 2,000 years ago, using evidence from archaeological excavations. There are thatched round houses and a forge, and staff in period dress demonstrate different activities typical of Iron Age peoples.

### Ceredigion Museum Aberystwyth D5

Housed in a former Edwardian music hall, this museum contains a large collection of items relating to the area's past. It features re-creations of an old pharmacy, a dentist's

surgery and a dairy, as well as model ships, penny farthings and Welsh furniture including a fine 19th-century dresser (*above*).

### Glynn Vivian Art Gallery and Museum
Swansea D8

Displays here feature fine examples of Swansea's 'Cambrian' porcelain, produced during the 18th and 19th centuries. The gallery also contains European paintings, drawings and sculptures, including work by local artist Ceri Richards (1903–71). The venue is used regularly for touring exhibitions.

### Gwent Rural Life Museum Usk G8

Items donated by local people make up this fascinating assemblage of everyday

19th- and 20th-century objects from the Welsh Marches. There is a re-created cobbler's shop, as well as milling equipment and vintage tractors, and displays on the rural crafts of thatching and cheese-making. The old Malt Barn contains a display on the agricultural year.

### Museum of Welsh Life near Cardiff F9

Buildings from all over Wales have been re-erected on this 100-acre site centred on St Fagans Castle. From Merthyr Tydfil there is a row of miners' cottages, each decorated from a different period between 1805 and 1985, while from Lampeter is a Victorian school where lessons are re-enacted. The gas-lit farmhouse is the only building remaining from the original estate; today it is used for demonstrations of Welsh cookery. Craftspeople such as a cooper, woodturner, baker and saddler work on site, and many of their products are for sale. The farmyard contains a noisy collection of old breeds of animals.

### National Cycle Exhibition
Llandrindod Wells E6

Some 250 models, as well as cycling memorabilia and tributes to past heroes, embrace all aspects of the evolution of the bicycle. On show are examples ranging from an 1818 hobby horse—the first-ever bicycle, which was propelled by scooting along the ground—through bone shakers and penny farthings up to the latest models.

### National Museum and Gallery Cardiff
Cardiff F9

This all-embracing collection is the leading museum of its kind in Wales. The galleries feature Britain's largest collection of paintings by Monet, a portrait of Dylan Thomas by Augustus John (*right*) and works by such 20th-century British masters as Stanley Spencer and David Hockney. The 'Evolution of Wales' exhibition is a journey

from the big bang through the dinosaur age to the present. Other highlights include Celtic treasures, Welsh ceramics and fossils.

### Newport Museum and Art Gallery
Newport F8

This wide-ranging museum includes exhibitions on Newport's Chartist uprising

**ABOVE** *At Techniquest, a bright and stimulating museum for all ages, interaction with exhibits is encouraged as a way to learn about science.*

of 1839 and the growth of the town as an industrial port, as well as finds from the nearby Roman town of Caerwent. The Art Gallery houses mostly British works plus changing exhibitions of contemporary visual arts. The John Wait Teapot Collection contains no fewer than 300 teapots, complemented by the pepperpot collection in the Iris Fox Room.

### Anglesey Heritage Gallery
near Beaumaris D2

This gallery illustrates Anglesey's history and natural history, and includes wildlife paintings by celebrated bird artist Charles Tunnicliffe, whose studio at Malltraeth is reconstructed here. The gallery also features changing exhibitions of arts and crafts.

### Techniquest Cardiff F9

Techniquest (*pictured above*), a 'Science Discovery Centre', delves into the world of science with some 160 hands-on activities and challenges. Visitors can try launching a hot-air balloon or making an animated film. In the Discovery Room, which gives a bird's eye view of the exhibition area, are 'curiosity' boxes on such subjects as bridges and fossils. The museum also houses a planetarium and a theatre which hosts educational shows on scientific themes.

# HOUSES AND GARDENS

### Aberglasney near Carmarthen C7

A tunnel of overarching yews (reputed to be 1,000 years old) is the most remarkable feature of this spellbinding garden in the Towy Valley east of Carmarthen. Aberglasney's orchards, vineyards and oaks were praised in a bardic ode of 1471, but much of today's garden was laid out in the early 17th century by Anthony Rudd, Bishop of St David's. The house, now only a shell, was extensively modified a century later in Queen Anne's time, and the eight-column Ionic portico dates from the early 19th century. Lovingly restored and replanted after years of neglect, Aberglasney was the subject of a 1999 BBC documentary series, *A Garden Lost in Time*.

### Bodelwyddan Castle near Rhyl E1

Set amid rolling parkland, and complete with turreted battlements, this Victorian mansion houses a superb selection of 19th-century paintings from London's National Portrait Gallery. Furniture from the Victoria and Albert Museum and sculpture from the Royal Academy add to the aura of opulent splendour. William Holman Hunt and John Singer Sargent are among the painters represented at Bodelwyddan; subjects include eminent Victorians such as Robert Browning, John Millais and Florence Nightingale, as well as Queen Victoria herself.

### Bodnant Garden near Conwy D2

Wales's most striking formal garden was created on the east side of the Conwy Valley

in 1875. Between the two world wars the second Lord Aberconway developed the site further when he carved a series of stately Italianate terraces and a vast lily pond from a wide, sloping lawn. Extending over 80 acres, with majestic views of Snowdonia, Bodnant also embraces the Dell, a deep

wooded valley cut by a tributary of the River Conwy. From March until the end of June camellias, magnolias and rhododendrons bring great splashes of colour to the leafy Dell, which also contains a pine grove, a wild garden, a waterfall (*above*) and a 180-foot-long laburnum arch.

### Dyffryn Gardens near Cardiff F9

Dyffryn Gardens were landscaped in the late 19th century around a prosperous merchant's house (not open to the public). Set in 70 acres of parkland in the Vale of Glamorgan, the

gardens are famed for their rare and exotic plants, especially those introduced from eastern Asia. Glasshouses support a host of tropical and subtropical species, including orchids and palms. The Dragon Bowl, an oriental bronze fountain, is a fitting centrepiece for Dyffryn's spectacular water-lily canal, and among other attractions are the Italianate Pompeiian garden and an arboretum.

### Erddig Hall and Gardens near Wrexham F3

Life 'below stairs' is imaginatively evoked at Erddig Hall, a grand 17th-century mansion restored to 1920s condition. The bakehouse, kitchen, laundry, stables, smithy and other workshops—some still in use—can all be visited, and the Servants' Hall is lined with portraits of 18th- and 19th-century members of staff. Owned for nearly 250 years by the Yorke family, Erddig and its fine collection of 18th-century furniture were acquired in 1973 by the National Trust, since when the ornamental garden has been returned to its former glory.

### National Botanic Garden of Wales near Carmarthen C7

The former Middleton Hall estate in Carmarthenshire, developed by William Paxton in the late 18th century, is the site of Wales's new national botanic garden, opened in May 2000. Original walled gardens, lakes and waterfalls have been restored, and numerous new features developed, dedicated to illuminating the theme of plants as sustainers of life. Highlight of the 568-acre garden is the Great Glasshouse (*pictured left*)—at 333 feet by 198 feet the largest single-span oval greenhouse in the world—designed by Sir Norman Foster to house a collection of flora from Mediterranean-type climates around the globe.

### Penrhyn Castle near Bangor D2

Overlooking the Menai Strait from its parkland setting, Penrhyn Castle is an extravagantly ostentatious example of the early 19th-century taste for neo-Norman architecture. Built by Thomas Hopper between 1820 and 1840, the house has more than 300 rooms, many crammed with luxurious fittings. Among its most interesting features are the full-size slate billiard table in the library, a one-ton slate bed frame designed for Queen Victoria, and the stained-glass windows in the great hall. Exhibited paintings include works by Rembrandt, Canaletto and Gainsborough.

**ABOVE** *Ancient olive trees, over 100 years old, are quarantined in the Great Glasshouse at the National Botanic Garden of Wales. The glasshouse is home to many Mediterranean species.*

ABOVE *Most people who come to Welshpool visit striking Powis Castle. The gardens include four 17th-century Baroque terraces sloping away from the red sandstone castle walls.*

### Scolton Manor Museum
near Haverfordwest B7

Life in a Victorian country house is vividly recalled at Scolton Manor, where the comfort and luxury of the family rooms stand in stark contrast to the simplicity of the servants' working areas. The Victorian theme continues in Scolton's costume gallery, and there is also an interactive display on Victorian life. In the grounds are a stable and smithy, and carpenter's and wheelwright's workshops. The manor house is surrounded by a country park with a visitor centre.

### Tredegar House near Newport F8

An imposing Victorian front belies the fact that Tredegar dates largely from the Restoration period, and for more than 500 years was the ancestral home of the Morgan family. The interior is distinguished by gilded carvings and elaborate ornamental ceilings. With grounds extending over 90 acres, Tredegar embraces walled gardens and an orangery, as well as an adventure playground, parkland and lakeside walks. Craft workshops provide the setting for demonstrations of traditional skills such as leatherwork and pottery.

### Tretower Court near Abergavenny F7

Framed by the Brecon Beacons, Tretower Court is a rare example of a substantial Welsh manor house surviving from late medieval times. The restored family rooms and beamed great hall face in on a cobbled courtyard entered through a stone gatehouse. Exceptional craftsmanship is evident in the design of the wooden gallery with its sliding wooden shutters overlooking the courtyard. A short walk away are the remains of Tretower Castle, a 13th-century round tower, which replaced an earlier Norman fortification.

### Plas Newydd near Beaumaris D2

Classical and Gothic styles are combined in this magnificent mansion on the shores of the Menai Strait, built in the 1790s by James Wyatt and Joseph Potter for the Paget family, later the Marquesses of Anglesey. As well as fine collections of furniture and portraits, there is an exhibition devoted to the work of Rex Whistler; his largest painting, 58 feet long, hangs in the dining room. Military relics include the artificial leg of the 1st Marquess of Anglesey, who led the British cavalry at Waterloo. The gardens were laid out in the early 19th century by Humphry Repton.

### Powis Castle and Garden Welshpool F4

Built as a border fortress by the Princes of Powys, this medieval castle was bought by Sir Edward Herbert in 1587. Late 16th-century plasterwork still adorns the ceiling of the Long Gallery. The Great Staircase was designed in the 17th century by the architect William Winde, who also laid out the spectacular terraced gardens (*pictured above*). The gardens, overhung with yew trees, contain colourful borders, an orangery and an aviary. The Clive Museum—named after Edward Clive, a son of Clive of India who married into the Herbert family—is a fascinating collection of treasures from the subcontinent.

### Tudor Merchant's House Tenby B8

Tenby's past prosperity in its days as a thriving port is reflected in the Tudor Merchant's House, built for a wealthy local trader in the late 15th century. A rare survivor of its architectural type, this rambling three-storey house retains some important early features, though it is furnished with fixtures and fittings from the 16th century and later periods. Original fireplaces and chimneys—one in the 15th-century Flemish style—survive on all floors, and the remains of a fresco dating from the mid 1700s, now in three parts, can be seen on the interior walls.

# CASTLES

**W**ALES HAS FACED *several waves of invaders over the centuries, most of whom built castles to establish a firm foothold and frighten the natives into submission. Consequently, the land is dotted not only with Welsh-built castles but also with Roman forts, imposing Norman strongholds and the grandiose fortresses built by Edward I in the 13th century to show the Welsh that he was King of their land.*

### Beaumaris D2
Begun in 1295, this castle was the last of the 'iron ring' of fortresses built by Edward I to subjugate the Welsh. Edward's military architect, Master James of St George, created two symmetrical concentric rings of walls punctuated by sturdy towers and circled by a moat linked to the sea. Although never completed, his scheme represents the pinnacle of medieval castle design in Britain.

### Caerleon Roman Fortress near Newport F8
At this site are a well-preserved rectangular walled fortress together with a barracks and a 5,000-seat amphitheatre. Caerleon is one of the most evocative Roman sites in the country, and artefacts depicting daily life in the fortress are on display at the Roman Legionary Museum.

### Caernarfon C2
Edward I built this magnificent castle in 1283, and his son, the first English Prince of Wales, was born here the following year. The castle served as a royal palace, fortress and seat of government. In 1969 Caernarfon was the setting for the investiture of Prince Charles as Prince of Wales. The Queen's Tower contains the regimental museum of the Royal Welch Fusiliers, Wales's oldest regiment.

### Caerphilly F8
Somewhat incongruous in the surrounding modern town, this 13th-century castle is the largest in Wales. An outstanding example of medieval military architecture, it was built with concentric walls and further defended by a water-filled moat, together with artificial lakes and islands. The towers and walls stand to their original height (having been partly rebuilt in the 19th and 20th centuries), although one tower leans spectacularly. There are full-size replicas of medieval siege engines on display.

### Cardiff F9
The Normans incorporated the remains of a Roman fortress into this castle, which has

expanded over the centuries. From 1865 much of the castle was extravagantly remodelled by the fabulously wealthy 3rd Marquess of Bute, who employed the architect William Burges to transform it. Burges created a series of extraordinary interiors, resplendent with gilding, murals and stained glass.

### Carew B8
Built between 1280 and 1310, Carew Castle is a classic example of a medieval fortress that has been turned into a mansion. In Elizabethan times it was adapted for domestic use by Sir John Perrot, who was probably an illegitimate son of Henry VIII; he built the north wing, which looks out across a millpond. Besieged in the Civil War, Carew is now a fascinating ruin.

### Carreg Cennen near Carmarthen C7
High above the rolling countryside near Black Mountain, Carreg Cennen occupies a seemingly impregnable perch on the edge of a sheer 300-foot limestone cliff. A passageway

leads into the cliff face to a natural cave thought to have been inhabited by prehistoric settlers. Centuries of strife and warfare between the Welsh and English have left the castle an atmospheric, weather-beaten ruin.

### Castell Coch Cardiff F9
This extravagantly romantic castle was the creation of the 3rd Marquess of Bute during the 19th century. His architect William Burges created a three-turreted, medieval-style fantasy that would look more at home in central Europe than South Wales. Burges died in 1881, and Castell Coch was completed by his colleagues. There is a working portcullis, and the ceilings and walls of the domed drawing room are exuberantly decorated with murals of scenes from *Aesop's Fables*, paintings of flowers and carvings of butterflies. (*For pictures see page 106.*)

### Chepstow G8
The original keep of Chepstow Castle was built within a decade of the Norman Conquest

on a cliff-edged spur above the River Wye, guarding one of the most important routes into Wales, and was one of the earliest stone castles in the country. It was in use until 1690, and was repeatedly altered throughout its active history, with gatehouses, barbicans, towers and curtain walls gradually added to further enhance its natural defensive position.

## Cilgerran B6

Romantically placed on the wooded banks of the Teifi gorge, this Norman castle has been painted by many artists, including J. M. W. Turner. Cilgerran has impressive twin round towers and a curtain wall, with forest views from the battlements.

## Conwy D2

Edward I's castle, together with the town walls of Conwy, forms one of Britain's greatest fortified sites (*see picture on pages 142–3*).

Its natural defensive qualities derive from its situation on a rock beside the Conwy estuary. From the eight round towers and the battlements there are superb views over the town and across to the jagged peaks of Snowdonia.

## Criccieth C3

Llywelyn the Great established this stronghold in *c.* 1230 on a lofty promontory on the Lleyn Peninsula; the design for its gatehouse may have been copied from contemporary English castles. In 1283 Edward I's men captured Criccieth; in 1404 it was besieged, recaptured and razed by Welsh freedom-fighter Owain Glyndwr, and only the scorch-marked ruins remain.

## Denbigh E2

Denbigh Castle was built by Henry de Lacy on behalf of Edward I, and the spectacular

three-towered gatehouse may have been designed by the King's architect, Master James of St George. The castle affords fine views of the Vale of Clwyd.

## Dolwyddelan near Blaenau Ffestiniog D3

This 13th-century castle was erected by Llywelyn the Great but fell to the English in 1283. The scale is modest—it comprises a rectangular tower, restored in the 19th century, beside a fragmentary curtain wall—but it enjoys a splendid position on a hill looking across to the peak of Moel Siabod.

## Harlech D3

Seemingly impregnable on its vertical cliff perch, Edward I's mighty fortress (*pictured below left*) guards a majestic sweep of the peaks of Snowdonia and Cardigan Bay. It did fall in 1404, however, to Owain Glyndwr, and again during the Wars of the Roses, when a long siege at the castle inspired the song *Men of Harlech*.

## Manorbier near Tenby B8

This Norman castle, with its 13th-century round tower and stately gatehouse, commands fine views of the Pembrokeshire coast. In 1146 the great Welsh scholar and chronicler Gerald of Wales (*see feature on page 111*) was born here; he described Manorbier as 'the pleasantest spot in Wales'. Life-size models of Gerald and other historical figures are on display.

## Pembroke B8

Dwarfing the town, and surrounded on three sides by water, Pembroke Castle was the mightiest of the Norman strongholds built to control the Welsh. Despite a long and bloody history it defied all assaults until the Civil War, when it was taken by Cromwell's forces. Its rounded keep stands almost 80 feet high and at its base the walls are nearly 20 feet thick; the towers are linked by battlemented walkways. Margaret Beaufort, the wife of Edmund Tudor, came to the castle for safety during the Wars of the Roses and gave birth to the future Henry VII here in 1457 (*see feature on page 166*).

## Raglan near Usk G8

With its moat and turrets, Raglan Castle looks the epitome of a medieval fortress, but it belongs in fact to the closing stages of Welsh castle building: work probably began in 1435 for Sir William ap Thomas on the site of a much earlier Norman motte. More of a domestic residence than a fortress, the castle

**BELOW** *Harlech Castle, on a crag overlooking the sea, occupies a natural defensive position. Accordingly, it was the last fortress to fall during the Wars of the Roses.*

# CASTLES (CONTINUED)

was built to impress. Thomas and his son William Herbert created an opulent palace containing state apartments, an imposing great tower and a fine gatehouse. In 1646 Raglan finally served a military purpose when it endured a long siege before succumbing to Cromwell's forces in the Civil War.

## Rhuddlan near Rhyl E1

Although Rhuddlan is set back three miles from the sea, Edward I ensured that the castle had coastal access by engaging 1,800 men to divert into a canal the nearby River Clwyd. A pair of massive towers flanks the gatehouse, and remains exist of a defensive river gate. In 1284 the castle was the venue for the signing of the Statute of Rhuddlan, which annexed Wales to the English Crown. Designed both as a garrison and a royal residence, Rhuddlan was partly destroyed by Parliamentary forces during the Civil War.

## Segontium Roman Museum
### near Caernarfon C2

The layout of this Roman auxiliary fort, dating from AD 77, can be seen on the edge of Caernarfon beside the Menai Strait. Until about 394 Segontium was the military and administrative centre of northwest Wales, defending the Roman Empire against rebellious tribes. A museum contains finds from the site and gives an insight into Roman life in Wales.

## Weobley near Llanelli C8

This now largely roofless castle was built by the de la Bere family in the 13th and 14th centuries and overlooks the estuarine marshes on the northern coast of the Gower peninsula. Always a fortified manor house rather than a defensive stronghold, Weobley was well designed for comfortable living, with an array of private rooms as well as garderobes (toilets) and a great hall with a fireplace.

## White Castle near Abergavenny F7

With Skenfrith and Grosmont castles, White Castle completes a triangle of medieval fortresses known as the 'Three Castles' or the 'Welsh Three', which together controlled entry into this part of Wales. Refortified during the reign of Henry III in 1263, White Castle is the most impressive of the trio. It is named after the white plaster that originally covered its masonry as a stone preservative, traces of which can still be seen. The castle is enclosed by a water-filled moat, and its round towers are linked by high curtain walls.

# RELIGIOUS SITES

## Bangor Cathedral Bangor D2

Founded in AD 548, Bangor is thought to have enjoyed the longest continuous use of any British cathedral. It was largely rebuilt in the late 15th and early 16th centuries, and heavily restored by Gilbert Scott in the 1860s. Inside is the 16th-century wooden figure known as the Mostyn Christ, thought to have been hidden by the Mostyn family during the Reformation, and a memorial to Owain of Gwynedd, King of North Wales, who died in 1169 and is thought to be buried here. The nearby Biblical Garden is planted with flowers, shrubs and trees mentioned in the Bible.

## Carew Cross Carew B8

This outstanding 14-foot-tall Celtic cross bears an inscription to Maredudd ap Edwin, an 11th-century Welsh king. It is carved with an intricate reef knot design, and its well-preserved wheel-head was chosen as the symbol of Cadw, the body responsible for the 'built heritage' of Wales.

## Lamphey Bishop's Palace
### near Pembroke B8

This former bishop's residence dates from at least the 13th century, but Henry de Gower, Bishop of St David's from 1328 to 1347, remodelled parts of the building. Here the high-status medieval bishops of St David's could retreat to a life of luxury, and the palace became a firm favourite with them. Although the palace is now a ruin, the 70-foot-long Great Hall hints at past splendour.

## Llandaff Cathedral near Cardiff F9

Llandaff Cathedral, serving the city of Cardiff, is a 6th-century foundation, but was rebuilt in medieval times and restored once again in the 1800s when windows and panels by the pre-Raphaelite artists Edward Burne-Jones and Dante Gabriel Rossetti were incorporated into the building. The most immediately striking feature is a 20th-century concrete arch, surmounted by a cylindrical organ case to which is attached Jacob Epstein's huge aluminium sculpture *Christ in Majesty* (*left*).

## Partrishow Church near Abergavenny F7

Hidden away in the Black Mountains close to a holy well, this little church seems far removed from the modern world. Founded in the 1000s and restored in the 13th and 14th centuries, it has a fine 15th-century rood screen and loft and a rare pre-Reformation wall painting of a figure of Death. A few miles away are the beautifully situated ruins of Llanthony Priory and the tiny Church of St Martin at Cwmyoy, where subsidence has tilted the tower, altar, roof and arcades into somewhat drunken angles.

## Rug Chapel near Llangollen F3

This private 17th-century chapel, little changed through the centuries, displays a richly carved rood screen and a beamed roof painted with rose motifs. The gallery, family pews, altar rails and bench ends are similarly elaborate. Near by, Llangar Church is an impressive medieval building with 15th-century wall paintings, box pews and a minstrels' gallery.

## St Asaph Cathedral near Rhyl E1

This, the smallest cathedral in Britain, has a memorial in the churchyard to Bishop William Morgan, who made the first Welsh translation of the Bible in 1588. The Privy Council later ordered that Welsh Bibles be placed in every church in Wales. Today only a handful of his Bibles survive; one of them is displayed in the north transept of the cathedral.

## St Brynach's Church near Fishguard B7

In the churchyard of St Brynach's is one of the most perfect of all Welsh Celtic crosses: dating from the 10th century and standing at a height of 13 feet, it is carved with elaborate interlacing designs (*see picture on page 136*). Amid the avenue of yews leading to the church is a tree known as the 'bleeding yew' because of the sticky red sap that oozes from it.

## St David's Cathedral and Bishop's Palace St David's A7

The greatest cathedral in Wales is approached by a downward flight of 39 steps or 'Articles'. Highlights inside are the choir stalls (including a unique stall reserved for the monarch) and the delicately carved 16th-century oak roof. The nearby ruined Bishop's Palace was largely built by Bishop Henry de Gower in the 14th century. Many decorative elements survive, including the wheel window of the Great Hall, superb arcading and a medley of stone carvings.

### St Non's, St Justinian's and St Govan's Chapels St David's Peninsula A7

Tucked amid the coastal cliffs of Pembrokeshire are these three primitive hermitage chapels. Close to the city of St David's is St Non's, named after David's mother; according to tradition its well sprang when St David was born here in the 6th century. Nearby is the romantic ruin of St Justinian's, named after a 6th-century Breton saint. Farther south, near Bosherston, steps lead down to the 11th-century chapel of St Govan's, reputedly founded by the saint in gratitude after the rocks split open to provide a hiding place as he was fleeing from pirates. St Govan may have provided the model for the knight Sir Gawain of Arthurian legend.

### St Winefride's Well near Denbigh E2

Legend tells of an incident in the 7th century when a local chieftain tried to rape Winefride; failing, he decapitated her, and a spring miraculously appeared where her head fell. Her uncle Bueno replaced her head on her shoulders, and she came back to life, living on to become an abbess. With its reputation for healing properties, the well has long been a place of pilgrimage: Henry V visited it before and after the Battle of Agincourt. The well is housed in St Winefride's Chapel, a handsome example of the 15th-century Perpendicular style.

### Strata Florida Abbey near Aberystwyth D5

The abbey's remote position amid lonely hills epitomises the kind of site favoured by the Cistercian order. Founded in the 12th century, Strata Florida ('Vale of Flowers'), became a key centre of Welsh culture and was visited by princes and poets. Now a ruin, the abbey retains its west doorway and a medieval tiled pavement.

### Tintern Abbey near Chepstow G8

Dating mostly from the late 13th and early 14th centuries, this Cistercian house is the most intact of the abbeys of Wales. The walls stand to their original height, and the graceful archways have survived virtually unscathed. Its romantic setting in the Wye Valley inspired William Wordsworth to write his '*Lines composed a few miles above Tintern Abbey*'.

ABOVE *The shell of Tintern Abbey is a majestic sight, its arches soaring heavenwards.*

### Valle Crucis Abbey near Llangollen F3

A 9th-century Christian cross, known as Eliseg's Pillar, gave its name to Valle Crucis ('Valley of the Cross') Abbey, which was founded by Cistercian monks in 1201. Much of the fabric has been preserved, notably the chapter house with its rib-vaulted roof. The abbey church retains a beautiful west façade, while its eastern end is reflected in the monks' fishpond.

## THE HEAVENLY SCENT OF CALDEY

SITUATED JUST OVER two miles south of the coastal resort of Tenby in Dyfed, Caldey Island with its small village and monastery is an oasis of spiritual calm.

Celtic monks first arrived on the tiny island—it measures about one and a half miles long and one mile wide—in the 6th century AD. Little is known about this early era and not much remains except for a stone inscribed with ogham, an ancient Gaelic script.

By the early 12th century, King Henry I had seized the island and given it to one of his barons, Robert Fitzmartin. From him it passed into the hands of Benedictine monks, who began building a priory in the 1130s. Its visible remains include a church which was partly rendered with pebbles from the beach.

ABOVE RIGHT *A perfumer-monk on Caldey distils scent from the island's abundant crop of herbs and flowers.*

LEFT *The monastery on tiny Caldey Island has been home to an order of Belgian Trappist monks since 1928.*

The Benedictines remained on Caldey until Henry VIII dissolved the monasteries in 1536. After this, the island remained in lay hands until Anglican Benedictine monks—another branch of the order—bought it in 1906 and built the monastery that can be seen today. They stayed for only 22 years before selling the island to Belgian Trappists of the Reformed Cistercian Order, who are the current owners. These monks support themselves by farming and by selling their dairy produce and—more unexpectedly—their exquisite, handmade perfume, which they make from the lavender, gorse and other wild plants in which the island abounds. In this way they are able to maintain their austere way of life and perpetuate Caldey's 1,500-year-old spiritual tradition.

# INDUSTRIAL HERITAGE

**W**ALES IS BLESSED WITH *abundant mineral wealth, and from the 1700s the copper, lead, tin, iron and slate industries boomed. Even more spectacular was the rise of the coal industry. The First World War brought an end to this astonishing growth, however, and the 20th century was marked by industrial decline. A few remaining working sites—and some newer ones—have opened their doors to the public, and many former mines and mills have reopened as tourist attractions.*

## MILLS AND POWER

### Aberdulais Falls near Swansea D8
These beautiful falls, painted by, among others, J. M. W. Turner, and owned by the National Trust, have powered industry since 1584. In early times copper smelting took place here; the site later became a corn mill and then, in the 19th century, a tin-plating plant; remains of the latter are still visible. Today a hydroelectric plant harnesses the power of the falls. There is an interpretative centre in the turbine room, which houses a fish ladder that allows salmon to bypass the main cascade.

### Carew Tidal Mill Carew B8
The only intact tidal mill in Wales, the present four-storey building next to Carew Castle dates from the early 19th century. Rising water enters the millpond and is stored until being released through sluices at the ebb tide, when the outflow of the water drives the millwheels.

### Centre for Alternative Technology
near Machynlleth D4
*See feature, right.*

### Electric Mountain Llanberis D2
This pumped storage station, beneath a mountain, in Europe's largest artificial cavern, is a remarkable feat of engineering. It has one of the world's fastest turbine generators, which can raise power output from zero to 1,800 megawatts in seconds. The visit begins with a sound-and-vision show, explaining how pumped storage meets consumer demands, and concludes with a minibus tour of the power station's tunnels.

### Museum of the Welsh Woollen Industry
near Cenarth C6
This is the largest of some 40 water-powered woollen mills that once operated in the village of Drefach Felindre, which was known as the 'Huddersfield of Wales'. The noisily clattering mill is geared towards modern production but still uses 19th-century Jacquard looms, which are operated by a card system like a primitive form of computer.

The museum illustrates the technological advances that have been made since the early Industrial Revolution and takes visitors past demonstrations of such processes as separating, spinning and dyeing.

## VILLAGE OF THE FUTURE

**T**HREE MILES NORTH of the town of Machynlleth, towering trees hide a disused slate quarry where a community of architects, engineers, scientists, gardeners, teachers and volunteers are working towards a brighter environmental future.

The Centre for Alternative Technology (CAT) is the successful brainchild of Gerard Morgan-Grenville, a rich, educated man who, in 1975, having tired of the commercial and industrial world, chose to live by the principles propounded by the alternative-lifestyle groups that he had seen in America in the 1960s. Against the background of spiralling fuel prices in the 1974 oil crisis, and a rising public awareness of the pollution being caused by the traditional energy industry, Morgan-Grenville set up his own eco-friendly community in this remote corner of mid Wales.

**RIGHT** *CAT makes recycling fun—these tin-can men and women are a great photo opportunity!*

From this, CAT grew. The centre combines an 'opted-out' lifestyle for its residents with scientific research into sustainable energy methods to end reliance on finite fossil fuels. Six self-sufficient families live here, producing organic food and powering the village through wind, water and solar power—CAT is not linked to a public supply. One of the centre's most famous innovations is a wind-operated telephone, and the sewage system recycles human waste to produce methane gas which the villagers use for cooking.

The centre informs the public about recycling, organic farming and energy conservation and is a living demonstration of how people can live in harmony with technology and nature.

**ABOVE** *Turbines at CAT harness the natural energy of the wind to provide the power to run the site.*

**LEFT** *The organic gardens at CAT contain flowers, greenhouses and solar panels to catch the rare Welsh sunshine.*

# METAL

### Blaenavon Ironworks Blaenavon F8
Dating from 1788, these ironworks were at the forefront of modern technology, using steam power rather than water wheels for blasting the furnaces. The works were eclipsed by the coming of steel in the 19th century, and the ruins survive as one of the best-preserved 18th-century ironworks in Europe. The workers' cottages are still standing.

### Dolaucothi Gold Mines near Lampeter D6
The Romans were the first to exploit the golden riches of the Cothi Valley, and their workings have left pits and channels in the area around Pumsaint. The mines lay dormant until activity resumed in the 19th century; it lasted until 1938. Today the mines offer a fascinating glimpse of both the Roman and modern workings, and there are displays of 1930s machinery from a North Wales lead mine.

### Dyfi Furnace near Machynlleth D4
A gushing waterfall on the River Einion powers a replica water wheel at this restored charcoal-burning blast furnace of 1755. It was in use for some 50 years refining silver and producing iron, until coke became the preferred fuel for smelting. Dyfi is one of the best-preserved furnaces of its kind in Britain, and visitors can see inside the blast furnace and bellows room.

### Great Orme Mines near Llandudno D1
These Bronze Age copper mines were first worked some 4,000 years ago, and are the oldest metal mines in the world to be open to the public. There are displays of stone hammers and other finds, and visitors can glimpse a huge cavern which is itself only a tiny fraction of the vast workings. Weather permitting, it is possible to watch archaeological excavations in progress.

### Llywernog Silver-Lead Mine Museum
near Aberystwyth D5
For nearly 2,000 years, peaking in the 1800s, mining for silver-rich lead ore was an important industry in mid Wales. Lead mining formed the bulk of the industry, and the silver was the icing on the cake, being used mainly for coinage. The mine closed in 1886 but briefly reopened from 1907 to 1910 for zinc extraction. A trail explores the site, which has water wheels, old machinery and tramways, and there is also an underground tour.

### Sygun Copper Mine
near Blaenau Ffestiniog D3
A walk through the tunnels and chambers of this 19th-century mine reveals delicate stalagmites and stalactites, and veins of copper ore. The mine is reputed to be Roman in origin; it finally closed in 1903. Visitors emerge blinking from below ground to a superb view over part of the Snowdon Horseshoe.

# COAL

### Big Pit Mining Museum Blaenavon F8
This colliery opened in 1880 and was a working pit for 100 years. Led by former miners, visitors don helmets and cap lamps and descend by the pit cage to underground roadways. On the surface are a winding-engine house, a blacksmith's workshop, pithead baths and exhibitions about coal.

### Cefn Coed Colliery Museum
near Swansea D8
A huge winding engine is the centrepiece of this exhibition, which focuses on life in the mines. Also on display is a passenger tram that operated in Neath until 1920.

### Elliot Colliery Winding House
near Merthyr Tydfil E8
The colliery here closed in 1967, but the steam-powered winding engine has been restored to working order and an exhibition charts the rise and fall of the local coal industry. Nearby, Drenewydd Museum re-creates life in a Victorian mining household, and has a centre charting the demise of the iron industry.

### Rhondda Heritage Park near Pontypridd E8
Exhibitions here tell the story of three generations of a mining family, with reminiscences about life and work and events in the Rhondda Valley's history, such as mining disasters and the fight for a minimum wage in 1920. The Fan House portrays the social and cultural heritage of the Valley, including its choirs, chapels, carnivals and brass bands. The underground tour re-creates the mine as it was in the 1950s, with smells, sights and sounds, including mock explosions and an exciting simulated ride through the tunnels.

# SLATE

### Inigo Jones Slateworks near Caernarfon C2
This, the only fully operating slateworks in North Wales to be open to the public, dates

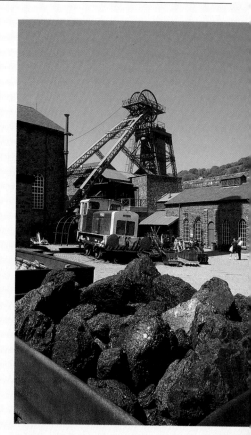

**ABOVE** *The Rhondda Heritage Park, previously the Lewis Merthyr Colliery, shows visitors what life was like in the mines in years gone by.*

from 1861. There are opportunities to watch craftsmen cutting, shaping, polishing and working slate slabs into such products as hearths and plaques. There is a self-guided tour and a video presentation, and visitors can try their hand at doing calligraphy on slates.

### Llechwedd Slate Caverns
Blaenau Ffestiniog D3
There are two tours exploring these historic caverns: Britain's steepest passenger railway descends a sharp gradient for the start of the

Deep Mine Tour, after which a walk is accompanied by sound-and-light sequences giving the story of a Victorian boy miner. The Miners' Tramway Tour, led by guides, includes a tram ride (*left*) and looks at how slate was worked and used. There is also a re-created Victorian slate-workers' village at the site, including a bank,

# INDUSTRIAL HERITAGE (CONTINUED)

## STEAMING THROUGH WALES

WELSH GEOGRAPHY was a powerful challenge for the pioneer railway builders. Rather than face the cost and difficulty of blasting routes through the mountains, the main line network followed the flat coastal land instead. But the coal and slate mines needed transport, and so cheaper narrow-gauge lines were built through the mountains to the steepest and remotest areas of North and mid Wales.

On the Blaenau Ffestiniog Railway, opened in 1836, horses hauled empty slate wagons from Porthmadog harbour to the mountain quarries. Loaded trains ran back down the line using gravity, carrying the horse in a wagon. When steam power arrived, engineer James Fairlie built special double-ended articulated locomotives to haul heavy trains around the line's sharp curves.

But from the 1920s, falling slate prices began to kill off the narrow-gauge lines, and when the government charged Richard Beeching with closing unprofitable railway routes in the 1960s, most Welsh cross-country lines disappeared.

Volunteer enthusiasts had already started to reverse this trend, however, and the lovingly restored Talyllyn Railway became the first to be reopened in 1951. The Ffestiniog line proved more of a challenge, as the route had been blocked by a hydroelectric scheme: parts of the railway were reopened in 1955 but restoring the whole route meant digging a tunnel and raising the track above the new lake, an undertaking that took 36 years. Other rescued lines include the Welshpool and Llanfair Railway; the Welsh Highland Railway; the Bala Lake Railway; the Vale of Rheidol Railway and the Brecon Mountain Railway—all of which carry passengers through the beautiful scenery of Wales.

**RIGHT** *On the Vale of Rheidol Railway, which runs from Abersytwyth to Devil's Bridge, car drivers are warned of the possible approach of a train at full steam.*

DOLGOCH STATION
ON THE
**TALYLLYN RAILWAY**
TOWYN MERIONETH WALES

**LEFT** *Dolgoch Station on the Talyllyn line is a romantic subject for Terence Cuneo's oil painting, which was made into a poster.*

**BELOW** *Passengers on the Welshpool and Llanfair Light Railway cruise through the countryside on a restored steam train.*

shops and pub with staff in period costume. In 1836 the Blaenau Ffestiniog Railway line (*see feature, above*) was opened to carry slate from the area's quarries to the sea; today it carries holidaymakers on a scenic ride to Porthmadog.

## Welsh Slate Museum Llanberis D2
An ambitious working museum occupies the site of Dinorwig Quarry, which employed up to 15,000 men and boys until 1969. Slate was transported via a narrow-gauge railway, which has been restored to working order. The Victorian workshops contain displays, and quarrymen's cottages from Blaenau Ffestiniog have been furnished in varying styles from periods between 1831 and 1969. There is an interactive museum for children, and former quarrymen demonstrate methods of slate cutting and dressing.

## INDUSTRIAL MUSEUMS

### Kidwelly Industrial Museum
near Llanelli D7
This former tin-plate works demonstrates for visitors the process of making tin plate by hand, and has exhibits on Carmarthenshire's industrial past.

### Maritime and Industrial Museum
Swansea D8
This fascinating museum is home to Wales's largest collection of maritime exhibits, including a lightship and a steam tug. The transport display includes a 1929 electric tram from the world's first horse-drawn passenger railway—from Swansea to Oystermouth—which opened in 1807. The Abbey Woollen Mill shows the process of manufacturing wool from raw fleece to finished goods.

# WILD WALES

WALES OFFERS SOME OF *the most dramatic scenery in the British Isles: famously green valleys, craggy, mist-veiled mountains and spectacular plunging waterfalls. Much of this countryside has been given national park status in honour of its wild beauty. While parts of Wales do get crowded, there are still some areas off the beaten track where you will have only the mountain sheep for company.*

## Brecon Beacons National Park E7
The Brecon Beacons National Park consists of four mountain ranges: the Brecon Beacons themselves; Fforest Fawr; Black Mountain (in the west); and, confusingly, the Black Mountains on the English–Welsh border. The peaks of the Brecon Beacons, south of the town of Brecon, are linked by curving, precipitous ridges and edged by deep valleys. This Old Red Sandstone range rises to its loftiest points at Corn Du (2,863 feet) and Pen-y-Fan (2,906 feet), which is the highest point in Wales outside Snowdonia. The eastern part of the national park is dominated by the Black Mountains, a range of long ridges alternating with deep, green valleys. Through these a road follows a scenic route past the ruins of Llanthony Priory and over the Gospel Pass, a short distance below the summit of Hay Bluff, where the view opens out northwards over the upper Wye Valley and across much of mid Wales. In contrast, Black Mountain is an aptly named brooding wilderness. Fforest Fawr is a former royal hunting ground: once populated with deer and wild boar, today it is a bleak area inhabited by hardy mountain sheep. Along the park's southern border lies the 'Waterfall Country' of the rivers Neath, Heptse and Mellte, which steer courses through great gorges and tumble over some of Britain's most dramatic waterfalls. One of these, Sgwd yr Eira, flows over a rock overhang so deep that a path passes behind the curtain of the fall.

## Clwydian Range F2
The Clwydian hills form a broad ridge looking across Snowdonia, the Berwyn uplands and Liverpool Bay. On the 1,818-foot summit of Moel Famau are the ruins of an Egyptian-style tower built in 1810 to commemorate the golden jubilee of George III. The lower summit of Foel Fenlli is crowned by the impressive ramparts of an Iron Age hill-fort.

## Elan Valley E6
Constructed from 1893 to 1904 to provide water for Birmingham, the chain of four reservoirs in the Elan Valley is a grand gesture

**ABOVE** *The Bronze Age stone circle known as Bedd Arthur (Arthur's Grave) in the Preseli Hills predates the 6th-century king, and was possibly used as an astrological observatory or religious site.*

of Victorian engineering, with dams adorning the huge, unpopulated expanse of the Cambrian Mountains. This 'Welsh Lake District' gives excellent opportunities for spotting the scarce red kite, while the oak woods on the hillsides are the haunts of a variety of other birds. Guided walks start from the visitor centre. Beyond the reservoirs, the mountain road to Aberystwyth passes the three-tiered Devil's Bridge, where a trio of roads cross the River Mynach.

## Pistyll Rhaeadr near Llanfyllin F4
'An immense skein of silk agitated and disturbed by tempestuous blasts', wrote George Borrow of this, the tallest waterfall in Wales, during his tour of the country in the mid 19th century. The water plunges spectacularly some 240 feet from the heather-clad Berwyn Mountains and is broken in mid-flight by a rock arch. (*See also page 133.*)

## Plynlimon E5
High on the slopes of this massif, which encompasses five peaks, are the sources of the rivers Wye, Severn, Rheidol, Llyfnant and Dulas. Plynlimon is best seen from Nant-y-Moch

Reservoir to the west, or from the monument to Wynford Vaughan-Thomas on a lonely road near Dylife to the northeast. From the 2,468-foot summit of Plynlimon the view includes Snowdon, the Preseli Hills, the Brecon Beacons, the Black Mountains and the Wrekin Hill in Shropshire.

## Preseli Hills B7
Rising to 1,760 feet and forming part of the Pembrokeshire Coast National Park, these bleak hills were the source of the bluestone that was transported over 200 miles to Wiltshire and used in the building of Stonehenge some 5,000 years ago; archaeologists are currently debating whether the stone was moved by human muscle or by glaciers during the Ice Age. The area is rich in ancient remains, including Iron Age hill-forts, Bronze Age stone circles (*see picture above*) and Neolithic cromlechs. In particular, the long ridge of Mynydd Preseli has a remarkable concentration of cairns and other sites, while on Carningli is the substantial Neolithic cromlech of Pentre Ifan, consisting of uprights supporting a massive 16-foot-long capstone. Through these hills runs the attractive,

# WILD WALES (CONTINUED)

**ABOVE** *A light dusting of snow on its peaks adds to the grandeur of Cadair Idris, seen across the Mawddach Estuary in winter. For those seeking solitude, this isolated range is ideal walking country.*

wooded Gwaun Valley, gouged out during the Ice Age by the action of fast-flowing glacial meltwater.

## Snowdonia National Park D2

Snowdonia National Park covers much of northwest Wales, including Cadair Idris (*pictured above*), the Rhinogs, the Arennigs and most of the coast from Porthmadog to Aberdyfi. Snowdon, or Yr Wyddfa, is the highest mountain in England and Wales at 3,560 feet. It is unique among British mountains in having a railway running to its summit, but the walk along the knife-edge ridges of the Snowdon Horseshoe provides the most exciting and most demanding route to the top. Long-abandoned copper- and slate-mine buildings are scattered beside the lakes of Llyn Glaslyn and Llyn Llydaw beneath Snowdon's eastern slopes, and by the Watkin Path.

North of Snowdon and the dramatic Pass of Llanberis, the Glyder range features the Cantilever Stone—a flat slab improbably balanced on boulders. Below the Glyders is the glacial lake Llyn Idwal, which became Wales's first national nature reserve in 1954. Here the variation of rock types and climatic conditions gives rise to a remarkable range of flora. Stretching some six miles northwards from here, the Carneddau Range forms the longest stretch of terrain above 3,000 feet in England and Wales,

before merging into lower peaks shelving down towards the northern coast.

The area around Betws-y-Coed is a particularly attractive terrain of forests, lakes, waterfalls and valleys, opening out in places to reveal rugged mountain backdrops.

Cadair Idris, in the south, is an isolated range of five summits reaching nearly 3,000 feet and, in fine weather, commanding views as far as Ireland. To the north of Cadair Idris rise the lower peaks of the Rhinogs, a boulder-strewn wilderness. From the remote lake at Cwm Bychan, a flagstoned path known as the Roman Steps (probably medieval rather than Roman in origin) provides access to the heart of the Rhinog range. There is much gentler walking to the north, along a disused railway track beside Mawddach Estuary.

## Welsh Wildlife Centre near Cilgerran B6

Owned by the West Wales Wildlife Trust, this 270-acre nature reserve beside a tidal stretch of the River Teifi embraces seven different habitats including primary woodland, a disused slate quarry, freshwater marsh and salt marsh. Special hides and microcameras enable close sighting of a range of wildlife, including otters, owls and one of Britain's largest colonies of the elusive Cetti's warbler (*left*). Guided walks, courses and other events are held, and there are five miles of paths.

# ISLANDS OF WALES

R OUGH THOUGH THE CROSSING *may be, a boat trip to one of Wales's offshore islands is well worth braving. These enchanting places are home to large sea bird colonies; the cliffs they frequent are bright with wild flowers in spring and summer, while seals bask on the rocks below.*

## Anglesey C1, C2, D1 & D2

Also known as Mam Cymru, 'the mother of Wales', this fertile lowland was economically important for centuries because of its grain harvests and copper reserves. The eastern and southwestern shores have expansive dune-backed sands, while to the north is a succession of more secretive coves. Early settlers left numerous monuments, such as the superb Bronze Age tomb of Bryn-celli-ddu near Llanddaniel Fab. Edward I's castle guards the Menai Strait at Beaumaris, Anglesey's most attractive coastal town. Here you can visit the courthouse of 1614 (still occasionally used, and the oldest active court in Wales), and view the dank cells of the nearby gaol. Near the eastern tip of Anglesey is the mostly Norman ruin of Penmon Priory. The village of Llanfairpwllgwyngyllgogerychwyrndrobwllllantysiliogogogoch ('St Mary's Church in the hollow of white hazel near a rapid whirlpool and the Church of St Tysilio near the red cave')—unremarkable in all but name—was named by a tailor in the 1880s who added to the original five syllables

**ABOVE** *The pretty resort of Amlwch, on the north coast of Anglesey, served as a port for the island's copper works from the 18th century.*

## SKOMER AND SKOKHOLM

THE STRANGE NAMES of Skomer and Skokholm—two rocky islands guarding the southern entrance to Pembrokeshire's St Bride's Bay—are pure Norse, given to them by Vikings during raids along the Irish Sea coast in the 9th century.

But the modern fame of Skomer and Skokholm rests on an entirely different type of visitor—the thousands of sea birds that breed on the rugged cliffs and flower-decked headlands after wintering out at sea or in warmer climes. The 759-acre island of Skomer (a National Nature Reserve, Site of Special Scientific Interest and the centre of a Marine Nature Reserve) is one of the most important wildlife sites in northwest Europe, and attracts large numbers of nature lovers every year.

A 15-minute boat trip from Martin's Haven on the mainland brings you into the sheltered bay of North Haven, whose slopes are riddled with the burrows of the underground-nesting Manx shearwaters. Around 100,000 breeding pairs nest here, but most visitors are unlikely to see them

as they only emerge from or return to their burrows at night.

More gregarious are the comical, clown-like puffins; the puffin colony on Skomer is home to 6,000 of these birds. Cliff-nesting birds that may be seen from the footpaths encircling Skomer include guillemots, razorbills, kittiwakes and fulmars.

Further out to sea, low-lying Skokholm is famous as the site of Britain's first bird observatory, which was set up in 1933. This idyllically secluded island shelters a similar range of bird life to its larger neighbour. As well as its ornithological delights, Skokholm is home to rabbits and a colourful array of wild flowers such as thrift and red campion.

**ABOVE** *Skomer houses a huge puffin colony; the birds nest in cliff-side burrows and the first chicks hatch in June.*

**RIGHT** *Skokholm Island is a paradise for bird photographers, who may snap razorbills, puffins, kittiwakes or guillemots.*

in order to make the place better known and thereby boost trade. Thomas Telford's suspension bridge provides a grand link with the mainland, while just to the west is the mansion of Plas Newydd (*see entry on page 149*).

### Bardsey Island B4
This island off the Lleyn Peninsula has been a place of Christian refuge and pilgrimage since the 6th century, and the bell tower of a 13th-century Augustinian abbey still stands. So many holy men were buried here that it became known as the 'island of twenty thousand saints'. Declared a National Nature Reserve for its status as a sea bird habitat, the island has accommodation for holidaymakers and hosts religious retreats. Day visits can be made from Aberdaron in summer.

### Caldey Island B8
*See feature on page 153.*

### Cardigan Island B6
Some 4,000 pairs of lesser black-backed gulls live in this wilderness haven near the mouth of the River Teifi. There is no access to the island, but fine views can be had from the mainland at Cemaes Head and from a toll path that leads through Cardigan Island Coastal Farm Park.

### Holy Island C1 & C2
Holy Island is part of Anglesey, lying just off the larger island's coast. In 1821 Thomas Telford put it firmly on the map with his new toll road from London, now the A5. Holyhead, the largest town in Anglesey, is a busy port with ferries leaving for Dublin's terminal Dun Laoghaire. The scenery is the island's most compelling attraction, however, and there are magnificent views to be had from the 720-foot summit of Holy Mountain. Sea birds frequent the cliffs by South Stack lighthouse, and the RSPB runs the cliff-top Ellin's Tower Seabird Centre.

### Puffin Island D1
The birds after which this tiny island off Anglesey is named appear in summer, although numbers are declining. Shags, cormorants and seals still proliferate, however. Fishing and scenic cruises can be taken from Beaumaris, though landing is not permitted.

### Ramsey Island A7
Across Ramsey Sound lies this spectacular RSPB sanctuary, where 400-foot cliffs provide nesting sites for guillemots, kittiwakes and razorbills, and choughs feed on ants in the short turf. Also on the island are dwindling numbers of red deer, while grey seals bob in the water close to shore. Summer boat trips depart from St Justinian's.

### Skokholm Island A8
*See feature, above.*

### Skomer Island A7
*See feature, above.*

# BESIDE THE SEASIDE

THE WELSH COASTLINE *encompasses some of the most diverse scenery in Britain, from the beautiful golden beaches of Pembrokeshire, beloved of surfers, to the marshes of the Dee Estuary, inhabited by wildfowl. Although the sun may not always shine on the beaches of Wales, there are many delights—including walking, birdwatching, shell-seeking and beachcombing—to be had on these shorelines, whatever the weather.*

## Cardigan Bay C3 to C6

This huge bay in mid Wales is a haunt of porpoises and bottle-nosed dolphins. South of Aberystwyth the seclusion of the cliffs is interrupted by only a handful of coastal villages and remote coves, while to the north three broad estuaries punctuate the coastline. Mwnt is a tiny National Trust-owned village with a sandy cove and, perched above it, a whitewashed church formerly used by pilgrims bound for Bardsey Island (*see entry on page 159*). An Iron Age fort stands on the cliffs above Llangranog, where the village squeezes into a narrow valley giving onto a beach; there is another fort at Cwmtydu, as well as a disused lime kiln backed by cliffs of spectacularly buckled shale strata.

## Carmarthen Bay B8 to C8

Extending for six miles along the bay are Pendine Sands, the setting for many early attempts at the world speed record: Malcolm Campbell set a new land-speed record of 174.88 mph here in 1927, and the story is told in the Museum of Speed at Pendine. Dylan Thomas's Laugharne faces the River Taf where

it converges with the Rivers Tywi and Gwendraeth to form a great estuary dividing the bay.

## Dee Estuary F1 to F2

Waders and other wildfowl are drawn to the salt marshes and mud flats of this river estuary, and Europe's largest concentration of pintails winters here. The River Dee was once an important shipping route into Chester, but this had to close when the river became silted up. A new port was founded at Connah's Quay in the 18th century and the river was canalised; although the docks have since closed, the area is still predominantly industrial. Remains of Edward I's castle can be seen at Flint, while beyond the mouth of the estuary, by Point of Ayr, are some 20 miles of holiday camps and seaside resorts, the largest of them being Prestatyn, Rhyl, Colwyn Bay and Rhos-on-Sea.

## Glamorgan Heritage Coast E9

Stretching from Breaksea Point westwards to the edge of Porthcawl, much of this rugged coast displays candy-striped cliffs made up of alternating layers of shale and limestone and riddled with fissures and blow-holes created by vertical joints in the rock. The cliff-top path has views across the Severn Estuary as far as Exmoor, and passes medieval St Donat's Castle, restored by American newspaper magnate Randolph Hearst in the 1920s and now used as a college. Near the thatched village of Merthyr Mawr are two more castles, Dunraven and Ogmore, guarding the Ogmore estuary.

## Gower C8 to D8

Although rich in prehistoric tombs and Iron Age forts, this peninsula is probably more popular for the superb sequence of golden sandy bays backed with jagged limestone cliffs—such as Three Cliffs Bay and Rhossili Bay—on its south and west sides. On the north coast are salt marshes punctuated by muddy creeks. West of Mewslade Bay lie the enigmatic rocks of Worms Head (*see picture on page 39*).

## Great Ormes Head D1

From the edge of Llandudno a cable car takes visitors onto this headland, which rises to 679 feet and gives views over Conwy Bay and the mountains of Snowdonia; the summits of the southern Lake District are sometimes visible to the north. Another way up is by the tram which has operated since 1902, and

LEFT *Rhos-on-Sea, in Colwyn Bay, North Wales, is a traditional family seaside resort.*

which passes copper mines once worked by Bronze Age settlers (*see entry on page 155*). The Marine Drive toll road makes a scenic five-mile loop round the headland.

## Lleyn Peninsula B3 to C3

This long, tapering peninsula is a land of windswept headlands, narrow lanes between high banks, and white farmhouses set against green pastures. A trio of peaks known as Yr Eifl, meaning 'the Fork' but known as 'the Rivals', comprise the highest ground, rising to 1,849 feet above the impressively preserved Iron Age hill-fort of Tre'r Ceiri. Pilgrims on their way to Bardsey Island used to stop at the Church of St Bueno at Clynnog-fawr, and modern-day visitors may want to make a detour to view it. Mynydd Mawr, a 524-foot hill by the Llŷn's western tip, gives a superb view of Bardsey Island. Southern Lleyn has surfing and bathing beaches in the vicinities of the fishing-village resorts of Aberdaron and Abersoch.

## Menai Strait C2 to D2

This narrow 14-mile stretch of tidal water running between Conwy and Caernarfon bays separates Anglesey from the mainland.

**ABOVE** *Three Cliffs Bay, named after its trio of jagged rock formations, is one of the finest beaches on the Gower peninsula. Fringed by sand dunes, it is relatively inaccessible and rarely overcrowded.*

Turbulent rip tides, which make for a difficult ferry crossing, led to the construction in 1819–26 of Thomas Telford's majestic iron suspension bridge, the Menai Bridge, across the Strait.

### Morfa Harlech near Harlech D3
Beneath the gaze of Harlech Castle, Morfa Harlech is an area of grazing land reclaimed from the sea, flanked by dunes and salt marshes which attract wading birds. Glorious sands, backed by the Lleyn Peninsula and the peaks of Snowdonia, extend southwards to lonely St Tanwg's Church. Near Llanbedr, Dyffryn Ardudwy is one of a cluster of prehistoric burial chambers in the area, while Shell Island, accessible only at low tide, is named after the more than 200 kinds of shell (*pictured right*) carried there by offshore currents.

### Pembrokeshire Coast National Park
B6 to B8
The 230-square-mile National Park extends from Amroth in the south to Cemaes Head at the mouth of the Teifi estuary in the north, making inroads inland only to include the Preseli Hills. Keen walkers can take the Pembrokeshire Coast Path which winds 186 miles through the park (*see entry on page 162*). The coast west of Tenby is marked by a succession of scalloped coves and dune-backed sands. Close to Manorbier Castle is the 5,000-year-old burial chamber known as King's Quoit, comprising two uprights supporting a bulky capstone. Ministry of Defence artillery ranges extend westwards from St Govan's Head, and there is no public access to the cliff path when red flags are flying. Guillemots, kittiwakes, herring gulls and other sea birds can be seen at Elegug Stacks, two towering limestone pinnacles. Immediately north from the sandy beach of Broad Haven, Bosherston boasts beautiful lily ponds (*pictured on page 19*), part of the estate of the long-since demolished Stackpole Court. The village of Angle lies by the mouth of Milford Haven, a deep natural harbour skirted by the national park. This is one of Europe's largest oil ports, with huge tankers serving endless refineries. Upstream from Neyland the scene is an unspoilt world of wooded creeks dotted with pleasure craft. Wooltack Point near Marloes gives views of Skomer and Skokholm islands. In clear conditions the Wicklow Mountains of Ireland can be seen from St David's Head, or from the moorland summit of Carn Llidi just inland. Northeast from here, the coast twists and turns around countless headlands and secret bays, which stand in striking contrast to the level-topped cliffs of southern Pembrokeshire. North of Garn Fawr, a steep-sided coastal hill crowned by ramparts of an Iron Age fort, Strumble Head is another haunt of sea birds. A lighthouse stands on its own island, while to the east a memorial on Carregwastad Point marks the site of the abortive French invasion of Pembrokeshire in 1797 (*see feature on page 38*). Despite its name, the prominent headland of Dinas Island is part of the mainland; from here there are wonderful views to be had up the coast.

# THE GREAT OUTDOORS

THE GREAT OUTDOORS *is there to be enjoyed, and there are many different ways of enjoying it in Wales. Long-distance footpaths wind their way across the country, passing through some spectacular scenery en route—as does the Welsh National Cycle Route. Another way to take in the view at a leisurely pace is on horseback. More of a challenge are the mountain and water sports on offer in Wales's peaks and valleys.*

## LONG-DISTANCE PATHS

### Cambrian Way (274 miles) F9 to D2

On its journey from Cardiff on the south coast to Conwy in the north, this walk crosses the highest and wildest terrain in Wales, ascending the Black Mountains, the Carmarthen Vans, Plynlimon, Cadair Idris, the Rhinogs and Snowdon—the highest mountain in England and Wales. The route is not waymarked and is suitable only for fit, experienced walkers with good navigational skills. The Cambrian Way Walkers' Association organises transport and accommodation along the route, as well as guided walks.

### Dyfi Valley Way (108 miles) D4 to E3

The River Dyfi winds through a majestically broad valley, explored by this looping route from Aberdovey along the north bank of the estuary to the southern tip of Bala Lake. From there it follows the south bank of the Dyfi to its finishing point at the sandy beach by Borth on Cardigan Bay.

### Glyndwr's Way (128 miles) F5 to F4

Setting off from Knighton on the Welsh–English border, Glyndwr's Way visits sites associated with the Welsh freedom fighter Owain Glyndwr, including Machynlleth, where he called a parliament in 1404. The walk follows a loop through mid Wales, finishing at Welshpool, and encompasses rolling uplands, reservoirs, quiet farmlands and unspoilt river valleys en route.

### North Wales Path (48 miles) E1 to D2

The North Wales Path takes in the best of the hills and headlands of the north coast between Prestatyn and Bangor, passing through Llandudno and Conwy. Walkers can enjoy spectacular panoramas of the Dee Estuary, Snowdonia and Anglesey.

### Offa's Dyke Path G8 to E1

*See feature opposite.*

### Pembrokeshire Coast Path (186 miles) B6 to B8

Encompassing virtually the entire seaboard of Pembrokeshire (*including Penberi, pictured below*), the coast path provides the most consistently beautiful coastal walking in Wales. The path weaves along cliff tops and around coves, and overlooks offshore islands. It takes

in a variety of superb wildlife habitats, including those of the rare chough and peregrine falcon, and in spring and summer the cliffs are covered in wild flowers.

### Severn Valley Way (210 miles) E5 to G8

This route takes the River Severn as its guide, following it from its source on Plynlimon near Aberystwyth and on through mid Wales. It finishes in dramatic style, passing under the Severn Bridges to reach Severn Beach beyond Bristol.

### Usk Valley Walk (50 miles) E7 to F8

From Brecon this mostly low-level path follows the Usk as it skirts the hills of the Brecon Beacons National Park. Beyond Abergavenny and the town of Usk itself it reaches the Severn Estuary at Newport.

### Wye Valley Walk (144 miles) G8 to E5

From Chepstow this walk heads upstream along the wooded gorge of the lower Wye, which gives a spectacular show of colour in autumn. The route scales the Wyndcliff viewpoint—famous for a panorama extending over the Severn Estuary and the Forest of Dean—and drops down to the riverside near

Tintern Abbey. From here the going is mostly level past Monmouth, beneath the Seven Sisters Rocks and Symond's Yat and into pastoral Herefordshire. At Hay-on-Wye, the walk re-enters Wales for a finale at Rhayader, as the upper Wye Valley becomes increasingly wild.

## CYCLING

### The Welsh National Cycle Route

The well-signposted Welsh National Cycle Route (Lôn Las Cymru) crosses Wales from north to south and was one of the first parts of the British National Cycle Network to be completed. Funded by the National Lottery, by 2005 the network will link much of Britain via traffic-free and traffic-calmed routes for cyclists and walkers.

The Welsh Cycle Route comprises several alternative, interlinking routes of varying difficulty through the industrial valleys of South Wales, the national parks of Snowdonia and the Brecon Beacons, and across the idyllically tranquil uplands of mid Wales—an area with almost limitless scope for both on- and off-road cycling.

One leg of the southern portion to Builth Wells starts from Chepstow and follows quiet roads and lanes over hilly country, via Abergavenny, the Gospel Pass in the Black Mountains, and the upper Wye Valley. The other leg sets out from Cardiff and takes a much gentler course along the 53-mile Taff Trail (*pictured below*), mostly on traffic-free tracks. It leads along the Taff Valley, through industrial Abercynon and Merthyr Tydfil, and skirts Pontsticill and Talybont reservoirs

in the Brecon Beacons National Park. Beyond Brecon, where the Taff Trail ends, the route becomes far more demanding, taking roads over the Eppynt massif.

The northern section to Holyhead has some tough off-road stretches, including the forests of the Cambrian Mountains, as well as easier rides between Builth Wells and Llanidloes, and across Anglesey.

## THE OFFA'S DYKE PATH

STRETCHING FOR AROUND 170 miles and passing through glorious valleys, rolling hills and woodland, the Offa's Dyke Path is one of the most attractive walking routes in Britain.

Opened in 1971, the path runs between Chepstow in Gwent and Prestatyn on the Clwyd coast. It takes its name from the massive earthwork or dyke with which King Offa (757–96) of the midland kingdom of Mercia attempted to fortify or demarcate his western border with Wales. Work on the dyke began in about 784: deep ditches were dug out and the soil piled up to form earthworks some 20 feet high. In some places the width of the ditch and earthwork was more than 70 feet. Although scholars doubt whether the dyke could have kept out determined Welsh chieftains, it probably deterred cattle raiders and, more to the point, in an age when constructions spoke louder than words, it proclaimed Offa's power and stature.

From its southernmost point, the path heads north, passing close to the ruins of Tintern Abbey and Monmouth. It then branches northwest towards Hay-on-Wye and continues north through Radnor Forest to Knighton, a small town with an Offa's Dyke Heritage Centre. The area around Knighton boasts some of the best-preserved sections of the earthwork. From here, the path runs along the top of the dyke itself, passing near the historic towns of Clun, Montgomery and Oswestry before reaching Llangollen. The path then runs west of the dyke before closing with it at Gop Hill, where the dyke ends; the path itself continues for a couple of miles into the seaside resort of Prestatyn.

**ABOVE** *A stone commemorating the start of Offa's reign marks the point where his dyke is crossed by the Knighton–Presteigne Road.*

**LEFT** *Walkers on the Offa's Dyke Path enjoy spectacular views across the Lugg Valley at Discoed near Presteigne.*

# OTHER ACTIVITIES

## Caving

The Brecon Beacons area is home to some of Britain's finest cave systems, including those at the Llangattock escarpment above Crickhowell, and Fforest Fawr, where a cave entrance can be seen from a path at Porth-yr-Ogof. These are the preserve of the experienced caver, but the three spectacular Dan-yr-Ogof show caves are open to the non-caving public. They form part of a huge limestone cave system and include Bone Cave, which was inhabited by humans some 3,000 years ago, and the vast Cathedral Cave.

## Climbing

The summits of Snowdonia provide some of the best terrain for climbing in Britain. Non-climbers can witness the experts at work at Idwal Slabs, the rock buttresses overlooking Llyn Idwal beneath Glyder Fawr. The Welsh International Climbing Centre at Merthyr Tydfil and the Llangorse Riding and Rope Centre both have facilities for indoor climbing, with instruction available for total beginners.

## Pony trekking

There are stables scattered throughout rural Wales offering guided treks, often at a very gentle pace suitable for inexperienced riders. Mid Wales is particularly good for riding, with minimal traffic on the roads, and plenty of gentle drovers' tracks giving splendid views, while in Pembrokeshire you can enjoy glorious rides along the beaches. The Black Mountains offer abundant unfenced country, excellent for trekking or more energetic riding.

## Water sports

Total beginners can learn the basics at one of the many water-sports centres dotted around Wales. The beauty and variety of the coast attract numerous pleasure craft, while inland Bala Lake is the longest and deepest body of water in Wales. Pembroke, the Menai Strait, Aberystwyth, Tenby and Swansea Bay are among numerous sailing areas. Surfing and windsurfing haunts include the beaches of Gower and Pembrokeshire, as well as Hell's Mouth (Porth Neigwl) on the Lleyn Peninsula. Canoeing and kayaking can be enjoyed on the calm waters of the Dee and Teifi, or on estuaries such as the Cleddau and Towy, while there are more adventurous white-water runs (*right*) along the Rivers Usk, Wye, Conwy and Llugwy.

# THE FAME OF WALES

WALES IS, *to most people's minds, synonymous with rugby and singing. No wonder then, that a list of the country's most famous sons and daughters should include a fair sprinkling of representatives from both these arenas. The famous Welsh lilt has also contributed to the success of actors and politicians, poets and broadcasters alike. Meet some of them below in our selective guide.*

### Shirley Bassey
Singer

(Born 1937 in Cardiff) Bassey began singing in local working men's clubs as a teenager but was discovered and put on the stage in 1955. Her career took off and she had a string of hits, including the theme songs to two James Bond films, *Goldfinger* (1964), and *Diamonds Are Forever* (1972). Her big, vibrant voice and glittering stage presence made her a huge cabaret star. In 1999, Bassey sang at the opening ceremony of the Rugby World Cup in Cardiff.

### Aneurin Bevan
*See feature, right.*

### Richard Burton, born Richard Walter Jenkins
Actor

(1925–84, born in Pontrhydyfen) Burton first appeared on stage in 1943 but his acting career was put on hold while he served in the RAF. By the mid 1950s he was Britain's leading Shakespearean actor, and his rich Welsh voice was put to perfect use in the radio production of Dylan Thomas's *Under Milk Wood*. On screen, Burton specialised in historical film roles, and he achieved superstar status in 1963 when he played Mark Antony to Elizabeth Taylor's Cleopatra. The sparks flew offscreen as well as on, and he and Taylor were twice married.

### Charlotte Church
Soprano

(Born 1986 in Cardiff) This teenage singing star's career took off with the launch of her first album, *Voice of an Angel*, in 1998; the collection of traditional hymns and Welsh and Irish folk songs sold over 3 million copies worldwide and made her Britain's top female solo artist. The schoolgirl from Cardiff has performed live for the Queen, the Pope and US President Clinton, and has also received film offers from Hollywood.

### Gareth Edwards
Rugby player

(Born 1947 in Gwaun-cae-Gurwen, near Swansea) Edwards won his first cap at the age of 19, and at 20 became the youngest-ever captain of the Welsh team. The Cardiff scrum half never missed a game for his country, and won 53 caps. He was awarded an MBE in 1975, and now works as a commentator.

### Sir George Everest
Engineer

(1790–1866, born in Gwernvale) For the best part of his career Everest worked on the trigonometrical survey of India, first as

## NYE BEVAN AND THE NHS

**LEFT** *Aneurin Bevan meets a group of nurses on July 5, 1948, the day the National Health Service came into being.*

ANEURIN—better known as Nye—Bevan, founder of the National Health Service, was born in Tredegar in 1897. The son of a miner, Bevan himself began work in the pits at the tender age of 13 and soon became a passionate trade unionist, going on to lead the Welsh miners in the General Strike of 1926. Three years afterwards he began his parliamentary career as Labour MP for Ebbw Vale.

Bevan became Minister of Health in the new Labour government of 1945, and it is for his work in this role that he is most celebrated. Before the war, medical care in Britain could only be obtained by payment or by undergoing stringent means testing. Bevan was the architect of the 1946 National Health Service Act—inspired by the 1942 Beveridge Report, recommending a welfare state for Britain—which brought the NHS into being two years later, promising free medical and dental services for all, paid for by taxation.

But in 1951 the outbreak of the Korean War led the government to propose a rearmament programme, to be funded by cutbacks in social expenditure—including the introduction of charges for prescriptions and dental and opthalmic treatment. Bevan argued that this was destructive of a key socialist principle framed in the National Health Service, and resigned his post in protest.

Bevan is commemorated in Wales by four large monoliths standing on a windswept hilltop near Tredegar: three represent the towns of his constituency and the fourth, slightly bigger, represents Bevan himself. But the National Health Service remains Bevan's enduring legacy to the people of the United Kingdom.

superintendent and then as surveyor general. He completed the survey in 1843, and it was used to map the subcontinent. In 1865 the world's highest peak, then known as Peak XV, was re-named Everest in his honour.

### Geoffrey of Monmouth
Writer

(*c.* 1100–55) Although the exact facts of his life are unknown, Geoffrey was raised in Wales and served in one or two religious posts. He earned fame with his *History of the Kings of Britain*, a chronicle of the founding of the nation, which described a long and glorious Welsh past. The *History* was later shown to be based on legend rather than fact but remains a great work of literature, and is the source for most stories about King Arthur.

### Henry VII

*See feature on page 166.*

### Sir Anthony Hopkins
Actor

(Born 1937 in Port Talbot) After graduating from the Royal Academy of Dramatic Arts,

Hopkins went on to become a member of the National Theatre company in 1966 and appeared in his first film the following year. He won an Oscar (*left*) for his portrayal of a cannibalistic serial killer in *The Silence of the Lambs* (1991). He was knighted in 1993 and made his directorial debut in 1995 with *August.*

### Colin Jackson
Athlete

(Born 1967 in Cardiff) At the 1993 World Championships, Colin Jackson set a world record which still stands for the 110-metre hurdles. After a period of injury in the mid 1990s, he made a triumphant comeback at the World Championships in 1999, where he regained his world champion title, becoming the first male athlete and first Briton ever to achieve the double.

### Augustus John
Painter

(1878–1961, born in Tenby) John studied at the Slade School in London with his elder sister Gwen and shared his first studio with

**ABOVE** *Tom Jones sings with a Welsh male voice choir at Wembley Arena in 1999 as the Welsh rugby team prepare to take on great rivals England in the Five Nations tournament.*

her in Tenby. By the age of 23 he was a professor in Liverpool, living in a ménage à trois with two women by whom he had six children. He then spent some time living in a Gypsy camp; Gypsies, landscapes and women were his most frequent subjects. His bohemian lifestyle endeared him to London society, for whom he embodied the flamboyant Celt, and he became one of the most celebrated portraitists of his day.

### Gwen John
Artist

(1876–1939, born in Haverfordwest) As quiet as her younger brother Augustus was loud, John spent most of her life in Paris where she studied with James McNeill Whistler and became Auguste Rodin's mistress. After converting to Catholicism in 1913, she became ever more reclusive. She enjoyed little success in her lifetime, but her subtle, muted paintings, mostly of interiors and lone women, have enjoyed an increasingly favourable reputation in the years since her death.

### Tom Jones, born Thomas Jones Woodward
Singer

(Born 1940 in Pontypridd) Jones started his career as a club singer in the early 1960s, but his vocal talent was spotted by the songwriter Gordon Mills, who wrote Jones's trademark

song, *It's Not Unusual,* for him in 1964. It was a huge chart hit; several more hits followed but Jones's powerful voice and sexy stage shows made him more at home singing at nightspots and cabarets than on the pop scene. He was wildly popular with women, who often threw their underwear at him on stage. After several years in semi-retirement, during which he settled in California, Jones re-entered the charts in the 1980s with the song *Kiss*, and in 1999 released an album of duets with some of the biggest names of 1990s pop, including the Welsh bands Catatonia and Stereophonics.

### Neil Kinnock
Politician

(Born 1942 in Tredegar) Neil Kinnock, the son of a miner and a nurse, was elected to Parliament in 1970. Many felt that he lacked gravitas, but his gift for oratory ensured him a meteoric rise through the ranks of the Labour Party under the patronage of leader Michael Foot. Although he had never held ministerial office, Kinnock replaced Foot as leader in 1983, becoming the youngest person ever to hold the post. Kinnock tackled two potentially vote-losing problems by ridding Labour of the extreme left-wing organisation Militant Tendency, and persuading the party to drop its commitment to unilateral nuclear disarmament. Nonetheless, Labour suffered a surprise general

# THE FAME OF WALES (CONTINUED)

## HENRY VII

WALES IN THE 15TH CENTURY was a dissatisfied country: in 1400 Owain Glyndwr's last bid for independence from English rule had been crushed, and the Welsh had consequently become second-class citizens. And since 1455 the Marcher Lords (who controlled the border lands) had embroiled their part of the country in the Wars of the Roses, the battle between Yorkists and Lancastrians for the throne. Then in 1485 the unthinkable happened—a Welshman became King of England and Wales.

The Welshman in question was Henry Tudor, son of Edmund, a Welsh knight, and Margaret Beaufort, a Lancastrian heiress. Three months before Henry's birth, Edmund was killed fighting for the Lancastrians, and the 14-year-old Margaret sought refuge at Pembroke Castle, the home of Edmund's brother Jasper. It was here, on January 28, 1457, that Henry Tudor was born, and here too that he spent his childhood, learning Welsh and enjoying music, poetry and sport.

**ABOVE** *A 16th-century Italian bust of King Henry VII of England and Wales.*

But this happy existence in the protective shadow of the castle walls was not to last: Henry was the Lancastrians' main claim to the throne, and after the Yorkist Richard III seized the crown in 1471, he fled to France. Henry returned to Wales in 1485, landing at Milford Haven, where he gained support by promising to deliver the Welsh from the servitude they had long suffered under the English. Henry's army marched forth under the banner of the red dragon of Wales, and defeated Richard at the Battle of Bosworth Field. Shortly afterwards, clad in the Welsh colours of green and white, he was crowned Henry VII in Westminster Abbey.

Henry didn't forget his roots, including the red dragon in the royal arms and appointing Welshmen to government posts. But he never returned to the country of his birth, and it was his son, Henry VIII, who brought Wales completely under English rule with his Acts of Union of 1536–43.

**ABOVE** *An illustration in Raphael Holinshed's 1577 Chronicle of England depicts the Battle of Bosworth Field where Henry Tudor defeated Richard III to become King.*

**LEFT** *King Henry VII was born and brought up at Pembroke Castle, the seat of his paternal uncle Jasper Tudor. The castle was granted to Jasper in 1452 by Henry VI.*

election defeat in 1992 which led to Kinnock's resignation. Ironically, for a previously anti-Europe politician, Kinnock became a European Union Commissioner in 1995 and four years later was European Commission Vice President. His wife Glenys was elected to the European Parliament in 1994.

### The Ladies of Llangollen
#### Eccentrics
(1739–1829, 1755–1831, born in Ireland) Eleanor Butler and Sarah Ponsonby, better known to the world as 'The Ladies of Llangollen', were two Irish lesbians who fled their native country on horseback disguised in men's clothes to escape marriage and the reprobation of society. The ladies settled in Llangollen at a house they named Plas Newydd ('new place'); although they had planned to live as recluses, Sarah and Eleanor in fact entertained some of the great figures of their day, including the Duke of Wellington.

### David Lloyd George
#### British Prime Minister
(1863–1945, born in Manchester) David Lloyd George was born to Welsh parents, and was only two when his father died and the family returned to Wales. He started his career as a solicitor, but in 1890 was elected as Liberal candidate for Caernarfon Boroughs, a seat he retained until 1945. From 1905 to 1906 he was President of the Board of Trade and he became Chancellor of the Exchequer in 1908. He was a social reformer, and his 'People's Budget' the following year levied taxes on large incomes and luxury items to pay for old-age pensions, while his National Insurance Act of 1911 laid the basis of the welfare state. After a brief spell as Secretary of War, Lloyd George became coalition Prime Minister in 1916. Acclaimed as 'the man who won the war', his government was overwhelmingly returned to power in 1918 and he retained the premiership until 1922. But a decline in personal popularity caused by his womanising and dubious financial dealings led to his resignation. Towards the end of his life Lloyd George was made 1st Earl of Dwyfor.

### Merlin
#### Mythical wizard
Merlin makes his first appearance in early oral traditions as the Welsh poet Myrddin, but he is more famous as the wizard and soothsayer at King Arthur's court. This incarnation is mostly the work of Geoffrey of Monmouth (*see entry on page 165*), whose *History of the*

*Kings of Britain* is one of the major sources of Arthurian legend.

## Jan Morris
### Journalist
(Born 1926 in Somerset) A journalist, historian and travel writer of Anglo-Welsh parentage, Morris was *The Times*'s correspondent on the 1953 Everest expedition, and broke the historic news that man had conquered the mountain. In 1974, James became Jan with a much-publicised sex-change operation; her book *Conundrum* is a memoir of this event. Morris's writings include books on Wales, Venice, Oxford and Spain, and in 1986 her fictional *Last Letters from Hav* was shortlisted for the Booker Prize. She was awarded a CBE in 1999, and lives in Wales.

## Robert Owen
### Philanthropist
(1771–1858, born in Newtown) Owen became apprenticed to a clothier at the age of 10; nine years later he was manager of a Manchester cotton mill. As he rose through the ranks he lost none of his empathy for the plight of the workers. In 1798 he bought the New Lanark Mill in Scotland, where he established a model community, including the world's first infant school and a welfare programme. His ideas were influential in the development of trade unions, and his followers, known as Owenites, were the early forerunners of the socialist movement.

## Sir Henry Morton Stanley, born John Rowlands
### Explorer and journalist
(1841–1904, born in Denbigh) An illegitimate child, Stanley grew up in the local workhouse.

In 1859 he went to the United States where he was adopted by a merchant named Stanley. While Stanley was working as a journalist on the *New York Herald*, his editor set him the assignment of finding David Livingstone, a missionary and explorer believed to be lost in Africa. Stanley did find him—and greeted him with the famous words 'Dr Livingstone, I presume?'. This encounter inspired him to become an explorer, and he embarked on an expedition across Africa during which he traced the course of the Congo River and established the beginnings of the Congo Free State.

## Dylan Thomas
### Writer
(1914–53, born in Swansea) Thomas started his career as a journalist and published his first book of poems, known simply as *18 Poems*, in 1934. He married Caitlin Macnamara three years later, and the Thomases settled in Laugharne. Here, while working for the BBC, he wrote from a boatshed near his home overlooking the Taf estuary. His collection of autobiographical short stories, *Portrait of the Artist as a Young Dog*, came out in 1940. But Thomas aquired a reputation as much for his drinking as for his writing and two weeks after the first radio performance of his 'play for voices', *Under Milk Wood*, he died of alcoholism.

## R. S. Thomas
### Poet
(Born 1913 in Cardiff) Thomas was ordained into the Church of Wales in 1936 and spent his working life as a minister. His first volume of poetry, *The Stones of the Field*, was published in 1946. Thomas's early work takes a bleak look at the Welsh landscape and the problems encountered by small Welsh communities. His later poems are more spiritual, reflecting on an inner landscape and the nature of the poet's relationship with God.

## Wynford Vaughan-Thomas
### Writer and broadcaster
(1908–87, born in Swansea) Wynford Vaughan-Thomas—author of the chapters at the heart of this volume—joined the BBC as a reporter in 1937 and in the same year covered the coronation of George VI. During the Second World War he became a war correspondent, reporting from the front line in Europe. After 30 years at the BBC he returned to Wales and worked for Harlech Television, where he was director of

programmes until 1972. Just outside Dylife there is a slate memorial carrying a depiction of this popular television and radio broadcaster, hand outstretched over the valleys and peaks of his beloved Wales.

## J. P. R. Williams
### Rugby player
(Born 1949 in Ogmore) John Peter Rhys Williams won the Wimbledon Junior Tennis Championships in 1966 before joining the London Welsh rugby team while studying medicine in London. After graduating he played for Bridgend and was selected for the Welsh side. J. P. R., as he is affectionately known, played 55 games for Wales and made two tours with the British Lions in the 1970s, when he was rated the best fullback in the world. He captained his national team in his final season, and after retiring from the game in 1979 became an orthopaedic surgeon.

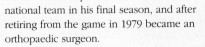

## Richard Wilson
### Painter
(*c.* 1714–82, born in Penegoes, near Machynlleth) Wilson studied as a portrait painter but in 1750 went to Italy and began painting landscapes in the classical style. On returning to Wales, he painted the mountains of his childhood, and he is now considered the first great British landscapist. Wilson was a co-founder of the Royal Academy in 1768 but shortly afterwards his career went into decline; taking to drink, he died a forgotten man in 1782.

## Catherine Zeta Jones
### Actress
(Born 1969 in Swansea) Catherine Zeta Jones was drawn to performing as a child, and at the age of 10 won the grand final of a Butlin's holiday camp competition singing a medley of Shirley Bassey numbers. She appeared in several West End musicals as a teenager but really hit the big time when she played Mariette in the television adaptation of H. E. Bates's *The Darling Buds of May*. She subsequently moved to Hollywood to make her name on the big screen. Superstardom was not long in coming as Zeta Jones landed roles starring alongside such Hollywood heavyweights as Antonio Banderas and Sean Connery.

# HISTORIC HOTELS INNS AND PUBS

**The Bear** near Abergavenny F7

This historic coaching inn, which dates back to 1432, remains an ideal watering hole for the travel-weary: plush, cushioned armchairs, leather easy chairs and a generous sofa are positioned round a great open fire, with a window seat overlooking the market square and a medley of antiques along the walls. Local food, however, is the Bear's key attraction: Welsh rarebit, Welsh lamb and Welsh cheeses are all served, alongside more exotic dishes. Staff here were reputedly moved to tears when the Bear was voted Pub of the Year 2000 in a survey of 6,000 British pubs.

**The Blue Anchor Inn** near Barry F9

The old-world charm of this archetypal pub, established in 1380, is famous throughout Wales. Inside is a rambling warren of passageways, alcoves and cosy, low-beamed

rooms with open fires and heavy oak doors. Outside, Virginia creeper climbs the ancient stonework towards the thatched roof. In summer, the pub is adorned with flowers in troughs and hanging pots. A new terrace has been built, with a path leading down towards the shingle flats that are the most southerly point of Wales.

**The Dinorben Arms** near Denbigh E2

Whisky fans will warm to this characterful village inn, with its three flagstoned rooms and open fires: it offers a range of no fewer than 300 malt whiskies. Others may be lured by the magical qualities attributed to a renovated Roman well, glassed over and housed in the Well Bar. The lunchtime smorgasbord is also popular, especially if you can claim a table on one of the landscaped, brick-floored terraces, which cling to the flanks of the Clwydian Range and overlook the Vale of Clwyd.

**Dolmelynllyn Hall** near Dolgellau D4

This remote country hotel in Snowdonia has the air of a retreat; indeed, the great poet

Shelley is said to have found inspiration here. The 16th-century house with mock-Tudor additions is surrounded by 1,200 acres of National Trust land. The food, in particular, is exceptional. You can nibble on leek fritters in a lounge that looks out onto formal gardens, before moving into the high-ceilinged, mahogany-panelled dining room for, say, braised, stuffed quails or roast loin of Anglesey lamb.

**Hotel Portmeirion** Portmeirion D3

This opulent waterside curiosity was dreamed up by eccentric architect Sir Clough Williams-Ellis, who spent around 50 years developing the village into a jigsaw of domes and pastel façades. The hotel, resembling a tycoon's holiday mansion, stands as the centrepiece of Sir Clough's work. It is a Victorian house transformed to combine a hotchpotch of styles from around the world. Eating here is a real pleasure: the sweeping curve of the 1930s dining room allows magnificent views of the Snowdonia foothills and the shoreline of the Traeth Bach estuary.

**The Radnorshire Arms** Presteigne F6

For two years of the English Civil War, the Radnorshire Arms hid a Catholic priest from the Roundheads; or so claims a diary, which, along with secret passageways and priests' holes, was found during recent renovations to the building. These discoveries have only

added to the already-significant charm of this old-fashioned inn, with its oak panelling, latticed windows and heavy black beams hung with horse brasses. During the day, guests can drink on the flower-bordered lawn (previously a bowling green); and for those who can't tear themselves away, there are several cosy bedrooms upstairs.

**The Walnut Tree** near Monmouth G7

This famous pub combines the sophistication of world-class cuisine with the informality of a whitewashed country inn. Hopeful diners queue before opening time for the pleasure of sampling the many hybrid dishes created by an Italian cook working in the shadow of the Brecon Beacons. If a drink is all you're after, you'll not be turned away: an outstanding wine list is complemented by an array of local ales.

**Ye Olde Bull's Head** Beaumaris D2

Samuel Johnson came here, and so did Charles Dickens—a fact acknowledged upstairs, where the bedrooms are named after characters from his novels. The cosy interior is carefully cluttered with interesting antiques: there is a rare 17th-century water clock, a chilling collection of cutlasses and the town's old ducking stool. The oak door that guards the entrance to the courtyard lays claim to being the largest 'simple-hinged' door in Britain. For the connoisseur, there are more than 220 wines to choose from.

**ABOVE** *The renovated Victorian mansion of Hotel Portmeirion, overlooking the flats of the Traeth Bach estuary at low tide. Beyond rise the mountains of Snowdonia.*

# CALENDAR OF FESTIVALS AND EVENTS A SELECTION

FOR A COUNTRY *that is renowned for its singing, it is wholly appropriate that many of Wales's festivals should revolve around music; and with a wealth of beautiful countryside to enjoy, fitting, too, that her rivers and mountains should provide the setting for action-packed, physically gruelling races. Wales also proudly celebrates its Celtic heritage at various events through the year, and its hill-farming tradition in livestock fairs and agricultural shows. Precise dates and timings may vary: tourist offices have more details of these and other events.*

## FEBRUARY

**RHONDDA HERITAGE PARK** CELTIC FESTIVAL

## MARCH

**THROUGHOUT WALES** ST DAVID'S DAY Celebrations across Wales commemorate the country's patron saint.

## APRIL

**CARDIFF** WELSH INTERNATIONAL CAR RALLY
**NEWPORT** DRAMA FESTIVAL

## MAY

**BEAUMARIS** FESTIVAL (late May to early June). Arts, music, drama, children's events and exhibitions.
**HAY-ON-WYE** FESTIVAL OF LITERATURE *See feature on page 144.*
**ST DAVID'S** CATHEDRAL FESTIVAL (late May to early June). International performers present a programme of classical concerts.
**VARIOUS LOCATIONS** URDD NATIONAL EISTEDDFOD The Youth Eisteddfod, the largest youth festival in Europe, with some 40,000 young people taking part. Alternates annually between North and South Wales.

## JUNE

**BARMOUTH TO FORT WILLIAM** THREE PEAKS YACHT RACE Crews of five sail the distance, with two from each crew scrambling up and down Snowdon, Scafell Pike and Ben Nevis—11,174 feet of ascent in all.
**CARDIFF** SINGER OF THE WORLD COMPETITION Held every two years, with a star-studded line-up of singers competing for the title.
**CRICCIETH** FESTIVAL (late June to early July) Music and arts events.

## JULY

**BUILTH WELLS** ROYAL WELSH AGRICULTURAL SHOW Features livestock exhibitions, trade stands and sheepdog trials.
**CARDIFF** WELSH PROMS Held at St David's Hall.
**FISHGUARD** MUSIC FESTIVAL
**GOWER** FESTIVAL Classical and folk music in churches across Gower.
**LLANGOLLEN** INTERNATIONAL MUSICAL EISTEDDFOD *See feature on page 98.*
**SNOWDON MOUNTAIN RACE** Ten-mile race from Llanberis to the summit of Snowdon and back.
**WELSHPOOL** MID WALES FESTIVAL OF TRANSPORT Rally for all types of vehicles from the early 1900s to the present, at Powis Castle.

## AUGUST

**BRECON** JAZZ FESTIVAL
**CARDIFF** FESTIVAL (late August to early September) Huge festival of music and the arts.
**CARMARTHEN** UNITED COUNTIES SHOW Agricultural show.
**CILGERRAN** CORACLE REGATTA A race on the River Teifi using coracles—small, portable craft formerly used for fishing, and little changed since the Iron Age.
**HOLYHEAD** ANGLESEY COUNTY SHOW Premier agricultural show for North Wales, with trade stands, falconry displays, showjumping, shire horse displays and a fairground.
**LLANDRINDOD WELLS** VICTORIAN FESTIVAL The townsfolk celebrate their Victorian past by dressing up in period costume and decorating the town.

**LLANWRTYD WELLS** WORLD BOG SNORKELLING AND MOUNTAIN BIKE LEAPING CHAMPIONSHIPS Competitors snorkel along a channel cut in a bog (*above*) and attempt to leap over it on mountain bikes.
**VARIOUS VENUES** ROYAL NATIONAL EISTEDDFOD OF WALES (*See also feature on page 98.*) Alternates annually between North and South Wales.

## SEPTEMBER

**TENBY** ARTS FESTIVAL Music and art in the seaside resort.

## OCTOBER

**ANGLESEY** OYSTER AND SHELLFISH FESTIVAL A three-day celebration of the island's shellfish bounty.
**LLANDUDNO** FESTIVAL Music, poetry, opera, jazz, dance, folk music, competitions and talks.
**SWANSEA** FESTIVAL OF MUSIC AND THE ARTS Held since 1948, this is the principal professional arts festival in Wales, with concerts, exhibitions and theatre.

## DECEMBER

**BUILTH WELLS** ROYAL WELSH AGRICULTURAL WINTER SHOW
**CENARTH TO CARDIGAN** CORACLE REGATTA Held on Boxing Day.
**MOUNTAIN ASH** NOS GALAN Race held on New Year's Eve in honour of a local runner.

## USEFUL INFORMATION

Listed below are the details of Tourist Information Centres for a selection of destinations. Please note that these details may be subject to change.

**ABERYSTWYTH**
Terrace Road
Aberystwyth
SY23 2AG
Tel. (01970) 612125

**CARDIFF**
Cardiff Central Station
Central Square
CF1 1QY
Tel. (02920) 227281

**HOLYHEAD**
Penrhos Beach Road
Holyhead
LL65 2QB
Tel. (01407) 762622

**LLANDUDNO**
1–2 Chapel Street
Llandudno
LL30 2YU
Tel. (01492) 876413

**SWANSEA**
Plymouth Street,
Swansea
SA1
Tel. (01792) 468321

*For general information contact:*

**THE WELSH TOURIST BOARD** at
Britain Visitor Centre
1 Regent Street
London
SW1Y 4XT
Tel. (020 7808 3838)

*The following websites may also be of interest (NB website addresses can change):*

Official Wales Tourist Board:
http://www.tourism.wales.gov.uk

Brecon Beacons National Park:
http://www.breconbeacons.org

Cymru Calling:
http://www.wales-calling.com

National Eisteddfod of Wales:
http://www.eisteddfod.org.uk

# INDEX

and acknowledgments

Note: page numbers in **bold** refer to captions for illustrations

# ACKNOWLEDGMENTS

The editors gratefully acknowledge the use of information taken from the following publications during the preparation of this book:

*Blue Guide: Wales* by John Tomes, A & C Black 1979

*The Brecon Beacons National Park* by J.M. Brereton, David & Charles 1990

*Castles in Wales* by Roger Thomas, The Automobile Association and the Wales Tourist Board 1982

*Castles of Britain and Ireland* by Plantagenet Somerset Fry, David & Charles 1996

*Celtic Art* by Ruth and Vincent Megaw, Thames and Hudson 1989

*Celtic Art* by I. M. Stead, British Museum Publications 1985

*Celtic Britain and Ireland* by Lloyd and Jennifer Laing, The Herbert Press 1995

*Cows, Cardis and Cockneys* by Gwyneth Francis-Jones, 1984

*The Dictionary of National Biography*, Oxford University Press

*The Drovers' Roads of Wales* by Fay Godwin and Shirley Toulson, Wildwood House Ltd 1977

*The Encyclopaedia Britannica*

*Encyclopaedia of Britain* by Bamber Gascoigne, Macmillan 1994

*England and Wales under the Tudors* by Sinclair Atkins, Edward Arnold 1975

*A History of Modern Wales* by Philip Jenkins, Longman Group UK Ltd 1992

*Insight Guides: Wales* edited by Brian Bell, APA Publications Ltd 1989

*Modern Wales: A Concise History* by Garth Elwyn Jones, Cambridge University Press 1994

*Ordnance Survey Leisure Guide: Brecon Beacons and Mid Wales,* The Automobile Association and the Ordnance Survey 1989

*Ordnance Survey Leisure Guide: Snowdonia and North Wales,* The Automobile Association and the Ordnance Survey 1989

*The Oxford Companion to British History* edited by John Cannon, Oxford University Press 1997

*A Short History of Wales* by A. H. Dodd, B. T. Batsford 1972

*Wales* by Peter Sager, Pallas Athene 1991

*Wales: The Rough Guide* by Mike Parker and Paul Whitfield, Rough Guides 1997

*Walking Round Wales: The Giraldus Journey* by Shirley Toulson, Michael Joseph 1988

*When was Wales?* by Gwyn A. Williams, Black Raven Press 1985

*Wild Wales* by George Borrow, Collins 1977

# PICTURE ACKNOWLEDGMENTS

*T* = top; *C* = centre; *B* = bottom; *L* = left; *R* = right

**Front Cover** The Photolibrary Wales/Chris Stock **Back Cover** *T* The Photolibrary Wales/Richard Davies *B* The Photolibrary Wales/Chris Warren **2** The National Trust Photographic Library/Joe Cornish **4** The Photolibrary Wales/Peter Venn **6–7** Woodfall Wild Images/David Woodfall **10** *BL* Windrush Photos/Colin Carver **10–11** Archie Miles **12** © The Skyscan Photolibrary **13** © The Skyscan Photolibrary **15** *T* Woodfall Wild Images/Jeremy Moore *B* Woodfall Wild Images/Mark Hamblin **16** Wales Tourist Board **17** By permission of the National Museums and Galleries of Wales/Museum of Welsh Life **18** Woodfall Wild Images/David Woodfall **19** The Photolibrary Wales/Dave Hart **20** *TL* Lake Vyrnwy Hotel *BR* Collections/Robert Hallmann **21** *T* The Photolibrary Wales/David Williams *B* Western Mail & Echo Ltd **22** Images Colour Library/Jeff Tucker **24–25** Gettyone Stone/Robin Smith **26** David Vaughan-Thomas **27** The Photolibrary Wales/Rex Moreton **28** *TL* The Photolibrary Wales/Steve Benbow **28–29** Woodfall Wild Images/David Woodfall **29** *TR* Derry Brabbs **30** *L* S4C *R* The Photolibrary Wales/Steve Benbow **31** © The Skyscan Photolibrary/Bob Evans **32** *T* By permission of The National Library of Wales *B* The Anthony Blake Photo Library/Anthony Blake **33** Celtic Picture Library **34** *T* The Photolibrary Wales/Steve Benbow *B* The Photolibrary Wales/Paul Kay **35** Wales Tourist Board **36** *L* The Photolibrary Wales/Louise Beddow *TR* Oxford University Museum *BR* Oxford University Museum **37** Windrush Photos/John Hollis **38** *T* The Photolibrary Wales/Rex Moreton *CL* & *C* By permission of the National Museums and Galleries of Wales/Department of Archaeology & Numismatics *CR* The Bridgeman Art Library, London/Ms 6 f.167v, Lambeth Palace Library, London, UK *BL* Carmarthenshire County Museum **39** The Photolibrary Wales/Richard Anthony Founds **41** The National Trust Photographic Library/Joe Cornish **42** *BL* The Photolibrary Wales/Mo Wilson *BR* By kind permission of Corus Group PLC **42–43** The Photolibrary Wales/Chris Warren **43** *BR* By kind permission of Sony Manufacturing UK **44** *L* By Courtesy of the National Portrait Gallery, London/Collection 12680 *R* The Photolibrary Wales/Steve Benbow **45** *TR* Glamorgan Record Office *BL* The Photolibrary Wales/Derek Rees *BR* By permission of The National Library of Wales **46** Fortean Picture Library/Paul Broadhurst **47** The National Showcave Centre for Wales—Dan-yr-Ogof **48** Collections/Michael Collier **49** *T* Aerofilms *B* Science and Society Picture Library/National Railway Museum **50** *CR* The Bridgeman Art Library, London/Private Collection *BL* Wales Tourist Board **51** Science and Society Picture Library/National Railway Museum **52** Newport Museum & Art Gallery **53** Science and Society Picture Library/National Railway Museum **54** *L* Photo by David Toase *R* The National Trust Photographic Library/Penrhyn/Douglas Pennant Collection/John Hammond **55** Photo by David Toase **56** *L* By permission of the National Museums and Galleries of Wales/Department of Industry *TC* Science and Society Picture Library/National Railway Museum *R* Celtic Picture Library **57** The Photolibrary Wales/Jeremy Moore **59** *L* Collections/Michael Collier *R* The Bridgeman Art Library, London/Add Ms 54782 f.40, British Library, London, UK **60** © The Skyscan Photolibrary **61** CADW: Welsh Historic Monuments. Crown copyright **62** CADW: Welsh Historic Monuments. Crown Copyright/By kind permission of the Vicar & Churchwardens, Tewkesbury Abbey **63** *L* Ancient Art and Achitecture Collection *R* The Photolibrary Wales/Billy Stock **64** *TC* By permission of The British Library/Roy.143.E.IV *C* The Photolibrary Wales/David Williams *BL* CADW: Welsh Historic Monuments. Crown Copyright *BR* CADW: Welsh Historic Monuments. Crown Copyright **66** *TL* © The Skyscan Photolibrary **66–67** *B* Woodfall Wild Images/David Woodfall **68** Ffotograff/Charles Aithie **69** *L* Topham Picture Library *R* The Bridgeman Art Library, London/Private Collection **70** *L* By permission of The National Library of Wales *R* By permission of the National Museums and Galleries of Wales/Department of Archaeology & Numismatics **71** *L* CADW: Welsh Historic Monuments. Crown Copyright *R* Ashmolean Museum, Oxford **72** The Photolibrary Wales/Steve Benbow **73** Woodfall Wild Images/David Woodfall **75** Photo by David Toase **76** *L* By permission of The National Library of Wales *R* Woodfall Wild Images/Jeremy Moore **77** The National Trust Photographic Library/Chris Warren **78** *TL* By Courtesy of the National Portrait Gallery, London **78–79** The Photolibrary Wales/Brian Woods **79** *TR* Collections/Michael St Maur Sheil *CR* Ffotograff/Patricia Aithie **80** Alpine Club Library **81** *T* Celtic Picture Library *B* Alpine Club Library **82** David Vaughan-Thomas. **83** *TR* The Longland family *CR* & *BR* John Cleare/Mountain Camera **84–85** Images Colour Library/Will Curwen **87** Gerallt Llewelyn/By kind permission of Jane Pullee **88** *T* Ffotograff/Patricia Aithie *B* Collections/Gena Davies **89** University of Wales, Swansea/South Wales Coalfield Collection **90** Robert Harding/Andy Williams **91** V. K. Guy Ltd/Mike Guy **92** Celtic Picture Library **93** Portmeirion **94** *T* Wales Tourist Board *B* Frank Lane Picture Agency/M. Nimmo **95** *L* Carmarthenshire County Museum *R* By permission of the National Museums and Galleries of Wales/Department of Archaeology & Numismatics **96** The Photolibrary Wales/Ray Wood **97** The Bodleian Library,

Oxford/MS. Gough Maps 231, fol. 127R **98** *TL* Royal National Eisteddfod of Wales *TR* Mary Evans Picture Library *CL* Llangollen International Musical Eisteddfod *BL* Llangollen International Musical Eisteddfod *BR* Llangollen International Musical Eisteddfod **100** *L* By permission of The National Library of Wales **100–101** *R* The Photolibrary Wales/Aled Hughes **101** *CR* © Reader's Digest/Richard Turpin **103** *L* © The British Museum *R* By permission of The National Library of Wales **104** The Photolibrary Wales/Neil Turner **105** By permission of the National Museums and Galleries of Wales/Department of Industry **106** *TL* By Courtesy of the National Portrait Gallery, London *TR* © The Skyscan Photolibrary *BL* Collections/John D Beldom **107** The Photolibrary Wales/Neil Turner **108** Hayes Davidson/John Maclean/John Maclean **109** Hulton Getty Images **110** *TL* By permission of The National Library of Wales *TR* Hulton Getty Images *BL* Western Mail & Echo Ltd **111** By permission of the Syndics of Cambridge University Library **112** *TL* By permission of The National Library of Wales *TR* From John Ogilby's 'Britannia' of 1675, reproduced by Alexander Duckham & Co. Ltd, 1939. *CL* By permission of The National Library of Wales *CR* Lloyds TSB Group Archives *B* Woodfall Wild Images/David Woodfall **114–115** Woodfall Wild Images/David Woodfall **116** *TL* The Photolibrary Wales/Martin Barlow *TR* The Photolibrary Wales/Janet & Colin Bord *C* Welsh Lamb and Beef Promotions Ltd *CR* Little Acorn Products *B* Melin Tregwynt/Tregwynt Mill **118** *TL* Hulton Getty Images *TR* Collections/Robert Deane *CL* The National Library of Wales/With kind permission of Sheila Hooper **120** Woodfall Wild Images/David Woodfall **121** Robert Harding/Adam Woolfitt **123** *L* Cover of *Wild Wales* by George Borrow. Published by Gomer Press, illustrated by Wil Rowlands *R* By Courtesy of the National Portrait Gallery, London **124** By permission of the National Museums and Galleries of Wales/Museum of Welsh Life **125** David Vaughan-Thomas **126** The Photolibrary Wales/Brian Woods **127** *L* The Bridgeman Art Library, London/Archives Nationales, Paris, France/Lauros-Giraudon *R* Woodfall Wild Images/David Woodfall **128** The Photolibrary Wales/David Williams **129** Derry Brabbs **130** *BL* & *TR* Woodfall Wild Images/Mark Hamblin *BR* Woodfall Wild Images/Steve Austin **130–131** Woodfall Wild Images/Jeremy Moore **131** *BR* OSF/John Paling **132** NHPA/Laurie Campbell **133** Woodfall Wild Images/David Woodfall **135** *T* The Photolibrary Wales/Janet & Colin Bord *B* David Tarn **136** The Photolibrary Wales/Steve Benbow **137** *T* The National Trust Photographic Library/Joe Cornish *B* Derry Brabbs **138–139** Robert Harding/Roy Rainford **140** *TL* © Reader's Digest/Robert Eames *CL* Collections/Gena Davies *CR* By permission of the National Museums and Galleries of Wales/Museum of Welsh Life *BL* The National Trust Photographic Library/Joe Cornish **141** *T* Images Colour Library/Peter Watson *TC* Science and Society Picture Library/National Railway Museum *BC* The Last Invasion Centre/© Elizabeth Cramp RWS/photograph by Miranda Walker *B* Robert Harding/Duncan Maxwell **142** *L* Celtic Picture Library *B* The Photolibrary Wales/Chris Stock **142–143** Robert Harding/Roy Rainford **144** *L* Collections/Gena Davies *R* The Photolibrary Wales/David Williams **145** *T* The Photolibrary Wales/Steve Benbow *B* © Reader's Digest **146** Treorchy Male Voice Choir **147** *TR* The Photolibrary Wales/David Williams *CL* Ceredigion Museum *BR* Bridgeman Art Library/London/National Museums and Galleries of Wales, Cardiff © Courtesy of the artist's estate **148** *T* The National Trust Photographic Library/Kevin J. Richardson *B* Archie Miles **149** Images Colour Library/Kevin Richardson **150–151** CADW: Welsh Historic Monuments. Crown Copyright **152** The Photolibrary Wales/Dave Williams **153** *TR* The Photolibrary Wales/Billy Stock *BL* Mick Sharp and Jean Williamson *BR* The Photolibrary Wales/Steve Benbow **154** *CL* The Photolibrary Wales/Steve Benbow *CR* Collections/Nick Oakes *BL* Robert Harding/David Hunter **155** *T* The Photolibrary Wales/Neil Turner *B* Photo by David Toase **156** *T* Collections/Alain le Garsmeur *C* Science and Society Picture Library *B* Collections/Alain le Garsmeur **157** Woodfall Wild Images/Jeremy Moore **158** *TL* The National Trust Photographic Library/Kevin J. Richardson *BL* OSF/Tony Tilford *BR* Neil Holmes **159** *L* Woodfall Wild Images/Mike Powles *R* Celtic Picture Library **160** *BL* Celtic Picture Library **160–161** Woodfall Wild Images/David Woodfall **161** *B* George A. G. Workman **162** *TC* David Tarn *BR* The Photolibrary Wales/John Kinsey **163** *TR* Collections/Gena Davies *CL* Archie Miles *BR* The Photolibrary Wales/Pierino Algieri **164** *TL* The Photolibrary Wales/Andrew Davies *TR* Popperfoto *BL* Topham Picture Library **165** *T* Western Mail & Echo Ltd *B* Rex Features Ltd/Eugene Adebari **166** *TL* The Bridgeman Art Library, London/Victoria & Albert Museum, London, UK *CR* By permission of The British Library/598.h.3–4 *BL* The Photolibrary Wales/Neil Turner **167** *TL* Hulton Getty Images *CR* Colorsport **168** *CL* The Photolibrary Wales/Neil Turner *BR* Topham Picture Library/George Wright **169** Jeff Morgan

SEPARATIONS Litho Origination Group plc, London
PAPER Périgord-Condat, France
PRINTING AND BINDING Printer Industria Gráfica SA, Barcelona, Spain

615009/1